Sport and Canadian Diplomacy

D0989666

Sport and Canadian Diplomacy

DONALD MACINTOSH
and
MICHAEL HAWES

with contributions from
DONNA GREENHORN
and
DAVID BLACK

McGill-Queen's University Press
Montreal & Kingston • Buffalo • London

© McGill-Queen's University Press 1994
ISBN 0-7735-1161-x

Legal deposit second quarter 1994
Bibliothèque nationale du Québec

Printed in Canada on acid-free paper

This book has been published with the help of a grant from the Social Science
Federation of Canada, using funds provided by the Social Sciences and
Humanities Research Council of Canada. Funding has also been provided by the
School of Physical and Health Education, the Department of Political Studies,
the School of Graduate Studies and Research, and the Faculty of Arts and Science
of Queen's University, and by Canada Council through its block grant program.

Canadian Cataloguing in Publication Data

Macintosh, Donald
    Sport and Canadian diplomacy
    Includes bibliographical references and index.
    ISBN 0-7735-1161-x
    1. Sports and state – Canada. 2. Canada – Foreign relations – 1945–   . I. Hawes,
Michael K., 1954–   . II. Greenhorn, Donna Ruth, 1952–   . III. Black, David R.
(David Ross), 1960–   . IV. Title.
    GV585.M26 1994   327.71   C93-090665-9

Some of the material in this book has previously appeared as "The IOC and
the World of Interdependence" in *Olympika: The International Journal of Olympic Studies*
1, 1992; "Trudeau, Taiwan, and the 1976 Montreal Olympics" in *American Review
of Canadian Studies* 21(4), 1991; "Canadian Diplomacy and the 1978 Edmonton
Commonwealth Games" in *Journal of Sport History* 19(1), 1992; and "Hockey
Diplomacy and Canadian Foreign Policy" in *Journal of Canadian Studies* 28(2), 1993.
Published by permission.
    The Gleneagles Declaration and the Code of Conduct are reproduced from the
1988 Constitution of the Commonwealth Games Federation. Reproduced by
permission.

This book was typeset by Typo Litho Composition Inc. in 10/12 Baskerville.

Contents

Acknowledgments

This book had its origins in a grant from the Social Sciences and Humanities Research Council of Canada to conduct a study of sport and Canadian foreign policy, and we are most grateful for this support. We also wish to acknowledge the monies provided by the School of Graduate Studies and Research and the Faculty of Arts and Science of Queen's University to help in the final preparation of this manuscript. As was the case with *Sport and Politics in Canada,* this book serves as a starting point for more detailed examinations of the many facets of sport and foreign policy in Canada. Our work covers only the federal aspects. There is much work to be done on provincial excursions into sport and foreign policy. The Quebec government's involvement in the Conference of Ministers of Youth and Sport of French-Speaking Countries, an organization that sponsors sport aid programs for third-world French-Speaking countries and the Francophonie Games, is a good example. Various other provincial and civic governments have also ventured into the world of international sport politics in efforts to bring events such as the Olympic and Commonwealth Games to their jurisdictions.

As is the case in all projects of this magnitude, there are many people whose contributions need to be acknowledged. John Hilliker, Anne Hillmer, Hector Mackenzie, and Ted Kelly in External Affairs and Abby Hoffman and John Scott in Fitness and Amateur Sport were all most cooperative in assisting us to gain access to relevant government files and documents. Many of the central actors in our story were kind enough to allow co-author Macintosh to interview them; most of them reviewed and commented on preliminary drafts of material related to their involvement. The names of these people appear in appendix A. Bruce Kidd deserves special mention. He was a great source of knowledge, was most generous of his time, and made his extensive files on sport and apartheid available to us.

Our team of research assistants at Queen's University contributed greatly to the final product. At various stages Lorna Porcellato, Samantha Scott-Pawson, Lisa McDermott, and Jill Smith all worked diligently on the project. Two persons deserve special mention on the title-page. Research assistant David Black prepared and wrote the material on Canada's relations with South Africa that was subsequently integrated into chapters 4, 6, 7, and 8. Long-time research associate Donna Greenhorn conducted the document research and wrote most of the material that appears as chapters 2 and 3 and much of chapter 4 as well. Without all these contributions, our book would be a lesser one.

EDITOR'S NOTE

Two separate reference systems have been used in this book. The first – conventional Chicago style – uses citations in the text for all standard references listed in the bibliography. All references to government documents, personal communications, confidential sources, and letters and memos, however, have been placed in endnotes according to chapter. This dual system allows the reader to identify standard references immediately, but move through the text without the excessive interruptions that would have occurred if all source material had been cited in the text.

Sport and Canadian Diplomacy

CHAPTER ONE

Introduction

In October 1987 Joe Clark, then secretary of state for external affairs, and Otto Jelinek, minister of state for fitness and amateur sport, announced that the government intended to make greater use of sport in promoting Canada's image abroad, and they confirmed a larger role for government in the international sport movement (Canada, 28 October 1987). Sport had come to play an important place in Canada's foreign relations. In many ways the announcement caught both the bureaucratic and the academic communities off guard. Little, if any, attention had been paid by Canadian political scientists to the role of sport in international politics. Trevor Taylor suggests that this is because many international relations scholars have viewed "their subject solely in terms of an inter-state struggle for security and power," with cultural and social issues playing only a modest role in this struggle (Taylor 1986a, 29). Indeed, he notes that there is not a clearly identifiable body of work in international politics dealing with social and cultural relations, a place in which sport might logically be located. However, an increasingly large amount of academic attention is being given to the study of "low politics," but primarily as they relate to economic matters.

Taylor suggests four reasons why sport should be of particular significance for students of international relations. First, he argues that it is a major element in world society and culture. Sport has increasingly attracted the attention of sociologists and historians, and thus deserves consideration by political scientists. Given this importance, he believes that political scientists should think "rigorously about the impact (either positive or negative) on the international political system dominated by states" (ibid., 38). Although our work sheds some light on this second point, we focus primarily on his third and fourth criteria. Taylor also claims that sovereign states sometimes "direct sport as part of their internal and external policies" (ibid.). Our purpose is to examine the ways in which sport has intersected with Canada's foreign-policy objectives since World War II and to trace the forces and events that led up to the Clark-Jelinek announcement. Taylor's fourth point is that sport also has significance in the study of international relations because it is based primarily on organization (ibid., 42) and as such, often works on a global basis through transnational actors and international non-governmental organizations (Taylor 1988a, 533). In one very important sense, international relations are about regularized, co-operative behaviour and the institutions and arrangements that exist to achieve that goal. In this book, we explore the relationship between sport and Canadian foreign policy, with full confidence in the fit and in the explanatory power of the transnational relations paradigm. Before setting the theoretical framework, however, we offer a brief overview of the dramatic changes in international sport following World War II, along with an abbreviated assessment of the Canadian government's response to these changes (for a full account of these events, see Macintosh, Bedecki, and Franks 1987).

SPORT AND
THE CANADIAN STATE

Prior to World War II, sport occasionally played an informal role in Canada's relationships with other countries. As early as 1883 two representative lacrosse teams – one a native people's team captained by Big John (Scattered Branches) and the other headed by W.G. Beers – toured the British Isles, acting as both athletes and "emigration agents" for the dominion government by attracting settlers to the Canadian West (Schrodt, Redmond, and Baka 1980). However, Canada's relative disinterest in sport as an instrument of foreign policy was summed up best by Prime Minister Mackenzie King, who, when questioned about Canadian participation in the 1936 Nazi Olympics, noted, "It is doubtful that anyone participating in the Olympic Games is a representative of the Government of this country" (HC Debates, 13 February 1936, 159).

At this point it should be remembered that it was not until the 1920s that Canada started slowly to shake itself loose from British influence and to establish itself as a fully independent state capable of managing its own foreign relations (particularly with the United States). Up until that time, all critical decisions about Canadian foreign policy, including going to war, were made in Britain. This transformation was gradual, beginning with the 1923 Canada–US Pacific Halibut Treaty, the first treaty negotiated by Canadian officials. Further ground was gained in 1927, when the Mackenzie King government opened a legation (embassy) in Washington. By the end of the decade, Canada had legations in Paris and London as well and had begun to pursue an independent foreign policy in earnest. Much of Canada's early diplomatic activity involved the United States – from policy co-ordination on prohibition, Ku Klux Klan activities, and commercial aviation, to disputes over the St Lawrence Seaway, the auto industry, and Arctic sovereignty. Prohibition aside, these became the enduring themes in Canadian-American relations. It was not until after World War II that Canada committed itself to multilateralism and internationalism as its principal foreign-policy thrust.

Sport assumed an increasingly important role in society after World War II. The Soviet Union's decision to use sport to promote its form of government and social organization abroad played a critical role in this development. Initially, Western nations were reluctant to follow this lead, partly because of the residual Victorian concept of the "amateur" athlete and the tradition of autonomy of sport from government, and partly because they did not feel the need to justify their forms of government in the same way as the Soviets did. However, the remarkable successes of Soviet athletes in international sport events soon swept aside these inhibitions. By the 1970s the governments of most developed (and some emerging) nations were actively supporting corps of "state" athletes with a view to promoting national unity and pride at home, as well as prestige and recognition abroad.

The advent of television in the 1950s also played an important role in the increasing visibility and popularity of sport. Television's unique affinity with sport meant that millions of people who hitherto had little or no interest in spectator sport became ardent viewers of televised sport. The potential for exploiting this large audience was not lost on television networks and corporate sponsors; both professional and so-called amateur sport increasingly became important vehicles to sell goods and services on television. This led to an intensification of the commercialization and professionalization of amateur sport to a point where it is now difficult to distinguish between amateurism and professionalism.

Canada was not immune to these developments. The emerging popularity of sport and a growing concern over the country's international performances, particularly in hockey, soon found their way into the media. Canada's role as the premier force in international hockey had been usurped in the 1950s by the Soviet national hockey team, which had come to dominate both the Olympics and the World Championships. Canadian ambassadors abroad were quick to inform the secretary of state for external affairs about the extent to which international sports events were used for political purposes in Europe, particularly in the Soviet Union and other Warsaw Pact countries.

Some had been struck by the political passion displayed at various competitions because of the presence of Soviet participants. It was obvious that the Soviets were attempting to use the success of their athletes to prove the superiority of the USSR, and Canadian ambassadors were becoming concerned about Europeans' sensitivity to this type of propaganda.[1]

In 1949 the secretary of state for external affairs, Lester Pearson, acknowledged that international contests were more than mere sporting events: they had grown into events of some political importance. He was quoted as saying, "International sport is the means of attaining triumphs over another nation," and he maintained that Canada needed to adapt itself in this respect.[2] Pearson, of course, was an avid sportsperson himself. He had received a Massey Foundation fellowship to attend the University of Oxford, where he played ice hockey and lacrosse (Pearson 1972). This exposure to "gentlemanly" amateur sport was to have an influence on him for the rest of his life.

The Canadian government soon found itself considering ways in which it might help improve the country's international sport performances. At about the same time, there was a growing concern among educators and fitness advocates over the apparently low level of physical fitness among Canadians. These two phenomena, along with other social and economic forces that were characteristic of the expanding welfare state in Western industrialized nations at this time, culminated in the federal government's enacting in 1961 a bill to encourage fitness and amateur sport.

During the first few years after the passage of this bill, the federal government was content to play a passive role in the promotion of fitness and amateur sport. It entered into cost-sharing agreements with the provinces and turned over its federal responsibilities to the National Fitness and Amateur Sport Advisory Council. This council made grants to national sport organizations (NSOs) on behalf of the federal government in the hopes that such monies would make Canadian athletes more competitive and result in more successes at international competitions. These measures, however, did little to improve Canada's stature in international sport. In the first place, other countries were also intensifying their efforts to better their performances. Second, Canadian NSOs did not have the technical and administrative resources necessary to help their athletes improve their performances. As a consequence, the clamour in the press and in the House of Commons that had characterized the 1950s continued unabated in the 1960s.

These worries over Canada's poor showing at international sporting events coincided in the late 1960s with certain larger forces and events in Canadian society. Pierre Trudeau, following his election as leader of the ruling Liberal Party, was searching for ways to counter what he saw as two strongly divisive forces in Canadian society. On the one hand, there was a growing francophone nationalism and calls for more independence in Quebec; on the other, the increasing demand for more autonomy from the other provinces. As an advocate of strong central government, Trudeau sought, in the federal election campaign of 1968, ways in which he could strengthen Canadian unity. It is significant that the first Canada Games, held in Quebec City in 1967 and one of the few initiatives that the federal government took in sport during the 1960s, had as their theme, "Unity through Sport." It was in this context that in an election speech in Castlegar, British Columbia, Trudeau mentioned sport as part of culture, connecting it with the theme of national unity and suggesting that sport had a role in harmonizing relations between Quebec and the rest of the country. He promised that, if elected, his government would establish a task force to investigate amateur sport in Canada.

These events all culminated in a new policy direction for the federal government in sport in the 1970s. It did not renew the federal-provincial cost-sharing agreement for fitness and amateur sport, in part because of the continued wrangling with the provinces over jurisdictional matters and in part because the federal government was not getting any political mileage out of these programs. Rather, it turned its attention to the promotion of what would become known as high-performance sport.

Improved international sport performances were essential if sport was to be effective in the promotion of national unity. To this end, the federal government took a number of steps in the late 1960s and early 1970s to bolster Canada's sport system. It established the National Sport and Recreation Centre in Ottawa to house and provide support to the NSOs and created a separate division within Fitness and Amateur Sport – Sport Canada – to deal directly with high-performance sport. Three quasi-independent bodies, designed to promote fitness and amateur sport in Canada, were also created: the Coaching Association of Canada, Participaction, and Hockey Canada. Our analysis of sport and foreign policy begins with the creation of Hockey Canada in 1969. But first we turn to the theoretical framework of the analysis.

TRANSNATIONAL RELATIONS AS A FRAMEWORK FOR ANALYSIS

Foreign-policy analysis and international relations theory have, for the most part, been focused on questions relating to state behaviour in general and international security in particular. In recent years, however, the study of international relations has become increasingly sensitive to the "low politics" of social and economic issues and the increasingly complex behaviour and interaction of various non-state actors. As the world becomes more interdependent, foreign-policy analysis has had to become more attuned to the vagaries of "world politics" as opposed to the logic of "inter-national relations." In other words, it has been necessary to come to terms with relations that take place across national borders (as opposed to those that take place simply between states), relations that involve sub-units of national governments, and those that involve various sorts of quasi-governmental and non-governmental actors. As will become clear, transnational organizations and actors, both quasi- and non-governmental, play an increasingly important role as our story of sport and Canadian foreign policy unfolds.

Accordingly, it is essential to have a clear and systematic understanding of how various ideological perspectives influence our thinking and direct the behaviour of political leaders and policymakers. While it is possible to locate many different analytic positions (and many variations on these positions), we have chosen to isolate the three main perspectives in the literature and argue for the logic of the transnational relations perspective. Scholars of international relations have referred to these competing perspectives in various ways, the most common distinctions being the realist, liberal, and Marxist positions (see, for instance, Dougherty and Pfaltzgraff 1990; Gilpin 1987; Rosenau 1982). The principal analytic differences among the three perspectives revolve around the structure of the international system, the underlying logic or fundamental principles that characterize the system, and the distribution of power and influence (i.e., the relative status of the main actors).

On the question of the structure of the international system, the basic difference is quite clear; realists posit a state-centric or interstate system; the liberal (transnational) perspective suggests a multi-centric structure; and the systemic perspective (often associated with Marxist theorizing) suggests a systemic or global-centric structure. James Rosenau has captured this distinction neatly in his analysis of the three perspectives. He contends, "The state-centric analysts presume a fragmented structure in which power is located in nation-states; those who adhere to a multi-centric approach picture an interdependent structure with power distributed among a variety of types of actors; and those who subscribe to a globalcentric perspective view the system as having an integrated structure deriving from patterns of power distribution that have been in place for centuries" (Rosenau 1982, 4; see also Rosenau 1990).

Likewise, the three perspectives can be distinguished according to the underlying logic to which they adhere. Traditional realists maintain that the international system is characterized by anarchy and by the political competition for power and influence. Proponents of the transnational relations perspective hold that the system is characterized by the notion of complexity and by cross-cutting alliances and other informal arrangements, although the system is basically orderly (Haas 1976; Pentland 1990). The systemic perspective, by contrast, is characterized primarily by its focus on historical patterns of state behaviour and by the persistence of various structural and bilateral relationships of dependency.

Finally, with respect to the composition of the system and the distribution of power within it, the differences among the three perspectives are equally clear-cut. Realists view the system as being fragmented, with power distributed unequally among the various actors (principally states). For them the notion of relative gains is a very important one. The transnational relations paradigm suggests that interdependence is the principal structural feature of the international system. Power is distributed (somewhat more equally) among nation-states, multinational enterprises, international organizations, and other transnational and/or transgovernmental coalitions. The third perspective sees the international system as being highly integrated, with power distributed according to the logic of long-established historical patterns of development, underdevelopment, imperialism, and exploitation.

While most students of international politics generally support the notion that there are three basic perspectives, there is a great deal of debate over the more subtle distinctions between the competing positions (indeed, this view is beginning to give way to new thinking in the field; see, for instance, Halliday 1991). With respect to the transnational relations perspective, for example, Robert Cox emphasizes adherence to the *status quo* and the "management of interdependence," focusing on the "liberal" character of the international system, rather than on the notions of multi-centrism and pluralism (Cox 1979). By contrast, Robert Gilpin views this perspective in terms of the challenge that systemic pluralism and complexity pose to the nation-state. He sees this view as one that is best understood in terms of the "sovereignty at bay" thesis, where the principal conflict of our time is between the political forces of nationalism and the economic forces of internationalism (Gilpin 1981, 1987). Others, such as Stephen Krasner, stress the societal (domestic interests) aspect of liberalism (Krasner 1985). The position we take here emphasizes the opportunities inherent in the interdependent environment and the need for national governments to find ways to co-ordinate domestic preferences and priorities within an increasingly complex and interconnected international environment.

Subtle differences in orientation help to underscore the complexity of each perspective and remind students of contemporary international politics how important it is to avoid simple ideological distinctions and to eschew single causal explanations for complex phenomena.

What follows is a somewhat more detailed review of the two principal competing perspectives – classic realism and transnational relations – along with a brief overview of the story we tell and how the two perspectives help us to understand the relationship between sport and foreign policy in Canada. First, we review the basic premises of classic realism. Then we proceed to an analysis of how the transnational relations paradigm came to challenge the dominant realist view and to draw our attention to "low politics" issues such as sport. We argue that for certain issues the logic of transnational relations (the so-called world politics paradigm) has replaced the logic of traditional realist thinking and, in other instances, has significantly extended the logic of realism. Finally, we offer a brief assessment of the importance of this paradigmatic debate.

Political realism, along with a preoccupation with the politics of power and security, emerged in the pragmatic and nationalistic period that followed World War II. Its initial prominence both in the academic community and in policy-making circles can be attributed to the decline of idealism and linked to the writings of Hans Morgenthau, George Kennan, E.H. Carr, and others (see Carr 1946; Morgenthau 1948; Waltz 1954). It characterizes the international system as an anarchic environment in which independent sovereign states are in constant competition for power and influence. In this formulation, the central goal of every state is the pursuit of its national interest and the maximization of its power relative to the other states in the system. The underlying premise here is that human society is inherently evil and that individuals (and socially constructed institutions such as the state) will attempt to enhance their relative position whenever the opportunity arises.

Realism portrays the international system as both state-centred and state-centric. States ultimately seek to maximize their influence, while achieving order through the balance of power process. Finding a systemic equilibrium, according the classical realists, is the main task of diplomatic activity. Balance of power theory, backed up empirically by the lessons of international relations in nineteenth-century Europe, goes hand in hand with the fundamental principles of realism. For realists, the international system has to be understood as a system of sovereign states that are in constant competition for scarce resources and political influence. From this perspective, international politics must be perceived as anarchy or, at the very least, as organized violence. The conflict over the distribution of power within the system will inevitably lead to war, as war becomes the ultimate arbiter – the means by which balance is restored. Nowhere is this point made more clearly than in Morgenthau's classic *Politics among Nations*, where he states that "all history shows that nations active in international politics are continuously preparing for, actively involved in, or recovering from organized violence in the form of war" (Morgenthau 1948, 36). Problems that do not relate to questions of war and peace are conceded to be of some importance by contemporary realist thinkers, but are ultimately still subordinated to security issues, broadly defined.

While this synopsis of the realist position is very brief, it is possible to summarize this perspective quite neatly by defining realism as an intellectual perspective that makes three interrelated assumptions. First, it assumes that states are the dominant actors, if not the exclusive actors, in international relations (the state-centric principle) and that states act as coherent units (the state-as-actor principle). Second, it assumes that force is a usable and effective instrument of foreign policy and that states will use force to enhance their relative position in the international system. Finally, it assumes that there is a clear hierarchy of issues in world politics, headed by the military-security issue. In short, it asserts that "high politics" (military issues) dominate "low politics" (economic, social, and technical issues).

The classical realist interpretation of world politics is both elegant and straightforward. Political and diplomatic interactions between sovereign states constitute the core of international relations. The outcomes of these interactions, according to realist theory, are largely determined by the distribution of power in the system. The now-famous billiard ball metaphor is a particularly apt representation of this view: "The realist model of world politics was simple and elegant. An image of states as billiard balls, interacting within a specific arena and according to established rules, became increasingly prevalent. Once the implication of the metaphor was grasped, that there are only a few immutable patterns of behaviour in politics – billiard balls, after all, are not very complex phenomenon – the principal preoccupation of statesmen became clear. They were to judge, by experience and intuition, the requisite amount of force to move one or another in a preferred direction" (Rothstein 1981, 389).

On the surface, realist theory would seem to help us understand the Canadian government's early interest in international sporting events and its potential (albeit modest) role in the ideological struggle between East and West. This is especially true in the case of Canada's rivalry with the Soviet Union over hockey and, to a somewhat lesser extent, with respect to the Taiwan issue during the run-up to the 1976 Olympic Games in Montreal. In addition, it would seem to be of some use in comprehending the decision taken by the Canadian government in support of the US–led boycott of the 1980 Olympic Games in Moscow.

At the outset, we identify the government's earliest interests in international sporting events with particular reference to Canada's declining fortunes in international hockey in the late 1950s and through the 1960s. We argue that the emergence of what we call "hockey diplomacy" and the importance of international hockey – both at a popular level and within the Canadian government – must be understood in the context of the Cold War realities that dominated the international system at that time. While the United States had no real interest in improving relations with the Soviet Union (since the anti-communist policy consensus which provided the *raison d'être* for US foreign policy actually required that Americans viewed the Soviet Union as an alien society and a dangerous adversary), Canada had every reason for cultivating relations with the Soviet Union. Realist theory holds that states will do whatever is necessary to maximize their relative power (and/or influence) in the international system.

Canada's real comparative advantage during the period we now refer to as the golden age of Canadian foreign policy lay in its role as a middle power: the honest broker or helpful fixer. Canada acted as a bridge between the Americans and the British in the formation of the North Atlantic community and defined the role of "peacekeeper and peacemaker" through its activities during the Suez crisis. Canadian diplomats believed that this role could logically be expanded to that of a mediator between the East and the West. After all, Canada had considerably more influence in this context than any objective assessment of its relative strengths would logically allow. Realist theory would expect nothing less; low-level linkages, which would elevate Canada's overall influence but not compromise its commitment to the Western alliance, made perfect sense. All sport exchanges, including the now-famous Canada–USSR hockey series in 1972, would become part of the larger drive to enhance cultural, scientific, and technical exchanges, thereby augmenting Canada's credibility and its influence.

The 1972 Canada–USSR hockey series was very successful for a number of reasons, not the least of which had to do with the realization that international sporting events had the potential to build or maintain a strong and coherent sense of national pride. Moreover, many people realized that sport had the capacity to be an effective instrument of foreign policy. This has to do largely with its tremendous popular appeal and with the fact that success (especially highly visible success) ultimately serves as a form of political and social validation.

The same lesson, in general terms, could be drawn from Trudeau's decision, in the early months of 1976, not to allow the Taiwanese to compete at the Montreal Olympics if they insisted on calling themselves the Republic of China. Ottawa chose to pursue its "one-China" policy despite considerable pressure from around the world, including Washington and London. The Canadian government in general and Trudeau in particular were criticized widely for politicizing the Olympics and for narrow nationalism. Not surprisingly, a realist interpretation of the events of 1976 would clearly suggest that Trudeau's position (however unpopular both at home and abroad) was entirely consistent with his new foreign-policy platform – one that saw Canada as a mentor state which could exercise considerable moral influence and a state which could and should provide some general moral leadership. All of this was in aid of enhancing Canada's overall position in the international system or at least, in aid of reducing its vulnerability *vis-à-vis* the United States.

Just a few years later, however, other nations would come to see the logic in "politicizing" the Olympic Games or, perhaps more accurately, could not avoid the natural and powerful opportunity to make a political statement. Following the lead of the US government, Canada decided in the early months of 1980 to support the boycott of the Olympic Games in Moscow as a response to the Soviet invasion of Afghanistan. The whole affair was coincident with what many political scientists saw as a dramatic return to the Cold War in the early 1980s. Realists were quick to point out that security issues still dominated the global policy agenda and that *rapprochement* between East and West was flawed in important ways. These issues are discussed at length throughout this book and especially in chapter 5, where some observations are offered with respect to the impact of the boycott on international sport and the connection with Canadian foreign policy.

The most compelling feature of the realist perspective – its profoundly simple, even parsimonious explanation of international political behaviour – proved in time to weaken its appeal. As our analysis of sport and Canadian foreign policy suggests, the realists' world of the 1950s and 1960s gave way to new realities in the early 1970s. The classic realist view seemed far too limited in a world characterized by a general relaxation in East-West tensions, a dramatically expanded level of international economic activity, the prominence of non-state actors, the increasing permeability of national borders, the breakdown of the Bretton Woods system (the post-war system of trade and payments), the decline of US hegemony, and the increasing focus on non-security issues. It goes without saying that the post – Cold War world of the 1990s is anything but a continuation of the realists' world of the 1950s and 1960s.

By the early 1970s, students and practitioners of international relations were actively looking for alternatives to the dominant realist view. The "world politics paradigm," pioneered and promoted by Robert

Keohane and Joseph Nye Jr (1972), emerged as a direct challenge to the logic of realism. It focused on the importance of transnational society, rather than interstate relations. The world politics paradigm was meant neither to replace the realist perspective nor to deny the relevance of interstate relations or the notions of power and national interest. Rather, this competing paradigm set out to extend the realists' understanding of contemporary international politics. It attempted to accomplish this task by introducing three specific amendments to realist theory. First, it maintained that states were not the only significant actors in world politics; various transnational actors (i.e., nongovernmental actors that operate across national boundaries) are also important in world politics. Second, the world politics paradigm added transgovernmental relations (i.e., direct interactions between agencies of different governments, where those agencies act relatively autonomously from central government control) to state-to-state relations. Finally, this perspective suggested that there is a multiplicity of issues on the global policy agenda and that the military-security issue no longer dominates that agenda. Even if the security issue was to dominate the agenda again, it would still be necessary to take into account other important issue areas.

By relaxing the state-centric assumption, the transnational relations perspective was successful in directing our attention to one of the most important structural problems in world politics: the extreme asymmetry of global actors. Where realism assumed a system of relatively equal actors (all of which were states), the world politics paradigm contends that the relations between the principal actors in world politics (both states and non-state actors) are highly unequal. Transnational business activity, for example, has traditionally been distributed very unevenly, with virtually all important activity originating in (or providing disproportionate benefits to) the developed market economies. The myth of state sovereignty and the emphasis on security issues (which were perpetrated by the realists) make the world seem less imbalanced than it is.

In addition to the assertion that states are not the only important actors in world politics, the world politics paradigm also relaxed the "state-as-actor" assumption, or the idea that national governments behave as single, unitary actors. The implication here is that international politics would include not only state-to-state relations and transnational relations but transgovernmental relations as well. Transgovernmental relations involve an increase in communications among governments. In particular, they draw attention to bureaucratic contacts that take place below the apex of power – pointing to the existence of a network of co-operative interactions among like-minded sub-units of different governments. Moreover, transgovernmental relations involve considerably more than simple transgovernmental policy co-ordination. According to this argument, regularized policy co-ordination often leads to changes in attitudes, where governments cease to be seen as closed decision-making units, and to the creation of transgovernmental élite networks. The resulting networks or coalitions amount to an alliance of sub-units of one government with like-minded agencies of other governments. International organizations, international regimes, economic summitry, and other forms of joint decision making have strengthened and legitimized this practice.

The transgovernmental dimension lends additional credence to three important features of the transnational relations perspective. First, the practical realization that conflict exists among various sub-units of national governments in the foreign-policy decision-making process challenges the realists' claim that national governments make decisions unitarily and rationally. In fact, the world politics paradigm is more in keeping with the bureaucratic-politics model of decision making, which suggests that national decisions are the result of a policy process characterized by conflict, compromise, and confusion among the constituent units of a national government. Some scholars see this connection as the crux of the transnational relations perspective.

Finally, transgovernmental relations underscore the increasing permeability of the nation-state. While transnational activities make societies more sensitive to one another and to systemic factors, national governments are pressed to control this non-governmental behaviour. Ironically, one possible result of these attempts to co-ordinate national policy is the further increase in direct bureaucratic contacts between sub-units of different governments. These transgovernmental relations add to the external threat posed by transnational organizations by challenging the autonomy of the state from within.

In sum, the challenge posed by the world politics paradigm introduced a number of important new factors to the study of world politics. These factors, which include the introduction of transnational and transgovernmental actors, the realization that bureaucratic politics applies in situations where interactions are transnational, and the notion of asymmetry, constitute an entirely new way of looking at world politics. The single largest point of departure between the two perspectives resides in the fact that the realist perspective focused on the rhetoric of national security whereas the transnational relations perspective is noted for its direct association with the notion of economic interdependence and its emphasis on cultural and social issues.

After a great deal of careful assessment and interpretation, we came to the conclusion that understanding the relationship between international sport and Canadian foreign policy was only possible through the conceptual lenses of transnational relations theory. Even in the three cases, noted above, where the realist explanation seemed eminently plausible (in chapters 2, 3, and 5), our research suggests that the realist version of the story (the power maximizing – influence maximizing version) was possible but incomplete. In all three cases, the relative importance of popular opinion, quasi-autonomous organizations, and other non-state actors could not be ignored. In the hockey diplomacy case, for example, we conclude that the real importance of the 1972 hockey series had more to do with the government's commitment to use international sport as a symbol of national unity than with an opportunity for new foreign-policy initiatives or roles. The same lesson (learned differently, however) can be gleaned from the chapter on the 1980 Moscow Olympics boycott. While Canada could hardly refuse to support the boycott (given its relationship with the United States), the final decision caused a great deal of public concern in Canada and clearly involved some political costs. Moreover, other important members of the Western alliance opted to take a very weak position and ultimately to allow individual sport associations (and, in effect, individual athletes) to decide for themselves. These incidents indicate both the weakness of the realist interpretation and the increasing influence of non-governmental and non-state actors.

As Andrew Fenton Cooper argues in his book *Canadian Culture: International Dimensions*, "cultural diplomacy is no longer the neglected aspect of foreign affairs" and is, in fact, "an essential dimension of Canadian diplomacy" (Cooper 1985, 3). We suggest throughout this book that much of Canadian foreign policy has to do with projecting abroad the habits of mind of Canadians. This is clearly the case in terms of Canada's commitment to multilateralism and order; it is equally clear with respect to Canada's initiation into peacekeeping and its long and venerable tradition in that area. We also would argue that this interpretation is confirmed by the story that we tell about the relationship between Canadian foreign policy and international sport.

This connection is made clear in the rest of the book. Chapter 3 has a great deal to say about cultural diplomacy and the ability of Canada to swim against the tide (especially the big waves that emerge just south of the 49th parallel) when it sees that there is both a political and a cultural principle at stake. In fact, all of the more recent empirical evidence (along with the conclusions that we draw from them) can be understood more fully in the context of the transnational relations paradigm. In chapter 4, we see the influence of both governmental and non-governmental transnational organizations in Canada's successful efforts to avoid a boycott by third-world Commonwealth nations of the

1978 Games in Edmonton. In our assessment of the early 1980s and of Canadian policy toward the Commonwealth and South Africa, we also see considerable evidence that transnational and transgovernmental factors are at work. Following the call by black African and other third-world Commonwealth countries to boycott the 1986 Edinburgh Games, a fierce political battle began to take shape that pitted influential sectors of External Affairs (which naturally supported such a boycott) against other departments, the Commonwealth Games Association, and the Canadian sport community. Those opposed to the boycott saw it as a measure that would only harm Canadian athletes while doing little or nothing to end apartheid. Eventually, Canadian athletes did participate in the Games, but not before a great many lessons were learned on both sides about how and under what circumstances such decisions are taken.

All of this led to a situation where the government decided actively to pursue a policy on international sport and to concede (if only by deed) that sport could play some role in promoting Canada's foreign-policy goals and priorities. We go on to contend that the lessons drawn from the transnational relations framework argue for an expanded role for sport in Canadian diplomacy. This can be seen in the discussion of the cabinet decision of October 1987, the controversy over Secretary of State Clark's decision to restrict entry into Canada for South African athletes, the continuing debate over South Africa, and the broader international debate on sanctions and South Africa. This leads us to focus in later chapters on the most recent initiatives taken by the Canadian government with respect to the Commonwealth, and then to examine the International Olympic Committee (IOC) as a transnational organization. While not strictly speaking part of the story about sport and Canadian diplomacy, this penultimate chapter is nonetheless both essential to our overall argument and helpful in drawing lessons from the Canadian case. It is especially so in the sense that there is a direct relationship among transnational organizations such as the Organization of African Unity and the IOC, which have played a clear and often compelling role in the formulation of Canadian foreign policy.

BETWEEN THEORY AND PRACTICE

The contrast between a realist image and an interdependence image has been a powerful theme in international relations scholarship since the late 1970s. The emergence of the transnational relations perspective and the rebirth of the historically conditioned dependence perspective have proven to be both workable alternatives to the logic of classical realism and important tools in understanding a world that is increasingly characterized by rapid change and by structural uncertainty. Interestingly, given recent events in the Soviet Union, Eastern Europe, and the Persian Gulf, some work in the field has returned to more traditional forms of realist thinking. An increasing number of students of world politics have come to believe that the preoccupation with transnational and global concerns may have obscured some of the more important and more enduring elements of the realist position. As Kalevi Holsti has noted: "Analysts have been so impressed by growing interdependence that they have ignored a simultaneous or parallel process that results in increased international fragmentation ... while transactions between societies have indeed grown dramatically throughout this century, nationalism, separatism and international disintegration have also been prominent ... The two trends are taking place concurrently" (Holsti 1980, 23). Nonetheless, interdependence and transnational relations are especially useful in understanding extra-state, subnational, and other relationships involving economic, social, and cultural issues.

OVERVIEW

As we suggested above, the transnational relations theme runs through our entire examination of sport and Canadian foreign policy. We start our analysis in the late 1960s, when realist theories of international relations were at their peak and the Cold War was still very much a reality of international politics. Even so, international sport organizations played an important role in the events that led to the historical 1972 Canada-Soviet hockey series and to the establishment of an International Sports Relations desk in the Public Affairs Bureau in the Department of External Affairs. It is around these events, which we have coined "hockey diplomacy," that we commence our story in chapter 2.

In chapter 3 we examine the forces and events that led up to the confrontation between Prime Minister Trudeau and the IOC over the right of Taiwan to compete as the Republic of China in the 1976 Montreal Summer Olympics in the face of Trudeau's new one-China policy. An unanticipated event at the Montreal Games themselves was the boycott by twenty-two black African nations in protest over New Zealand's continued sporting contacts with South Africa. International anti-apartheid sport organizations played a central role in orchestrating this boycott and in thwarting the Canadian government's unsuccessful efforts to avert it.

In chapter 4 we trace the successful measures that the Canadian government took to woo these organizations and black African nations in order to ensure that such a boycott would not be repeated at the 1978 Commonwealth Games in Edmonton. Central to these efforts was the adoption by the Commonwealth heads of government in 1977 of the Gleneagles Declaration, designed to put an end to sporting contacts with South Africa by Commonwealth nations. Next, in chapter 5, we turn to the US–led boycott of the 1980 Moscow Summer Olympics. Here we speculate as to why, on this occasion, Trudeau was content to fall in line with the United States in its frantic efforts to impose a world-wide boycott of the Moscow Games in protest over the Soviet invasion of Afghanistan, while once again coming into conflict with the IOC and indeed with the Canadian Olympic Association.

Canada's international sport initiatives in the 1980s centred largely around the country's policies on apartheid in South Africa and its leadership ambitions in the Commonwealth. In chapter 6 we put Canadian policies about sporting contacts with South Africa in the first half of the 1980s in the perspective of world-wide efforts, both governmental and non-governmental, to isolate that country in order to bring down apartheid. Sport played an important role in this fight, and this chapter ends with one of its most significant milestones, the very successful boycott, led by international anti-apartheid organizations, of the 1986 Commonwealth Games in Edinburgh. Chapter 7 traces the forces and events that led up to the 1987 cabinet record of decision to use sport more extensively in the pursuit of Canada's foreign-policy initiatives. Shortly thereafter, Secretary of State for External Affairs Joe Clark was forced to take measures to ban South African professional sportspersons from playing in Canada in order to maintain his credibility as chair of the (Commonwealth) Committee of Foreign Ministers on Southern Africa (CFMSA). Both these events clearly illustrate the conflicts and compromises among governmental departments in establishing priorities and strategies for Canada's international sport initiatives.

Next we examine the sport initiatives that Clark took in the CFMSA, not only to help developing countries compete more equitably in the Commonwealth Games and to give them a better sense of ownership in the Commonwealth Games Federation, but also to create more harmony in the Commonwealth itself. We conclude chapter 8 with a discussion of more recent developments on the international sport scene, and in South Africa itself, that have changed the strategy of the international anti-apartheid sport movement from isolating South Africa to integrating sport in the country itself. In chapter 9 we examine the IOC in the light of transnational relations theory and conclude that it, indeed, is a transnational organization. In the last chapter we expand further on the transnational theme, relating it to the way in which sport and foreign policy have intersected in Canada in the 1970s and 1980s.

Finally, we turn to a discussion of sport and international politics in the new world of interdependence, drawing some conclusions about recent events and speculating about the rest of the century.

CHAPTER TWO

Hockey Diplomacy

Canada's declining fortunes in international hockey in the 1950s and 1960s contrasted sharply with the golden age of its foreign policy, when it occupied an influential "middle-power" role in the international system. Back home, both the lack of success and the tarnished image of Canada's representative hockey teams abroad caused considerable concern in governmental circles. Consequently the Department of External Affairs became involved, albeit reluctantly and reactively, in what we call "hockey diplomacy."

That hockey should have been the catalyst for a growing awareness of the role sport could play in Canada's foreign-policy initiatives should come as no surprise. The penchant that Canadians hold for their un-official national game has been well documented elsewhere (see, for instance, Kidd and Macfarlane 1972; Dryden and MacGregor 1989). The trade that sent Wayne Gretzky to Los Angeles in 1988 was one of that year's major news events; Canadians were most upset that their "national treasure" was lost to the United States.

RELATIONS BETWEEN CANADA
AND THE SOVIET UNION

Because "hockey diplomacy" is intricately tied to the Soviet Union, we commence with a brief overview of the relations between Canada and the Soviet Union in the immediate post-war period. Canada's woes in international hockey were inexorably tied to the Soviet Union's rising fortunes in the game. Hockey diplomacy found its ultimate expression in the Canada–Soviet Union series in 1972. This country's relations with the Soviet Union deteriorated dramatically in the immediate post-war period, as the world moved inexorably toward Soviet-American rivalry and Cold War hostility. Once the Axis powers had successfully been defeated, the uncertainty and confusion of the post-war world led quickly to a split between East and West. In the early Cold War period, between 1946 and 1952, mutual antagonism and belligerence seemed the order of the day. Virtually all international events – from the communist *coup d'état* in Czechoslovakia in 1948, the Berlin Blockade, the formation of NATO in 1949, and the rise of the communists in mainland China, through to the Korean War and the Taiwan Straits crisis that followed – were seen as part of the ideological crisis between East and West, between capitalism and communism. Canada, as the nearest neighbour and closest ally of the United States, was quickly drawn into this Cold War conflict. Moreover, even if it had been possible to maintain some objectivity, incidents such as the much-publicized defection of Soviet diplomat Igor Gouzenko made "normal" relations between Canada and the USSR virtually impossible.

These relations thawed somewhat with the conclusion of formal hostilities in Korea and the death of Joseph Stalin. Canada undertook a number of initiatives, such as exchanges of trade and fisheries delegations and the visit to the Soviet Union in 1955 of the secretary of state for external affairs, Lester B. Pearson. This was the first time that any NATO foreign minister had ever visited the USSR (Munro and Inglis 1973, 191).

Any positive atmosphere that had been created between Canada and the Soviet Union in the mid-1950s, however, was destroyed in 1956 when the Soviets suppressed the uprising in Hungary. Relations were further complicated by the Egyptian-Israeli conflict, armed intervention by Britain and France, and the danger of Soviet interference on behalf of Egypt (Ford 1989, 34). Bilateral relations between the two superpowers, the United States and the Soviet Union, deteriorated even further over the impasse created by the Vietnam War. This atmosphere of hostility and distrust was, of course, to have an effect on Canadian-Soviet relations as well, even though Canada was lukewarm about US involvement in Vietnam. Ultimately, Canada was firmly rooted in the Western camp and shared the common assessment of the Soviet Union as a threat.

Although the United States was not enthusiastic about improved relations with the Soviet Union during the 1960s, Canada had both an interest in doing so and greater flexibility in its foreign policy. Two opportunities to improve Canadian-Soviet relations presented themselves during that decade. First, the prospect of a crop failure in the Soviet Union in 1966 coincided with the expiry of the Canadian-Soviet trade agreement and led to the signing by Canada of a contract for nine million tons of wheat over a three-year period (ibid., 92). When the Soviets found out that they did not need that much wheat, the Canadian

Wheat Board decided to defer the contract in the interests of preserving its special relationship with Exportkhleb, its Soviet counterpart. Second, the Canadian government extended an invitation to the Soviets in 1966 to send a parliamentary delegation to Canada. This visit, led by Dmitri Polyansky, resulted in the consolidation of Canada's position in the Soviet wheat trade, an increased interest in Canada as an important capitalist country, and the beginnings of a thaw in Canadian-Soviet relations (ibid., 92–4).

Following the successful Canadian visit of Polyansky, Prime Minister Pearson wrote to Soviet premier Alexei Kosygin to express interest in expanding relations with the USSR through the signing of a two-year Cultural, Scientific, and Technical Exchange Agreement between the Soviet Union and Canada. Approval for such a move had been granted by cabinet in August 1966. Instructions were given to the Department of External Affairs, along with the Visits Panel (which consisted of departmental members and representatives of National Health and Welfare), to negotiate a draft exchange agreement with the Soviet Union for Cabinet approval.[1]

As a follow-up to Pearson's letter to Kosygin, the Canadian ambassador to the USSR, Robert Ford, called upon Foreign Minister Andrei Gromyko to seek Soviet concurrence in this proposal and to pave the way for the impending visit of the secretary of state for external affairs. It was during the Soviet visit of Paul Martin in November 1966 that formal agreement was reached to increase cultural, scientific, and technological exchanges between the USSR and Canada (Ford 1989, 97–9). The Canadian government took the position that linkages at the level of low politics – technical, social, and economic issues – could be pursued without compromising its broader commitment to Western ideals.

By 1967, as a result of initiatives from the Fitness and Amateur Sport Directorate,[2] the Department of External Affairs had proposed that sport exchanges be included in the Cultural, Scientific, and Technical Exchange Agreement between Canada and the USSR.[3] Consequently, by 1971 Article 14 of the agreement stipulated, "Both Governments will encourage and facilitate exchanges of athletes and athletic teams, and of specialists in the fields of physical education, recreation, and sport" (Canada 1974, 6).

DECLINING IMAGE OF
CANADIAN HOCKEY

These political developments, along with the events in the world of international sport outlined in chapter 1, all came together for Canada in the world of hockey. In the halcyon days of its diplomacy, Canadian fortunes in international hockey began to turn sour. The Soviet Union's spectacular successes in international sport were now extended to hockey, a sphere where Canada had had its own way for two decades. This ascendancy came to an abrupt end in 1954, when the Soviet team scored an upset victory over Canada in the World Hockey Championships. That this victory was no fluke became evident when the Soviet hockey team defeated Canada and won the gold medal in the 1956 Winter Olympic Games. Canada finished third, behind the United States. Dismayed Canadian fans and the news media reacted to these defeats as if they were national calamities.

At this time Canada's entries in international tournaments usually comprised the team winning the Allen Cup (emblematic of Canadian "amateur" hockey supremacy), strengthened with whatever other good players could be added. These teams played a different style of hockey than did their counterparts in Europe and the Soviet Union. Used to many of the more unsavoury tactics of the North American professional game, the behaviour of these Canadian teams, especially when they were losing, was unacceptable to the fans or press of European countries, particularly in Scandinavia. Canadian players often were described by the press as "dangerous" and "ruthless," and Canadian teams were frequently accused of "hooliganism."[4] In one instance, the Penticton Vees were portrayed by Jim Coleman (1987, 78) as a "rollicking" team of reinstated professionals and amateurs who had gone to West Germany in 1955 with the sole purpose of avenging Canada's defeat by the Soviets in the 1954 World Championships. "From the outset, the Penticton Vees didn't act like members of the Canadian diplomatic corps. On the ice, they hit anything that moved," conduct that prompted the European crowds to hoot and whistle their disapproval (ibid., 78–9).

Similarly embarrassing incidents disturbed many Canadian ambassadors, who conveyed their concerns to the Department of External Affairs. In 1960, for instance, the Canadian ambassador to Sweden was provoked to write that "the placid surface of Swedish-Canadian relations" had come to "an ignominious and abrupt end" with the collision of the Swedish and Canadian hockey teams on the ice at Squaw Valley. The Swedish press concluded that for sport-minded Canadians who followed the fate of "their" hockey team with keen interest, "the prevailing image of Canada and Canadians was probably at its nadir."[5]

Canadians, indeed, were becoming distressed about the decline in Canada's international hockey supremacy. Newspaper articles and remarks in the House of Commons deploring the performance of the country's representatives in these tournaments became more common. Member of Parliament J.R. Taylor, an advocate of government support for sport, drew the attention of the House to the fact that "after the Olympic games of 1948, 1952 and 1956 and after the event at Squaw Valley, considerable publicity was given to Canada's inadequate showing." He maintained that frustrations stemmed from the fact that Canada did not assemble and train its best players (HC *Debates*, 22 June 1960, 5270). Similarly, some Canadian ambassadors were beginning to suggest that the country should either send teams of its best players according to a national selection process or else stay out of European tours.[6] But the ironclad ban against professionals remained in force, both in the Olympics and at World Championships. This restriction left Canada sending its so-called amateur teams, bolstered by reinstated amateurs from the National Hockey League (NHL). In 1961 the Trail Smoke Eaters provided Canadian fans with a small ray of hope when they won the World Championships in Geneva, Switzerland.

Meanwhile, Father David Bauer, a priest who had played professional hockey himself, had a dream that Canada could develop a competitive international hockey team with amateur players if the players could be kept together year-round. Thus the Canadian National Team became a reality. Father Bauer's team stayed together from 1963 until 1969 and won a great deal of admiration, both at home and abroad, for its sportsmanship, as well as its grit and determination. But it could never quite win the "big" games and was unable to win either a gold medal at the Olympics or a World Championship. As a result, those concerned with Canada's international hockey fortunes began to look for alternatives to Father Bauer's team.

The problems surrounding Canadian hockey performances abroad were of sufficient concern to the Department of External Affairs that a memorandum was prepared in May 1966 to focus attention on the issue. This undertaking stemmed from the fear that hockey tours were having a damaging effect on Canada's image and the belief that the whole matter was of sufficient political importance to be drawn to the attention of the prime minister.[7] This memorandum pointed out that hockey was synonymous with Canada in many areas of Europe. It argued that because the sport was the most conspicuous element of the Canadian presence in these countries, it should be viewed as one of the country's chief diplomatic weapons.

The diminution of goodwill for Canada that stemmed from the "brutish" and "reprehensible" conduct of many Canadian hockey players was, of course, more distressing to the Department of External Affairs than the record of losses in international play. Incidents of Canadian players' body-checking techniques, displays of bad temper, repeated penalties, and defiance of referees were conveyed to television audiences at home, often numbering in the millions. In short,

External Affairs considered Canadian amateur hockey to have clearly failed as a goodwill exercise. Although the department proferred a few suggestions for dealing with some of the main problems, it concluded that the present system was "manifestly inadequate and deserving of a careful and thorough search for improvement."[8]

But little in the way of concrete policy came out of these exhortations. According to Lou Lefaive, the director of Fitness and Amateur Sport at the time, it was common practice at External Affairs in this period simply to pass on letters of protest from Canadian ambassadors in Europe about the hockey teams' behaviour to the Canadian Amateur Hockey Association, accompanied with a note of admonition.[9] One measure that John Munro, minister of national health and welfare (with responsibilities for fitness and amateur sport), and Lou Lefaive urged upon the Department of External Affairs in the late 1960s was the appoinment of hockey attachés in Canadian embassies in key Scandinavian and eastern European countries. Such attachés would help to establish good relations with the host country's hockey officials and the press and would act to introduce local customs and conventions, particularly about hockey, to visiting Canadian hockey teams. Nothing came of this proposal in External Affairs.[10]

The External Affairs memo of May 1966 did, however, stir up some government action. Shortly after its completion, the then minister of national health and welfare, Allan MacEachen, announced a wide-ranging study of amateur hockey in Canada. The review was conducted by the hockey committee of the National Advisory Council on Fitness and Amateur Sport, whose chairperson was Willard L'Heureux. The scope of the study included Canadian participation in international competition and the role of Canada's national hockey team.[11] The *Report on Amateur Hockey in Canada* was tabled in the House of Commons in January 1967, followed by *Minor-Age Hockey in Canada* in October 1967 and the *Final Report* in February 1968.[12] These documents provided an exhaustive examination of amateur hockey in Canada, including the identification of problems and recommendations for their solution.

EVENTS LEADING UP TO THE FORMATION OF HOCKEY CANADA

This time Pierre Trudeau was campaigning in the federal election of 1968. During a campaign speech delivered at Selkirk College in Castlegar, British Columbia, he publicly deplored Canada's showing in international hockey. Trudeau's promise in this speech to establish a task force to look at matters pertaining to "amateur" sport in Canada was fulfilled when he became prime minister. The Task Force on Sport for Canadians commenced work in August 1968; its major preoccupation, to the surprise of few, was with hockey. Because of the short time frame that had been established for the task force, its members took advantage of the work that had already been completed by the hockey committee of the National Advisory Council on Fitness and Amateur Sport, particularly the *Report on Amateur Hockey in Canada*. As well, the task force received briefs from knowledgeable hockey persons and held discussions with players, coaches, officials, business leaders, and politicians, and with ambassadors in Stockholm, Helsinki, and Moscow, where Canadian teams had been involved in international competitions (Task Force 1969, 25).

But before the task force could complete its work, the minister of national health and welfare, John Munro, asked its chairperson, Harold Rae, to get started on one of its key recommendations, the establishment of a body to oversee hockey in Canada. The concept of Hockey Canada, according to Douglas Fisher (who was intimately involved in its establishment), was Rae's brain-child.[13] Following Munro's request, Rae sent out invitations for a meeting, to be held in the Château Laurier in Ottawa on 10 December 1968, to discuss ways and means of placing Canada's most effective amateur hockey team in world competition. Invitees included representatives of the two Canadian professional hockey teams and the Canadian Amateur Hockey Association (CAHA), executives of Canada's National Hockey Team, the president of the National Hockey League (NHL), interested business leaders, and members of the Task Force on Sports for Canadians.[14] The meeting was unanimous in agreeing that the first essential step in resolving this problem was the formation of a corporation, to be known as Hockey Canada.

Hockey Canada became a reality in late February 1969 at a meeting convened by John Munro.[15] Three prominent Canadian businessmen were elected to the key executive posts: Max Bell, chairperson; Charles Hay, president; and Ian Sinclair, head of the finance committee. Alan Eagleson, a Toronto lawyer and executive director of the NHL Players' Association, was appointed to chair the public relations committee. Leighton "Hap" Emms, a former NHL player and a leading coach and entrepreneur in Ontario junior hockey, became the general manager of Canada's national team (Coleman 1987, 116).

Hockey Canada was to be a non-profit organization, at arm's length from the federal government and governed by a twelve-member board. Three board members were to be appointed by the federal government and two by the CAHA; two members were to come from the business community. One representative was to come from each of the two

North American professional hockey leagues and their respective player associations. The final group represented was the Canadian Intercollegiate Athletic Union (Buckwold, Caouette, et al. 1977, 13). This structure was intended to serve as a catalyst in bringing the various constituent hockey groups together under one "umbrella."[16]

Hockey Canada had two mandates: to manage and develop Canada's National Team and to foster and develop hockey in Canada (Manning 1974, 1). The latter function was never carried out because of jurisdictional disputes with the CAHA. That organization resented the intrusion of a new body into affairs that it saw as its sole prerogative. Initially, the CAHA even ignored Hockey Canada's edicts about club participation abroad.[17] But because it was becoming increasingly dependent on the federal government for its funds, it eventually had to give up its international responsibilities to Hockey Canada. However, another reason that Hockey Canada never carried out its domestic mandate was that there was little glamour attached to developing amateur hockey programs at home, especially in relation to the organization's international responsibilities. It should be noted, however, that in its early years Hockey Canada did provide scholarships to promising young players who wished to attend Canadian universities rather than accept hockey scholarships in the United States. This assistance did help add to the credibility of the Canadian university hockey program as a viable alternative to playing college hockey in the United States. Hockey Canada, and in particular its president, Charles Hay, also played a leading role in getting a Canadian hockey coaching certification program off the ground.[18] This was the precursor of the national coaching certification program, one which has been widely praised and often copied in other countries.

INTERNATIONAL HOCKEY NEGOTIATIONS

From its incorporation in 1969, Hockey Canada directed most of its energies towards achieving its international mandate. First, it assumed responsibility for Father Bauer's National Team. Then it moved forward to carry out one of the task force's most important recommendations: to persuade the International Ice Hockey Federation (IIHF) to declare the World Championship an "open" competition. This measure would allow Canada to field a team that included its best players, that is, professionals (Manning 1974, 2).

As executive director of the NHL Players' Association and chair of Hockey Canada's public relations committee, Alan Eagleson was ideally positioned to further Canada's efforts in getting the IIHF to agree to the use of professionals in future World Championships. According to Jim Coleman (1987, 131), Eagleson had been delegated by Prime Minister Trudeau and John Munro to be the Canadian government's official negotiator in all matters relating to international hockey. However, Fisher maintains that he and Sydney Wise (a historian at Carleton University who, along with Fisher, was a co-author of the task force report) were asked by John Munro to represent him at the upcoming IIHF meeting.[19]

Be that as it may, in the spring of 1969 Eagleson travelled to Moscow to explore with the Soviets the concept of a world cup in hockey. Through the intercession of Canadian ambassador Robert Ford, Eagleson was able to meet with V.I. Koval, chief of the International Relations Division of the Soviet Sports Committee, and Andrei Starovoitov, deputy chief of the Hockey Department. Eagleson presented the Soviet officials with a statement on the position of the NHL Players' Association, which made it clear that they would accept any challenge from the Soviet team. According to Ambassador Ford, what the statement lacked in "diplomatic finesse," it made up for in its vigorous rebuttal of any suggestion that the NHL was avoiding a match with the Soviet team.[20] The procedure, as established during the meeting, required that an initiative be made to the IIHF by the USSR, a move that was unlikely to happen immediately.

Hockey Canada made its international debut in Stockholm in April 1969, when the National Team, still under the tutelage of Father Bauer, finished fourth in a six-team tournament. At this time, the five other nations represented in the tournament's "A" group were keenly aware of Canadian government interest in the country's hockey future, and they realized that if they wanted to keep Canada as a member of the IIHF, they would have to be prepared to allow Canada to be represented by professionals from the NHL. Consequently, at the next IIHF meeting in Crans, Switzerland, delegates agreed that in all future world competitions Canada would be permitted to use nine minor league professionals as well as reinstated amateurs (Coleman 1987, 117). Douglas Fisher, who by now was one of the federal government's representatives on Hockey Canada, was present at this meeting, along with other Hockey Canada board members Charles Hay, Chris Lang, and Father Bauer. The CAHA was represented at these meetings by Gordon Juckes and Earl Dawson. There is no record of Alan Eagleson's attendance (ibid., 118).

During the fall of 1969, the Department of External Affairs learned that the Soviets were seeking a reversal of the Crans decision because their eligibility for the 1972 Winter Olympics might be jeopardized if they played a Canadian team that included professionals. The Soviets, according to Fisher, had received threats about the consequences of "tainting" (as amateurs playing against professionals was termed in those days) from Avery Brundage, president of the International Olympic Committee (IOC). This behaviour was certainly consistent with Brundage's abhorrence of professionals in Olympic sport. To deal with the issue, the president of the IIHF, Bunny Ahearne, called a special meeting of the IIHF council.[21] Ahearne, according to Fisher, was also opposed to the use of professional players, but for different reasons. He could see that if professionals came to dominate the IIHF, the presidential sinecure that he had carefully built for himself over the years would be jeopardized.[22]

But before the Canadian delegation departed for this crucial meeting of the IIHF, John Munro called the members together at the Toronto airport for a briefing. At this meeting, government and Hockey Canada officials made it clear to CAHA delegates that the only way the IIHF would be convinced that Canada was serious about open world hockey championships was to withdraw from the IIHF (thus giving up the right to host the 1970 World Hockey Championships) if it rescinded the Crans agreement on participation by professionals. Ahearne, according to Lou Lefaive, was convinced that the CAHA would never turn down the chance to make the anticipated large profit from these championships. At this meeting, Munro assured the CAHA that it would be reimbursed for all expenses that it had incurred in anticipation of these championships. However, he evidently refused the CAHA's request that the federal government also reimburse it for the anticipated profits. Munro ended the meeting by assuring all delegates of the unqualified support of the federal government. This meeting, according to Lefaive, was a critical step towards Canada's eventually persuading the IIHF to agree to open championships.[23]

At the IIHF meeting, convened in Geneva in January 1970, the Soviet position was supported by the Swedes, Finns, and Czechs, and the Crans decision was rescinded. Consequently, Canada withdrew from international competition, vowing not to return until the basis of eligibility was reduced simply to a player's nationality. When the country refused to change its position, the IIHF took the 1970 World Championships (along with about half a million dollars' worth of anticipated profit) away from Winnipeg and awarded the championships to Sweden.[24]

The federal government subsequently honoured the financial commitments made by John Munro and paid off the $160,000 loan that the CAHA had taken out to guarantee the deficit of the National Team from 1965 to 1969. It also paid the bills that had accumulated in anticipation of the World Championships in Winnipeg. Hockey Canada, knowing that it had the support of the federal government, made good its financial obligations to members of the National Team who had enrolled in university programs. All in all, the cost to the federal treasury in paying off CAHA and Hockey Canada obligations totalled more than $350,000 (Coleman 1987, 118–9).

While the 1972 Winter Olympics were pending, further negotiations directed toward Canada's re-entry into international hockey competition were seen as being futile. But by February 1972, negotiations had re-opened, and they included an immediate approach through Canadian diplomatic personnel,[25] presumably because of the importance attached to this endeavour by the Trudeau administration.

When Trudeau had become prime minister in 1968, *rapprochement* with Moscow had been an element in his new foreign-policy strategy. He believed that the Soviet Union had to be brought into the mainstream of world politics and that Canada had a unique opportunity to help in this process (Ford 1989, 134–5). Thus his visit to the Soviet Union in 1971, a trip that was regarded as highly successful in strengthening Canadian-Soviet relations, came as no surprise. Soviet premier Alexei Kosygin later remarked that no other Canadian leader had been as well known or as popular in the USSR.[26] Among the most important developments during this visit were the signing of the Canadian-Soviet Protocol on Consultations and an umbrella agreement on economic co-operation (ibid., 117–20). The protocol was an attempt to "regularize" Canadian-Soviet relations, and it provided for consultation on specific international problems of mutual interest, such as Arctic pollution, trade in natural gas, and family reunification. It also called for meetings whenever necessary and on not less than a yearly basis. According to Jack Granatstein and Robert Bothwell, Kosygin saw the protocol as one that "would embrace all situations, not only crises, [and that] regular diplomatic consultations were the best way to ensure that the protocol worked" (Granatstein and Bothwell 1990, 194). The Soviet premier expressed pleasure at how well relations between the two countries were proceeding, and later that same year, Trudeau invited Kosygin for a return visit to Canada.

It was during this exchange of visits that hockey relationships became a subject of intergovernmental discussions.[27] Both leaders realized that the sport formed a common bond between the two countries, which could be used to strengthen bilateral relations. The significance of this realization can be seen in Trudeau's personal view of foreign policy. According to Ivan Head, his advisor in this area, Trudeau regarded foreign policy for the most part "as the pursuit of Canada's domestic interests abroad" (Radwanski 1978, 183). This philosophy was clearly articulated in the federal white paper *Foreign Policy for Canadians*, released in 1970 (Canada 1970). For Trudeau, the conjunction of the national goal of re-entering international hockey competitions with the opportunity to strengthen relations with the USSR must have been irresistible. However, it was a curious juxtaposition – *détente* at the government level at the same time as Canadians were anxious to field a team in international hockey that was capable of defeating the Soviets.

When the time was ripe, in early 1972, to resume negotiations on re-entering IIHF competitions, the Department of External Affairs offered its services to the CAHA and Hockey Canada to help resolve the international hockey impasse. The department had come to recognize its interest in Canada's role in international hockey, particularly with respect to the Soviet Union, and it was increasingly aware of its responsibility for contributing to the planning for international hockey matters.[28] As a step in this direction, the director general of the Bureau of Public Affairs called a meeting in February 1972 with Charles Hay, president of Hockey Canada, Lou Lefaive, who by this time was also one of the directors of Hockey Canada, and Gordon Juckes, executive director of the CAHA. Discussions at the meeting focused on ways in which the Department of External Affairs and the Canadian embassies in Moscow, Prague, and Stockholm could take a more active role in liaison and negotiation, in order to get Canada back into top-quality international play. It was also agreed that a three-person committee consisting of Hay, Lefaive, and Joe Kryczka, president of the CAHA, would be responsible for Canadian dealings in international hockey.[29]

Earlier that month, Canadian officials in Moscow had met with Andrei Starovoitov and other prominent Soviet hockey officials to discuss the state of Canadian-Soviet hockey relations. All the Soviet officials present at the meeting were unanimous in wanting to re-establish hockey contacts between the two countries. Starovoitov was urged to contact the Canadian delegation at the Winter Olympics in Sapporo and to speak to the CAHA representative there.[30]

As a result of negotiations with the Soviets by the federal government, Hockey Canada, the CAHA, and Canadian diplomats, agreement was reached during an IIHF meeting in Prague in April 1972 for an eight-game series to be played in September between the Canadian and Soviet teams. Because individual countries were represented at IIHF meetings by the respective presidents of national hockey associations, Kryczka was Canada's spokesperson at these deliberations. According to Lefaive, Kryczka stood up admirably to the three days of gruelling meetings and was central to Canada's success in this endeavour.[31] The Letter of Agreement on the Canadian–USSR Exchange, signed in Prague on 18 April 1972, allowed the CAHA to select an "unrestricted" Canadian team to play in the series.[32] According to Fisher, Alan

Eagleson, although not present at these meetings or part of the Canadian negotiation team, was able to grab most of the publicity and credit by being the first to phone the news home to Canada.[33]

THE 1972 CANADA–USSR HOCKEY SERIES

The announcement from Prague of the Canada-Soviet series was greeted with jubilation by Canadian hockey fans. In Europe the press surmised that the prestige of Canada had been seriously damaged by previous defeats of Canadian teams and that the series was an endeavour to rehabilitate the country's tarnished hockey image. The Canadian press also implied that Canada's prestige was at stake.[34]

Because of the political importance of the series and the myriad of diplomatic details that arose as a result of the negotiations, the Department of External Affairs established an International Sports Relations desk in 1972 to deal with the preparations for the September series (Morse 1987a, 19). Another reason for the establishment of this desk, however, was that the Soviet Union insisted that negotiations and protocol be handled formally through the two countries' respective foreign offices.[35] Correspondence between the Canadian hockey delegation and Starovoitov was henceforth channelled through the Department of External Affairs and the Canadian embassy in Moscow. Hockey Canada called upon the Moscow embassy to finalize the agreement reached with the Soviets in Prague, to make television arrangements for both the Canada–USA and European parts of the series, and to plan for the Soviet and Canadian supporters who would be accompanying their teams.

In Ottawa, government officials met with representatives from Hockey Canada to discuss how senior political personalities might be associated with the series and which Soviet politicians to invite in order to emphasize the importance of this exchange for Canada–USSR relations. Of key importance in avoiding problems during these extensive preparations was the Bureau of Public Affairs, which was responsible for international liaison, government representation and hospitality, and co-ordination with the Prime Minister's Office.[36]

The Canada-Soviet hockey series in the fall of 1972 was one of the most memorable events in Canadian sport history. The series is still remembered for its dramatic finish in the eighth and deciding game in Moscow, in which Paul Henderson scored a last-minute goal to win both the game and the series for Canada. Most of Canada (or so it seemed at the time) followed this series on television, and thousands of Canadians travelled to Moscow to see the games there.

Canadian officials took advantage of the occasion by sending a governmental delegation, headed by the minister of veteran affairs, Arthur Laing, and scheduling an official visit of the under-secretary of state for external affairs, A.E. Ritchie. At the first game of the Moscow series, Leonid Brezhnev, Alexei Kosygin, Nikolai Podgorny, Dmitri Polyansky, Alexander Shelepin, and many other members of the Russian hierarchy invited the Canadian delegation to join them in the government box, and Kosygin later received them in the Kremlin for a discussion of Canada–USSR relations, which was favourably reported in the press. In a somewhat more subdued assessment of the series, Ambassador Robert Ford felt that considerable interest in Canada had been aroused, which might in future facilitate his task in other diplomatic fields.[37]

CONCLUSION

There are a number of lessons that emerge from our story of hockey diplomacy. The 1972 Canada–USSR hockey series was, in itself, significant in three respects. First, it revealed the enormous potential of international sport in general and hockey in particular to generate national interest, enthusiasm, and pride. The success of the series, along with the other measures that the federal government took in the early 1970s to improve Canada's international sport performances, increased its penchant for using sport as a symbol of national unity and as another means to promote its own interests. Sport was also beginning to be seen as a novel and potentially useful tool of diplomacy. One view, expressed by Eric Morse, former head of International Sports Relations for External Affairs, is that "the 1972 series really was seminal for External's appreciation of sport as an element of Canadian international relations" (Morse 1987a, 18).

Ironically, this subtle, but important realization by the Canadian government that sport had a useful diplomatic purpose was destined to take a back seat to more dramatic events. Sport was to become much better known in international affairs as a vehicle for making overt political statements. Boycotts and threats of boycotts became common phenomena in the 1970s and 1980s, in part because they represented a safe, but highly visible way of exerting international political pressure. Sport boycotts were particularly effective when used in connection with the Olympic Games because of the intense public interest and television coverage attached to them. These boycotts were to cause much anguish and frustration among international sport organizations and great heartbreak and disappointment for many world-class athletes. Outright terrorist activities would also be increasingly associated with international sporting events (see Franks, Hawes, and Macintosh 1988, for a more detailed account of the uses to which sport has recently been put by nations seeking to further their foreign-policy goals).

International sport organizations, and in particular, the IOC, were unable to develop effective strategies to combat the use of sport boycotts, in part because they refused to admit that sport had a clear and inexorable political dimension, both domestic and international. It was not until Juan Antonio Samaranch became president of the IOC that the organization began to take effective political action to head off boycotts. (We say more of this in chapter 10.)

Second, the series illustrated that hockey still had the potential to both help and hinder Canada's image abroad. Press coverage of the games criticized the conduct of Canadian players, and the Soviet fans demonstrated their disapproval of Canadian roughness with ear-splitting whistling.[38] In commenting on the Soviets' stunning victory over Team Canada by a score of 7 to 3 in the opening game of the series in the Montreal Forum, Scott Young wrote, "That part of the nation [Canada] that was not especially disgusted by the score was disgusted with the chippy, belligerent play Team Canada had shown in face of adversity" (Young 1976, 171). The two exhibition games Team Canada played against the Swedish national team prior to the second half of the series in the Soviet Union could be described as public-relations disasters, as they degenerated into ugly brawls. The Canadian ambassador to Sweden, Margaret Meagher, was reported to have taken it upon herself to go to the Canadian dressing-room to reprimand the team (ibid., 177–8), and the Stockholm papers exploited all the unpleasantness of the games by referring to North Americans as "savages" (Coleman 1987, 154). According to Douglas Fisher, Alan Eagleson, in his own inimitable style, gave the ambassador an abrupt and rude dismissal.[39]

Third, the Canada–USSR series provided the Department of External Affairs with its first taste of formal involvement with international sport. The department proved able to provide good advice in areas of international relations where most sports officials were not knowledgeable and to perform valuable co-ordinating functions for this event.[40] The series also provided the impetus for the creation of the International Sports Relations desk, which served to formalize the department's bureaucratic involvement in sport.

It is important to note, however, that this measure was largely a reactive one in response to the specific need to provide services and expertise for the hockey series. According to a number of the central actors in these events, there were very few people at this time in the higher echelons of External Affairs who saw the potential of sport in international relations. Consequently, the sports desk was to languish in relative obscurity until the 1980s. For the first two years it was filled by a part-time trainee; in late 1974 it was filled permanently with a sport liaison officer. Still, the desk laboured for years with a very small budget, and it remained a one-person operation until 1987. It was not involved in any significant way in Canada's first major brush with the politics of international sport, the dispute with the IOC over Taiwanese participation at the 1976 Montreal Olympics; rather, it was assigned instead such tasks as arranging sport exchanges with the Soviet Union.

The sports desk did, however, provide expertise in the next two international sport incidents in the 1970s that were to engage federal officials at the highest level: Canada's diplomatic efforts to avoid a boycott by black African nations of the 1978 Edmonton Commonwealth Games and its decision to support the US–led boycott of the 1980 Summer Olympics in Moscow. We document these two episodes in chapters 4 and 5 respectively. But first we turn to the confrontation between the Trudeau government and the IOC over the right of Taiwan to compete in the 1976 Montreal Olympics.

CHAPTER THREE

Trudeau, Taiwan, and the 1976 Montreal Olympics

Prime Minister Pierre Trudeau's announcement, just before the opening of the 1976 Montreal Olympics, that athletes from Taiwan would be denied visas to Canada unless they agreed not to represent themselves as the Republic of China provoked an international controversy and triggered an avalanche of criticism. He took this measure in the face of International Olympic Committee (IOC) regulations, which forbade the banning of competing nations by the host country, and in spite of claims by the IOC that Canada had given its assurance at the time it had been awarded the Games that it would abide by all IOC regulations. National news agencies and newspapers in the United States and around the world were overwhelmingly critical of Ottawa's stand. Even Queen Elizabeth was reported to have admonished Canada's external affairs minister, Allan MacEachen, over the Taiwan issue.[1]

Moreover, the dispute added a particularly corrosive element to relations between Canada and the United States. President Gerald Ford urged American Olympic officials to seek a reversal of the decision, asserting that "the games have now been totally corrupted by a politicization that reduces this international sports contest to a mocking of the Olympic ideal and to a mere sideshow in the ideological wars" (*New York Times*, 13 July 1976, 32). Democratic presidential nominee Jimmy Carter criticized Canada for "playing politics" with the Olympic Games (Whitelaw, 21 July 1976). The American press joined in the fray, calling the Canadian government "gutless" and "spineless," and describing Trudeau's political intervention as "stunning stupidity and unconscionable petulance."[2]

At home, the press lamented the "shame and almost universal condemnation for Canada" (*Ottawa Journal*, 17 July 1976), and repeated questions and criticism were voiced in the House of Commons (HC *Debates*, 5 July 1976, 15001, 15005–6; 8 July 1976, 15159–60).

Perhaps the most devastating attack on Trudeau's policy came from the *Economist*, which alleged that his action in ordering a Taiwanese team not to carry a banner representing the Republic of China was illegal.[3] The Taiwan issue can only be understood in the broader context of Canada's foreign policy and the IOC's "two-China" dilemma. So we first address the new foreign-policy initiatives that Trudeau instigated when he became prime minister in 1968.

TRUDEAU'S NEW FOREIGN POLICY

Pierre Elliott Trudeau's election as leader of the Liberal Party and, consequently, appointment as prime minister in 1968 brought a new approach to Canadian foreign policy. He was the only Canadian prime minister who had not, either prior to or during his term of office, held the post of secretary of state for external affairs. He had exhibited little interest in foreign policy in his early career as a journalist; neither had he had much to do with foreign affairs during his short stint in the Pearson cabinet in the years immediately before becoming prime minister. As a relative outsider, Trudeau was critical of Canada's foreign policy in the 1960s. He was concerned about both substance and process, arguing that the country's foreign policy was not reflective of its domestic political needs and that there was no rational basis for taking decisions. Moreover, he maintained that previous governments had been slow to recognize the rapidly changing international environment (von Riekhoff 1986, 251). In this last respect, Trudeau believed that Canada was still basking in the reflections of its halcyon days as honest broker and peacekeeper and was not coming to terms with the fact that the golden age of Canadian foreign policy had passed.

It came as no surprise, then, that one of Trudeau's first priorities as prime minister was to initiate a thorough review of the country's foreign policy. The resulting white paper, entitled *Foreign Policy for Canadians* (Canada 1970), was to guide Canadian foreign policy in the 1970s. The new position of the Trudeau government was clearly enunciated in this document, namely, that foreign policy is "the extension abroad of national policies" (ibid., 9). The six glossy booklets that constituted *Foreign Policy for Canadians* identified the six principal themes that were to guide the country's foreign policy: peace and security, national unity and identity, harmonious natural environment, economic growth, social justice, and the quality of life. It is instructive to note that the government explicitly avoided any attempt to identify priorities within this group (see Byers 1978; *International Journal* 1970–71, 1978).

While the Trudeau foreign-policy review recognized the tremendously important role that the United States played in Canada's foreign (and domestic) policy, the new policy was especially interested in offsetting the influence of the United States. Consequently, in 1972, a seventh theme was added in the form of a statement on Canada's relations with the United States by the secretary of state for external affairs, Mitchell Sharp. The "Third Option" strategy, as it came to be known, rejected both the *status quo* in the Canada–United States relationship and the prospects for greater continental integration. Instead, the Third Option set out what Trudeau considered a proper balance in the relationship. It involved an attempt to wean Canada away from excessive dependence on the United States by developing closer economic and political ties with other countries. This move was consistent with his belief in the need for "counterweights," which translated into the concept of equilibrium, and checks and balances to correct abuses and excesses in the functioning of political institutions (Radwanski 1978, 136–7).

While this approach was sometimes misinterpreted as simple anti-Americanism and Trudeau was regularly attacked in the US press and political media for his independent policy,[4] the real goal was to achieve a greater balance in foreign policy, thus affording Canada a longer reach in its international relations. Not surprisingly, Trudeau also asserted the country's independence by occasionally pursuing policies that defied pressures from the United States (ibid., 184–5).

It is important to remember that the Third Option strategy emerged immediately prior to the 1972 federal election and that the Trudeau brain trust believed the Liberals would lose that election. The Third Option strategy and the Sharp paper have been seen by some as a successful attempt to attract voter support that might otherwise have gone to the NPD and as explicit recognition that the so-called special relationship between Canada and the United States had ended (see Hawes 1989).

At least as important as the content of Trudeau's new foreign policy were the mechanisms that would be adopted in implementing it. Trudeau, having never been an "insider" and believing in the rational policy process, was distrustful of the Department of External Affairs and was determined to break the traditional "old-boy" style of foreign-policy making in Canada, that is in a close-knit coalition of the prime minister, the secretary of state for external affairs, and a few very senior departmental officials. Instead, he set about to establish a protocol in which his axiom of "rational planning" would be paramount.

The cabinet reforms that were instituted by Trudeau were to have an important impact on foreign policy. First, he implemented procedures whereby individual cabinet ministers were to have a greater input into the policy-making process. This was to be accomplished by more structured cabinet committees, working with more detailed briefing documents and tighter agendas. Trudeau also established the powerful Interdepartmental Committee on External Relations (ICER). Membership on this committee included the clerk of the Privy Council, the secretary of the Treasury Board, the deputy ministers of manpower and immigration and international trade and commerce, and the president of the Canadian International Development Agency. The undersecretary of state for external affairs chaired the ICER, but lacked overall authority (Nossal 1989a, 214). The committee was influential between 1970 and late 1974, but had fallen into disuse by the mid-1970s, when the Trudeau power base became more secure following the Liberal party's majority victory in the 1974 election.

Other reforms that Trudeau undertook, which fitted closely with his rational-planning mandate, included a greater effort at defining policy objectives, determining priorities among various policies, and tying these more closely to departmental programs. A central feature of this new process for developing rational policies through ministerial participation was the new omnibus Cabinet Committee on Priorities and Planning, chaired by the prime minister himself (von Riekhoff 1986, 254).

Because Trudeau had not developed close contacts with many senior public servants and thus lacked trust in their judgment, he chose to rely much more than his predecessors had on his own personal staff. As a result, the Prime Minister's Office doubled in size during his first two years in office. Among these personal advisors were a number of entirely new positions, including an advisor on foreign relations (Radwanski 1978, 148–9). These radical changes in the decision-making process were to have a great impact on the way in which foreign-policy decisions would be made. They became matters for discussion and debate at the cabinet level and were greatly influenced by the advice that Trudeau received from his personal staff.

Although Trudeau was initially cool to the notion that much good would come out of Commonwealth conferences, he soon changed his mind and became an ardent supporter of this organization (von Riekhoff 1986, 258), in part, because he saw in it the possibilities for improving economic and social conditions in third-world members of the Commonwealth. This view tied back to his personal interest in social justice, and along with his commitment it helped to explain his efforts to bring the South African sport issue to the agenda of the Commonwealth conference and his spearheading efforts to get the conference to reach an accord on the Gleneagles Declaration in 1977.

RECOGNITION OF CHINA

Trudeau's Third Option has been seen in retrospect as being unrealistic, and largely unaccomplished, in the face of Canada's strong economic, social, and political ties with the United States (see, for instance, Molot 1977; von Riekhoff 1986). It was, however, to play an important role in Canada's first major sojourn into the politics of international sport during the handling of the Taiwan issue at the 1976 Olympics in Montreal. One of the early foreign-policy measures that Trudeau had undertaken was to establish formal diplomatic relations with the People's Republic of China (PRC), a move that put Canada at odds with US policy and, in the case of the Montreal Olympics, with the IOC as well.

Trudeau's Liberal government had announced in 1968 its intent to initiate steps toward the recognition of mainland China (Radwanski 1978, 243). This initiative satisfied both aspects of his policy of independence *vis-à-vis* the United States; it involved closer economic and political ties with another country and it was being carried out at a time when the United States recognized and supported Taiwan. According to the Department of External Affairs guidebook on Pacific policy, "Strengthened relations with the Pacific will not only serve the broad objectives of Economic Growth, Social Justice, and Quality of Life, but will continue to contribute to the meaning and purpose of Canada's constant evolution as a unique and independent national community in North America."[5] In other words, it offered an important potential counterweight to US influence.

On 13 October 1970 the secretary of state for external affairs, Mitchell Sharp, was able to announce in the House of Commons that the Canadian government had formally recognized the PRC as the sole legal government of China. He noted that the Chinese government regarded Taiwan as an inalienable part of the territory of the PRC. Accordingly, Canadian officials in both Taiwan and Ottawa had taken steps to terminate formal diplomatic relations between Canada and Taiwan (Olafson and Brown-John 1986, 72). This announcement, according to External Affairs files, marked the first time that Canadian foreign policy had departed dramatically from American orthodoxy.[6] However, this fact was more troubling from a symbolic and political point of view than from a practical one, since the Nixon administration was by this time already moving on its own China policy. Moreover, the commercial implications of the new policy were not immediately apparent.

Following its withdrawal of diplomatic recognition of Taiwan, the Canadian government discouraged all official contact with the "Republic of China" in order to avoid compromising its policy of recognition of the PRC, at the same time it encouraged interchanges with mainland China.[7] The first incident from this policy was the removal of the Taiwanese flag from its pavilion at the British Columbia Trade Fair, held in Vancouver in June 1971. In the same year Canada's decision to support the admission of the PRC to the United Nations also demonstrated consistency with its new policy on China (Olafson and Brown-John 1986, 73). Private Taiwanese individuals and groups were allowed to enter Canada to take part in conferences, sports events, and other gatherings only on condition that they did not publicly proclaim themselves as representatives of the "Republic of China" or in any way promote the identity and claims of the regime in Taiwan.[8] Following Trudeau's visit to mainland China in 1973, an intensive program of cultural, educational, scientific, technological, and sport exchanges between Canada and the PRC was launched.[9] These initiatives set the stage for Canada's confrontation with the IOC over the right of Taiwan to participate in the Montreal Olympics.

THE IOC AND
THE "TWO-CHINA" DILEMMA

Appropriate Chinese representation at the Olympics had been a vexatious problem for the IOC ever since Chiang Kai-shek had been driven from the mainland to Taiwan by Mao Zedong's communist forces in 1949. This dilemma was complicated further by the IOC's traditional stance that politics should not be a part of the Olympic movement. Thus much of the IOC's efforts had been exerted to avoid taking a position on the issue of which of the two feuding governments legitimately represented the people of China.

China had first participated in the Olympics in 1932 under the auspices of Chiang Kai-shek's Republic of China (ROC).[10] The Chinese Olympic Committee remained in good standing with the IOC until the ROC's forced move to Taiwan (or Formosa, as it was then called in the West). From 1947 until 1951 the only Chinese National Olympic Committee officially recognized by the IOC was the one that was ostensibly situated in Nanking on the China mainland. But during this period, most members of the Chinese Olympic Committee, including two of the three Chinese members of the IOC, left Nanking with their files and resettled in Taipei on the island of Taiwan (Killanin 1983, 101–2). By July 1951, the National Olympic Committee was listed by the IOC as being located in Taiwan, even though no vote on this change had been taken. The IOC had simply acknowledged its move from Nanking to Taipei (Gilbert, 22 May 1975).

In 1952 the PRC lobbied for an invitation to the Helsinki Summer Olympics. Consequently, the IOC voted to let both Chinese teams participate, despite the fact that it had no constitutional basis for this decision because the PRC had no recognized national Olympic committee (Lyberg 1988–89a, 289). Be that as it may, thirty-eight men and two women from Beijing competed in the Helsinki Games (Killanin 1983, 102). The Taiwanese team left the Games in protest over the "illegality and impropriety" of the IOC's decision. Subsequently, at its meeting in Athens in 1954, the IOC did recognize the PRC Olympic Committee by a vote of 23 to 21 (Lyberg 1988–89a, 309).

The PRC thought that the issue had been resolved, but the following year the IOC president, Avery Brundage, noted that while China had been recognized at Athens, "the IOC also recognizes Taiwan."[11] Although this was a strictly unilateral announcement by Brundage (Gilbert, 22 May 1975), the PRC protested and refused to compete with the ROC, withdrawing from the 1956 Melbourne Olympics (Killanin 1983, 102). Two years later, the PRC officially withdrew from the Olympic movement, as well as from several international sport federations.[12]

The PRC's withdrawal did not end the debate. At the IOC's fifty-fifth session in Munich in May 1959, Soviet members Constantin Andrianov and Alexei Romanov put forward a proposal that the IOC recognize the PRC be recognized as having the sole Olympic committee for all of China. A long and confused debate ensued. At its conclusion, Avery Brundage announced that since the Taiwanese did not administer sport in China, the Republic of China was to be taken off the IOC membership list. The IOC did agree, however, that it would examine any subsequent request for membership from the ROC as the representative of Taiwan (*New York Times*, 29 May 1959).

This decision provoked an angry response from the United States. The State Department issued a formal statement labelling the IOC's action a "clear act of political discrimination" and protesting what it saw as "communist pressures" on the IOC (*New York Times*, 3 June 1959). Early in June the US House of Representatives voted to ban the use of army personnel and equipment at the 1960 Winter Olympics in Squaw Valley, California, if athletes from any "free nations" were excluded (*New York Times*, 4 June 1959). It was not surprising, then, that after negotiations with the members of the Taiwanese National Olympic Committee, Brundage proposed to the IOC that the ROC be readmitted as "the Olympic Committee of the Republic of China" (*New York Times*, 1 August 1959, 2). Brundage explained that the press had misinterpreted the IOC's decision at the Munich meetings.

Lord Killanin, who would succeed Brundage as president of the IOC in 1972, took an opposite view on this issue to that of Brundage; he was anxious to get both Chinas to compete in the Olympic movement, and in order to do so he favoured stripping Taiwan of its right to be called the Republic of China (Killanin 1983, 103). The majority of IOC members, however, supported the Brundage position.[13] Many of the older members still had close ties with the pre-revolutionary Chinese regime and had no real interest in pragmatic political positions (Gilbert, 22 May 1975). Consequently, at its fifty-seventh session in Rome in 1960, the IOC voted to recognize the Republic of China Olympic Committee, but insisted that the ROC participate in the 1960 Rome Olympics as "Formosa." The compromise represented an attempt to formulate a tentative two-China policy and to get the mainland back in the movement (Lyberg 1988–89b, 56).

Brundage's bias in the China membership dilemma is clearly illustrated by his actions ten years later. Despite the opposition of his entire executive board, he added the name of Henry Tsu, a Cantonese-born sportsman who was a strong supporter of the Chiang Kai-shek regime, to the list of new members to be approved by the IOC membership in Amsterdam in 1970. Over protests from executive board members, the general assembly approved the list of new members with Tsu's name on it, another indication of where the majority of the IOC membership stood on this issue (Killanin 1983, 103–4). At the IOC meetings in Luxembourg in 1971, Brundage responded to a statement by Reginald Alexander about ways to get the PRC back into the Olympics by declaring that "under no circumstances will Formosa be excluded in order to accept China" (Lyberg 1988–89b, 173).

Although the ROC threatened to boycott the Games over the 1960 decision, the IOC refused to reverse its decision, so the ROC was forced to march in the opening ceremonies under the name of Formosa. As the team was parading before the reviewing stand, the head of the delegation whipped out a second placard that read "Under Protest" (Killanin 1983, 103). Four years later, at the Olympic Games in Tokyo, the Taiwanese athletes were allowed to display "Republic of China" on their equipment (Lyberg 1988–89b, 80). For the Mexico Olympics in 1968, use of the title "ROC" by Taiwan was officially ratified by the IOC (ibid., 143). This, then, was the situation on the two-China issue when the IOC began considering Canada's bid to host the 1976 Summer Olympics in Montreal.

EVENTS LEADING TO
THE TAIWAN ISSUE
AT THE 1976
MONTREAL OLYMPICS

By 1969 the IOC was giving serious consideration to Montreal's bid. As part of its standard procedure, it requested government undertakings in response to Question G of the IOC rules, which reads, "Are there any laws, customs or any regulations in your city or your country that limit, restrict, or interfere with the Games in any way? Free entry must be accorded to teams from all National Olympic Committees recognized by the International Olympic Committee."[14] In response to this request, Prime Minister Trudeau wrote a short letter to Avery Brundage on 21 May 1969 in support of Montreal's application, offering on behalf of the government a "hearty welcome" and extending "to all who are associated with the Olympic Games a cordial invitation to visit us in Montreal in 1976."[15] The secretary of state for external affairs, Mitchell Sharp, also responded to the query of the IOC. His letter, dated 28 November 1969, assured the IOC that all parties would be free to enter Canada "pursuant to the normal regulations." Sharp added that he would be pleased to provide further information about these regulations upon request.[16]

The caveat "pursuant to the normal regulations" was appended because Canada foresaw the possibility of embarrassment with its NATO partners and wanted to prevent the kind of imbroglio that eventually transpired over Taiwan. At the time, however, the potential problem was seen as East Germany (GDR), which was constantly seeking international recognition from countries outside the communist bloc (Wilson, 22 July 1976). The IOC took the federal government's invitation at face value and did not ask for clarification of the "pursuant to normal regulations" clause. Lord Killanin was to say later that he thought Sharp's qualifications referred to "something like a cholera epidemic" (Janigan, 17 July 1976, A1, A11). When the Olympics were officially awarded to Montreal by the IOC in May 1970, Canada gave assurances that "there was nothing to hinder or restrict in any way the attendance of athletes" (*Korea Times*, 3 July 1976). The agreement was signed by the City of Montreal and the IOC. Sharp's letter of 1969, then, was the only written pledge the federal government made to the IOC.

In 1973 the PRC actively commenced to seek re-admission to international sport organizations because membership on at least five such organizations was a prerequisite of admission to the IOC. By 1974 the Canadian embassy in Beijing was relaying messages to Ottawa that the PRC was expressing concern over Chinese representation at the 1976 Olympics in Montreal, claiming that Canada would be violating its recognition of the PRC if it allowed Taiwan to participate. The PRC requested that the Canadian government deny entry under any circumstances to all Taiwanese Olympic participants (Nafziger and Strenk 1978, 265), and it intimated that bilateral relations (including trade) between the two countries could be affected if this request was not met.[17] Although the Canadian government protested that the matter was outside its jurisdiction, it was prepared to go to great lengths to safeguard its recent and major foreign-policy success in formalizing ties with the PRC (Morse 1987b, 11).

In the fall of 1974, in anticipation of possible political problems connected with the Montreal Olympics, the Department of External Affairs sharpened its focus by trying to foresee what negative scenarios might arise in 1976. By the end of the year, Ed Skrabec was assigned the task of pulling together the necessary background materials on potential political problems. He had been appointed in September as head of the Foreign Policy Section of the department's Information Division, which then included the sports desk.

The resulting series of reports, filed in the spring of 1975, were primarily concerned with South Africa and China, but they also contained a section on the history of political "intrusions" at the Olympics. These reports precipitated a series of meetings among officials in External Affairs, that included, at various levels and times: L.A.D. Stephens, former director-general of the Bureau of Public Affairs; Arthur Andrew, assistant under-secretary of state with responsibilities for China; Allan Rogers, director of the Information Division; Patrick Reid, the new director-general of the Bureau of Public Affairs; and Ed Skrabec.[18] The Taiwan–PRC rivalry was seen as the most serious potential problem. Thus the Canadian ambassador in Dublin was asked to find an occasion to enquire from Lord Killanin how the IOC intended to deal with the situation and to offer the services of the Department of External Affairs to the Canadian Olympic Organizing Committee (COJO in French) if Killanin seemed receptive to consultation and advice.[19]

In early April 1975 the minister of manpower and immigration, Robert Andras, amended the official instruments N and Z–4 to include Olympic identity cards in Immigration regulations. This action meant that persons entitled to receive Olympic identity cards would be allowed admission into Canada between 17 June and 31 August 1976 solely on presentation of the card.[20] As far as the IOC was concerned, the move was another indication of the federal government's good faith in abiding by IOC regulations and policies.[21]

In this same month (April), the PRC formally applied for admission to the IOC and at the same time called for the expulsion of Taiwan. By this time, with the assistance of other eastern Asian nations, in particular Japan, the PRC had gained membership in nine of the twenty-seven international sports federations recognized by the IOC (*Ottawa Citizen*, 17 July 1976). The PRC's legal documentation was provided by the National Olympic Committee of Iran, and its case was presented to the IOC by Prince Takeda of Japan, leader of the Asian bloc in the IOC (Gilbert, 22 May 1975).

Shortly after the PRC's application for re-admission to the Olympic movement, Arthur Andrew and Ed Skrabec met for the first time with

Lord Killanin in Toronto to discuss matters related to the Montreal Olympics. The minutes of this meeting have never been made public. James Worrall, a Canadian who was a member of the IOC and who attended the meeting at Lord Killanin's request, recalled that the meeting was held at the behest of the Department of External Affairs and was an informal and friendly session. Lord Killanin, according to Worrall, took the position that Canada had assured the IOC that all countries and their athletes would be admitted and thus that there was no issue to be discussed.[22]

However, a non-political source who studied the External Affairs records of this meeting claims that the Taiwan issue was raised at the meeting, not by Canada, but by the IOC. According to this version, when the representatives from External Affairs were asked what to expect in the case of Taiwan, they replied that there would be trouble if Taiwan's team attempted to enter as the "Republic of China." To the follow-up question of what would be necessary from the Canadian end to change this situation, the reply was that a ministerial decision would be necessary, but that this would be most unlikely (Wilson, 22 July 1976).

Whatever one makes of these conflicting reports, it subsequently became apparent that grave misunderstandings existed between Lord Killanin and Allan MacEachen, who was to take over the post of secretary of state for external affairs, regarding the substance of this crucial meeting. MacEachen would subsequently claim that Canadian officials had refused to give Killanin assurances that Taiwan would be admitted under the name "Republic of China," to which (according to DEA sources), Killanin had replied that he hoped the IOC could resolve the whole issue well before the Olympics. Killanin, on the other hand, recalled only that he had met about a year before the Montreal Olympics with Mitchell Sharp (whom he remembered as an "official" in the Department of External Affairs) who had inquired about the position of mainland China in the IOC (Killanin 1983, 136). Killanin must have been referring to his meeting with Andrew and Skrabec, because there is no record that he met with Sharp in the year preceding the crisis. Other sources say Killanin later maintained that he told Canada at the meeting there would be no change in the IOC position on Taiwan (see, for instance, IOC, July 1976a, 87; Janigan, 17 July 1976). Skrabec claims that Lord Killanin "knew of what we spoke," thus backing up MacEachen's side of the story.[23] Throughout the ensuing controversy surrounding the handling of the Taiwan issue, the discrepant views of this meeting were to remain a bone of contention.

The PRC's request for re-admission to the Olympic movement was formally considered by the IOC at its next meeting in May 1975. By this time, however, the PRC and the Soviet Union were political foes rather than allies, and their respective armies were posturing on the Chinese-

Soviet border. Thus, not only was the United States opposed to admitting the PRC to the IOC, but the Soviet bloc members were as well. The resulting debate split the IOC down the middle.[24] The outcome was delay; the IOC decided to postpone deliberations on the PRC application until further study could be carried out, including visits to Beijing and Taiwan by the IOC president, Lord Killanin (*Globe and Mail*, 24 May 1975). These visits, however, did not occur until after the Montreal Olympics (Killanin 1983, 105).

The decision placed Canada in an extremely awkward position. Taiwan was a member of the Olympic movement, but the PRC was not; the PRC was recognized by Canada, but Taiwan was not. External Affairs officials were left with the task of formulating recommendations to take to cabinet about the "China problem" at the Montreal Olympics. Consequently, in June of 1975, the department established a Special Olympics Coordination Unit and placed it in the office of the chief of protocol. This unit came within the responsibilities of Assistant Under-Secretary of State P. André Bissonnette, who would play a key departmental role in dealing with the IOC. Ed Skrabec was assigned in the first instance to head this special unit, but it was decided that a more senior official was needed. Accordingly, the former ambassador to Poland, J.A. McCordick, was appointed. But a short time after his appointment, McCordick retired from the public service and Skrabec was left to head up the unit after all.[25]

On 10 June 1975, at the request of Lord Killanin, COJO issued invitations to all member countries, including Taiwan. Killanin had previously requested that these invitations be delayed until he had had a chance to assess the overall situation.[26] But by the end of 1975, the Canadian government was taking steps to impose restrictions on Taiwanese teams wishing to enter Canada. It informed the IOC that Taiwanese boxers would not be admitted to the pre-Olympic meets to be held in Montreal if they tried to compete under the "Republic of China" banner. The Taiwanese decided that they could not accept the conditions imposed by Canada, and they declined to come.[27] In January 1976, COJO withdrew the invitation that it had extended to Taiwanese young people to stay in the Olympic Youth Camp in Montreal during the Games, much to the chagrin of the Olympic attaché from Taiwan.[28]

The next encounter between External Affairs and the IOC occurred in early February, when Ed Skrabec and A.J. Beesley, the Canadian ambassador to Austria, met with Lord Killanin at the Winter Olympics in Innsbruck, Austria, and warned him that the problem with China had to be resolved.[29] According to James Worrall, who was also present at this meeting, Killanin held to his previous position that Canada had given the IOC its assurance that the Games would be held according to IOC regulations and that the "two-China problem" was Canada's not the IOC's.[30] The fact that the issue of Taiwan participation had not surfaced during the Innsbruck Games probably had a reassuring effect on the IOC.

The February IOC meetings in Innsbruck adjourned without a decision on the China issue. According to Worrall, the matter was not even formally discussed.[31] The only reference to the China issue at the IOC executive board meetings was a report by Lord Killanin that he had not yet been able to arrange for his visit to the Republic of China (IOC, January-February 1976, 6). As a result, External Affairs officials began preparing proposals for the cabinet to examine. By early May 1976 the cabinet started to give serious consideration to the China problem. Eric Morse, who was head of International Sports Relations for External Affairs at the time, has suggested that the IOC assumed Canada would not risk criticism by being the first government to interfere directly in the staging of the Olympics in support of its own foreign-policy interest (Morse 1987b, 11–12). The IOC was soon to find out that that assumption was wrong.

THE CANADA–IOC CONFRONTATION OVER THE TAIWAN OLYMPIC BAN

Towards the end of April 1976, the secretary of state for external affairs, Donald Jamieson, had approved a policy recommending that the Taiwanese team be allowed to participate in the Montreal Olympics, providing that it agree to compete under a designation other than "Republic of China" or "China" and that it refrain from using the flags, anthem, or any other ROC symbols. Subsequently, this policy was approved by Prime Minister Trudeau.[32] Shortly after, on 26 May, Mitchell Sharp, who was then acting secretary of state for external affairs, and Ed Skrabec met with James Worrall to discuss the question of the participation of the "Republic of China" at the Montreal Olympics. The substance of the meeting was contained in a letter sent by Sharp to Lord Killanin on 28 May. In this letter Sharp stated that the Canadian government regarded the continuing membership of the "Republic of China" and the non-participation of the PRC in the Olympic movement as matters that could only be settled by the IOC. But since the problem had not yet been resolved, the government found it necessary, in light of its China policy, to apply to persons from Taiwan planning to participate in the Olympics the regulations that had been approved by Trudeau. Sharp suggested that the IOC might consider asking Taiwan to participate in the Games under another name, such as Formosa, as it had done in the 1960 Olympics in Rome.[33]

Killanin's response to Sharp, dated 8 June 1976, stated that Sharp's suggestions were "in complete conflict with Olympic rules and contrary to the conditions under which Montreal was allotted the Olympic Games."[34] Killanin argued that the letters sent to the IOC in 1969 by Trudeau and Sharp had confirmed that the IOC rules would be complied with fully, and he accused Canada of breaking Rule 7 of the fundamental principles of the Olympics: "No discrimination is allowed against any country or person on grounds of race, religion, or political affiliation."[35] Killanin maintained that "during the period of the Games the IOC is the supreme authority."[36] He concluded by saying that when he had explained his position to the Department of External Affairs officials during the meetings held in Toronto in April 1975 and subsequently at Innsbruck in 1976, no objection had been raised.[37] "On 24 June Killanin sent a follow-up letter to Sharp, stating that since he had not received any reply to his letter of 8 June, "I therefore presume that you are in agreement with my views and will comply with Olympic rules and traditions." Unless Canada confirmed its agreement with the contents of his letter of 8 June, Killanin threatened to inform the other parties concerned of Canada's position. He also requested that a meeting be arranged with representatives of the Department of External Affairs to discuss the situation.[38]

Lord Killanin's second letter precipitated further action in External Affairs. André Bissonnette, assistant under-secretary of state with responsibility for the Montreal Olympics, advised the minister on a strategy for dealing with the situation. The department had prepared a reply to Killanin's letter, reconfirming its position described in Sharp's letter of 28 May, but leaving the door open for further discussions. External Affairs also decided that the time had come to inform the government of Quebec confidentially of the situation through Bissonnette, because it suspected that Killanin would attempt to use public pressure to influence the Canadian government. A comprehensive statement of Canada's position was prepared for this eventuality. In the mean time, External Affairs continued to develop interdepartmental procedures in order to ensure that Canada would be capable of enforcing its policy.[39]

Subsequently, Allan MacEachen, the secretary of state for external affairs, for whom Sharp had acted, replied to the two letters from Killanin by stating that since the position of the Canadian government on the Taiwan issue involved the country's policy on China and reflected its national sovereignty, he was not able to confirm his agreement with Killanin's views. MacEachen, however, did agree that a meeting between External Affairs officials and the IOC was worth pursuing.[40] In the mean time, MacEachen asked Robert Andras, minister of manpower and immigration, to revoke the validity of the Taiwanese Olympic identity cards, a move that required an amendment to the ministerial instrument.[41]

At the end of June, External Affairs made a final attempt to resolve the impasse before it became a public issue. Bissonnette and Skrabec travelled to Frankfurt and informed Killanin that if the IOC continued to insist that Taiwan be allowed to participate in the Montreal Games, the department would have to take the issue to cabinet, where the most likely result would be the rejection of Taiwan participation. The outcome of the Frankfurt meeting was reported to Allan MacEachen by Bissonnette and Glen Shortliffe, MacEachen's departmental assistant. However, by the time Bissonnette and Skrabec had arrived back at the Toronto airport, the IOC had broken the story, accusing Canada of breaking its pledge to allow all athletes and officials authorized by the IOC to participate in the Montreal Games (*Facts on File*, 24 July 1976, 529).

An international furor ensued.[42] The first reports filtering out suggested that the IOC might withdraw its recognition of the Games if Canada did not yield on its stand (*Canadian News Facts*, 4 August 1976, 1601). Killanin made it known that Canada would never have been awarded the Games ahead of Los Angeles or Moscow if the IOC had had any indication of restrictions on the attendance of athletes (IOC, July 1976a, 1–2). In a prepared statement issued at its Château de Vidy headquarters on Lake Geneva, the IOC stopped just short of threatening to call off the Games, but a spokesperson said that it was considering disassociating itself from the Games by insisting the word "Olympic" be removed (*Korea Times*, 3 July 1976).

The dispute became even more complicated when the United States decided to enter the fray. In a telegram to the COJO on 2 July, Philip Krumm, president of the US Olympic Committee, stated that the United States would give serious consideration to withdrawing from the Montreal Games if the IOC withdrew its recognition. He urged Canada to reconsider its decision to restrict Taiwanese participation (Cady, 3 July 1976). A US withdrawal from the Games would have had serious consequences for the IOC, because the $25 million that the American Broadcasting Corporation (ABC) had paid to COJO for television rights for the Games would have been placed in jeopardy (Killanin 1983, 137–8; Janigan, 17 July 1976). The IOC's share of these payments, amounting to some $7 million (COJO 1978, 79), represented a major source of income for the IOC at that time (Strenk 1978, 24).

The negative ramifications of cancelling or moving the Games, how-ever, were too powerful even for some of the more vitriolic members of the IOC. It came as no great surprise, then, when Lord Killanin let it be known that the IOC would not pull out of the Games. His position was upheld a few days later when fifty-seven IOC members voted in fa-vour of continuing with the Games. There were nine abstentions and no votes recorded against the motion (IOC, July 1976b, 17). As a result, a spokesperson for the United States Olympic Committee issued the statement, "Since the President of the IOC has clarified his position that the IOC will not withdraw recognition, sanction or patronage of the Games, there should no longer be a question of United States' team participation in Montreal" (*New York Times*, 4 July 1976, 1). In the midst of a deluge of criticism of the Canadian position from around the world, counter-accusations flew back and forth between the IOC and the Canadian government. Killanin stated he was extremely upset that this matter had come up at the last minute and that there had never been any indication that it was going to be a problem until 28 May. MacEachen, however, maintained the Canadian government had in-formed Killanin a year earlier that there would be diplomatic problems with Taiwan attempting to represent all of China at the Olympics. "It was only when no action was taken by the IOC that we made it clear, in late May through the Acting Secretary of State for External Affairs (Mitchell Sharp) that we would apply a formula for the admission of athletes to Canada which would respect Canada's China policy" (Fox, 6 July 1976, 39).

On 5 July 1976 Trudeau, MacEachen, and Sharp launched a defence of Canada's stand on the Taiwan issue in the House of Commons, in interviews, and at press conferences. MacEachen referred to the letter from Sharp to the IOC in November 1969, in which all parties recog-nized by the IOC were assured of free entrance to Canada "pursuant to the normal regulations." The catch was "I should be pleased to provide you with any further information respecting these regulations should you desire it." MacEachen maintained, "It is obvious from that literal quotation that the undertaking ... was not an unqualified undertaking. At no point in making such an undertaking did Canada undertake to relinquish its sovereignty to an international organization, no matter how respected that international organization may be" (ibid.).

The minister pointed out that Taiwanese athletes could participate in the Montreal Games in the same way they had participated in the 1960 Rome Olympics, under conditions and regulations that had been approved at that time by the IOC.

In response to repeated questions in the House of Commons, the prime minister replied, "The government is right on this particular

issue" (Olafson and Brown-John 1986, 73). Debate in the House concluded on 12 July, when Trudeau noted:

Mr. Speaker, I think the best answer to the Olympic committee and indeed to
members of this House and the country who have shown concern, is that it is
not our policy nor our practice to bar any athletes from the games. We welcome
the athletes from Taiwan. We hope they will compete. We do not discriminate
on the basis of sex, race or, indeed, national origin. All we are saying, and it
seems to me this is a policy that would have the support of any member of this
House regardless of his party provided he believes in a one China policy, is that
we will not let athletes come into Canada ... to pretend that they represent a
country, China, that they do not represent. That is all we are saying. (*Canada
Report*, 22 July 1976, 1)

Trudeau's statement came shortly after a meeting of the Tripartite
Commission (representing the IOC, the international sports federations, and the national Olympic committees), which was held in
Montreal on 9 July and chaired by Lord Killanin. At the meeting, the
members had unanimously condemned the attitude of the Canadian
government in opposing the entry of a team of a national Olympic
committee under the name duly recognized by the IOC. It was decided
that the Tripartite Commission should commence talks immediately
with the Canadian authorities and representatives of the ROC National
Olympic Committee in order to avert cancellation of the Games.[43]

Lord Killanin met with External Affairs officials in a final attempt to
resolve the conflict. P. André Bissonnette, Glen Shortliffe, and Ed
Skrabec represented the department. But neither side would back
down at this tense meeting; Canada confirmed once again that it would
not admit athletes from Taiwan. On 10 July a bitter Killanin agreed to
the Canadian demands, and the IOC proposed to the Taiwanese that
they participate under the Olympic flag and the name of the IOC.
Although Canada agreed to the IOC proposal, it was turned down by
the Taiwanese (*Canada Report*, 22 July 1976, 2).

Killanin then reported to Trudeau on 15 July that the matter was at
an impasse (ibid.). Following a four-hour cabinet meeting, Trudeau ca-
pitulated on two of the three government conditions for Taiwanese
participation. The Taiwanese team could fly whatever flag and play
whatever national anthem it wanted, but he remained adamant that the
team not masquerade as the representative of the "Republic of China."
This compromise was accepted by the IOC and the United States
(*Houston Chronicle*, 16 July 1976).

In Taipei, however, an official of Nationalist China's Olympic committee said that the proposal was "completely unacceptable." Secretary-

General Niu Ping-yih reiterated that Taiwan would not take part in the Games unless its team was allowed to identify itself by the country's official name, which was recognized by the IOC. "To tell us now at the last minute that we cannot use the name is unwarranted political interference in an apolitical sporting event, so there is no way that we can accept this proposal" (ibid.). On 16 July 1976, the Taiwanese team officially pulled out of the Montreal Olympics.

THE AFTERMATH OF
THE TAIWAN ISSUE

Trudeau's government was caught in an extreme dilemma over the Taiwan-Montreal Olympics controversy. On the one hand was its official foreign policy, articulated in the 1972 "Options Paper," which advocated a more independent stance *vis-à-vis* the United States. One of the strongest expressions of this new stance had been Canada's recognition of the People's Republic of China as the legitimate government of China, a position that was in direct opposition to that of the United States. On the other hand was Canada's reputation in international circles as a consummate peacemaker and reconciler. In the end, Canada chose to stand by its one-China policy, but in doing so it incurred considerable damage to its international reputation and put its relations with the United States at some risk. Certainly, this incident was of particular interest to students of Canadian foreign policy since it confirmed the break that Trudeau had made with the foreign-policy priorities of his predecessors. Moreover, his persistence also points to the fact that decisions such as this one offered important opportunities to make foreign-policy statements and to take particular (and sometimes difficult) stands.

External Affairs Minister Allan MacEachen sought to justify Canada's position by stating that the policy had not been brought forward "to inject controversy or politics into the Olympic movement," but rather to prevent inconsistencies with Canada's recognition of the People's Republic of China (*Canada Report*, 22 July 1976, 3). The government believed that it had achieved "a reasonable and balanced position" by maintaining the integrity of its China policy, but at the same time fulfilling its obligations to the IOC.[44]

The federal government's position inevitably alienated much of the Canadian press and a good deal of the attentive Canadian public. Apparently it underestimated the widespread attraction of the Olympics and the emotional appeal of the concept that the Olympics should somehow remain apart from government, however unrealistic that concept might be. The mystique perpetuated by the IOC that the

Olympics should remain above politics and that a country's foreign-policy objectives should not be achieved at the expense of the Games prevailed in the minds of the press and the attentive public in this battle between Canada and the IOC. In defense of his government's position, Trudeau maintained that the spirit of the Olympics had changed because of the world's political atmosphere, pointing out that very few amateur athletes could exist without substantial state support and expensive facilities provided by government (*Montreal Gazette*, 19 July 1976).

Each side appears to have underestimated the other in this struggle. On the one hand, the IOC was convinced Canada was a country that would not risk international condemnation by banning another country from the Olympic Games in violation of the Olympic Charter. In the words of Ed Skrabec, who was present at all of the meetings over the Taiwan issue, the IOC "saw Canada as a mild-mannered, middle-power country that would eventually back down."[45] On the other hand, the Canadian government waited far too long to try to resolve the issue, either out of the misguided belief that the IOC would resolve the two-China dilemma itself or out of indifference to the potential gravity of a public stand-off with the IOC.

In the first place, the IOC had a long history of indecisiveness over political issues. In the earlier issue of South African participation in the Olympics, the IOC had waffled and had only made a final decision when it became obvious that unless it took a stand against South African participation, the 1968 Olympics in Mexico City would be placed in serious jeopardy. (These machinations are spelled out in more detail in the next chapter.) In addition, the IOC was split between the old-guard members, supported by those from the United States and some of its allies, who remained loyal to the Republic of China, and the communist bloc and many third-world members, who advocated membership for the People's Republic of China. The numerous long and inconclusive meetings that the IOC held over appropriate China membership certainly made clear its inability to resolve this problem.

The belief of many old-guard members, including Lord Killanin, that the IOC should remain aloof from international politics made finding a solution to this issue even more problematic. This belief, or at least the pretense at belief, was to prevail in the IOC under Killanin's leadership for another four years. It would not be until Juan Antonio Samaranch took over the presidency in 1980 that this attitude would change. (We return to that story in chapter 9, when we examine the IOC as a transnational organization.) Certainly, however, there were legitimate causes of concern in the IOC over Canada's stand. It marked the first time in Olympic history that a host nation had refused to allow entry to a recognized National Olympic Committee entry to the Games (IOC, July 1976a, 76). The next Summer Games were to be held in Moscow, the first time that a communist bloc country would host the Olympics. There was much concern among the old guard in the IOC that the Soviets would take advantage of this precedent by refusing admission to countries whose political views were an anathema to the Soviet Union.

For its part, the Canadian government seemed content to leave negotiations in the hands of middle-level External Affairs officials until very late in the affair. Perhaps the participation of high-level officials, or even cabinet ministers, earlier would have allowed the IOC and the government to come to some compromise before the matter became a public issue. James Worrall claims that the External Affairs officials who met with Lord Killanin on three occasions in the year preceding the crisis never made Canada's position clear, preferring instead to talk in "diplomatese."[46] The lateness of any action by the government was a sore point at home. The Canadian press complained that "it would not have been any excess of courtesy for the department to have made its policy clearly known before the Taiwanese left home" (*Halifax Chronicle Herald*, 28 July 1976, 6).

Certainly there was little prospect that Taiwan would change its position. The Taiwanese were still fighting hard for international recognition as the "Republic of China." Several long-range decisions had been taken by the PRC at a high-level party meeting in February 1975, and the decision that the PRC try to re-enter the Olympics was just one of these (Gilbert, 22 May 1975). The renewed vigour with which the PRC was seeking readmittance to the Olympic movement and expulsion of the ROC was just one more threat to the legitimacy of the ROC's claim to be the government of China. It was clear, Allan MacEachen surmised, that the Taiwanese were more concerned about making a political point than they were in actually participating in the Montreal Olympics.[47]

From the perspective of the United States, Trudeau's action was interpreted as yet another example of his application of an independent foreign policy, which Americans constantly criticized as interfering with Canadian-American relations. Trudeau had taken steps to recognize the country containing the world's largest population (PRC) at the same time that the United States was trying to keep it isolated. He could not understand why the Americans were so concerned about Canada's position in the controversy over Taiwan's status at the Olympic Games. In an interview with the ABC, he was quoted as saying, "I wonder what Americans feel we've done to them. We may have offended the China lobby in the United States, but the US itself hasn't been offended" (*Montreal Gazette*, 19 July 1976, 2). Besides the obvious reason that Canada's position was in direct contradiction to official US policy, there were two other factors involved in the violent reaction by the United States to the banishment of Taiwan. One was a fear that a Canadian ban on Taiwan might set a precedent for the 1980 Olympics (Trumbull, 16 July 1976) and cause a disruption of those Games. This concern would prove ironic because it would be President Jimmy Carter who would disrupt the Moscow Olympics. The second factor was the emotional commitment to Taiwan and the strong anti-communist feelings that Americans held at that time (Wilson, 22 July 1976).

The Canadian government was also accused of using the Olympic Games to enhance its diplomatic relations with the PRC to the exclusion of the ROC (Nafziger and Strenk 1978, 266). Ironically, even this development did not materialize. The PRC, believing it had a sympathetic ear with Trudeau, had certainly lobbied hard for the exclusion of Taiwan. Indeed, in February 1969 it had been successful in getting Canada to support its application for full representation in the UN. But in 1976 the China lobby did not get its way entirely. The Canadian government was prepared finally to admit the athletes from Taiwan as long as they did not call themselves representatives of the "Republic of China." In fact, government officials in Beijing made their opposition to this compromise known to the Department of External Affairs (*Canada Report*, 22 July 1976, 3). According to Jack Granatstein and Robert Bothwell (1990, 188), the Taiwan issue was "the only major crisis to trouble the waters of Canada-China [PRC] relations."

Commonwealth secretary-general Shridath Ramphal was one of the few who supported and praised Trudeau's stance on Taiwan's participation at the Olympics, asserting, "International sport cannot be immunized from matters of immediate and important international concern" (*Montreal Gazette*, 22 July 1976, 2). This praise was short-lived. At the same time that the Canadian government was grappling with the issue of Taiwanese participation at the 1976 Olympics, tensions were mounting over sporting contacts between South Africa and New Zealand. These tensions eventually resulted in a last-minute boycott of the Montreal Olympics by black African nations. Because attentions were focused elsewhere, the boycott took most Canadian and IOC officials by surprise and gave them little opportunity to prevent the exodus of black athletes from Montreal. This boycott was to negate what little credit Trudeau had received from influential third-world leaders, such as Ramphal, for his stand on Taiwan and to put a crimp in his considerable efforts to develop good relations with third-world countries. (We turn to the black African nation boycott of the Montreal Olympics and

Canada's subsequent efforts to avert a similar boycott of the 1978 Edmonton Commonwealth Games in the next chapter.)

In the end, Canada displayed "uncharacteristic toughness" (*Ottawa Journal,* 13 July 1976). For years the government had maintained a peacekeeping, mediative role in the international setting. When Canada abandoned its "Boy Scout" role and instead acted with a tough regard for long-term Canadian interests (Wilson, 22 July 1976), it caused dismay, outrage, and resistance. For the first time, it had stood firm in the face of international condemnation and in the process had maintained the integrity of its foreign policy on China. For this action, it paid a heavy price in image, both at home and abroad. As Granatstein and Bothwell noted in *Pirouette,* "it had been a curious crisis, but a crisis nonetheless" (Granatstein and Bothwell 1990, 189).

CHAPTER FOUR

The 1978 Edmonton Commonwealth Games

Although a quip attributed to a senior official in the Department of External Affairs that the department's efforts to avert a boycott of the 1978 Commonwealth Games in Edmonton led by black African nations generated more telex messages than did the entire Vietnam War may be apocryphal,[1] it is true that External Affairs went to considerable lenghts to prevent such a boycott. Canada's reputation as a leader in reconciling differences between developed nations and third-world members of the Commonwealth was at stake. This reputation had already been tarnished when twenty-two countries had supported the black African nations' call for a boycott of the 1976 Olympic Games in Montreal in protest over New Zealand's participation. New Zealand had drawn the ire of these nations because of its intransigence over sporting contacts with South Africa. A boycott of anything approaching the magnitude of the one in Montreal would not only be disastrous for the Edmonton Games, but would further damage Canada's reputation in the Commonwealth.

In this chapter we examine the steps that Canada took to ensure that the Edmonton Commonwealth Games were indeed successful, and we attempt to put them into the larger perspective of Canada's relations in the Commonwealth and its policy towards apartheid in South Africa. But first we set the stage by reviewing its foreign policy towards that country during the post-war period leading up to the Montreal Olympics and the sport sanctions it had imposed on South Africa during that time.

CANADA'S SOUTH AFRICAN POLICY, 1945–76

Canada's policy towards South Africa evolved gradually during the period 1945 to 1976, from a position of relatively close and friendly (although only marginally important) relations to one of increasingly vociferous criticism of South Africa's racist domestic policies of apartheid. This criticism, however, was tempered by a great reluctance by the Canadian government to back up its rhetoric with any concrete social, diplomatic, or economic measures. On those occasions in which South and southern Africa became major foreign-policy concerns, the politics of the Commonwealth were most often paramount. During this period, Canadian policymakers were deeply committed to the survival of the Commonwealth, and this motive was a primary force behind Canada's South African policy. The government's commitment to matters in southern Africa was consistent with its attempts to maximize its self-interests. As a major commodity exporter and a significant host for foreign capital, Canada was particularly sympathetic to "southern" concerns. Not surprisingly, it saw an opportunity to act as "honest broker" in north-south relations.

Underpinning these periodic Commonwealth imperatives, of course, was the genuine distaste that many Canadians felt for racism. But there were some abiding national interests and priorities that also dictated Canada's policy toward South Africa. One such priority was the desire to preserve and strengthen the multiracial Commonwealth as a bridge between the "Afro-Asians" and Western industrialized nations. Here, concern for Western interests in the Cold War was a primary, but not an exclusive motive. The government's interest during this period in expanding Canada's role as an international peacebroker in order to enhance its image as a relatively sympathetic and "progressive" Western middle power with Afro-Asian nations was another motive. These objectives often conflicted with a desire to maintain economic and social links with South Africa. Canada's economic relations with that country, although small in absolute terms, were nevertheless lucrative and weighted toward manufactured exports, a sector of the economy that was traditionally weak (Langdon 1978). A parallel confounding factor was the genuine – if naïve and misplaced – conviction held by many Canadian policymakers that economic and social ties were useful in influencing racial policies and strengthening liberal causes in South Africa (Tennyson 1982, 185).

During the immediate post-war period, Commonwealth connections, the recent wartime alliance, and trade relations, in which Canada enjoyed a healthy surplus, all contributed to the maintenance of relatively amicable relations between it and South Africa (Matthews and Pratt 1978, 165; Tennyson 1982, 112). In addition, there remained in Canada some nasty elements of racial prejudice, perhaps best manifested in certain "legal disabilities" imposed on Asians in British Columbia. Although these had been largely, if not entirely, eliminated in 1947 (Tennyson 1982, 121), racial prejudice still lingered in Canada. These residual attitudes had the effect of tempering Canadian criticism of South African policies during this period. But the two countries gradually diverged as Canada became more internationalist – as reflected in its strong commitments to the UN and the "new (multiracial) Commonwealth" – while South Africa was becoming increasingly isolated internationally. The election of the National Party in South Africa in 1948 and the subsequent legal imposition of apartheid structures put the country on a collision course with the movement towards decolonization in the rest of the world.

Nevertheless, until the early 1960s the Canadian government maintained that South Africa could best be influenced by quiet, behind-the-scenes approaches from a friendly government. In 1960, however, white South Africa's referendum vote to establish itself as a republic forced Canada out of its "studied aloofness" (Matthews and Pratt 1978, 165). Prime Minister John Diefenbaker was confronted at the Commonwealth meetings the following year with the prospect that support of South Africa's readmittance as a republic could result in the disintegration of a now predominantly non-white Commonwealth. Diefenbaker played a critical role in forcing Pretoria out of the Commonwealth by taking the position at these meetings that "Commonwealth membership must be tied to the acceptance of certain [non-racial] values" (Tennyson 1982, 164–70). This position set the stage for Canada's subsequent polic, shift to support UN resolutions condemning apartheid, although it was to continue for many years to oppose economic and other sanctions.

The one area in which Canada did adopt sanctions was in the sale of arms. In response to a non-binding UN Security Council resolution in 1963, Canada imposed an arms embargo on South Africa. However, this ban exempted trade in spare parts. As this was precisely the area in which the Canadian military industry specialized, the embargo had virtually no effect on the small volume of bilateral trade in arms with South Africa (Redekop 1984–85, 94). This glaring loophole was closed in 1970, but another, that of allowing the sale of dual-purpose equipment with civilian and military capabilities, was to remain open (ibid., 95).

In response to Rhodesia's Unilateral Declaration of Independence (UDI) in November 1965, Canada also imposed economic sanctions against that territory. These sanctions, however, were implemented in the context of Prime Minister Lester Pearson's diplomatic initiative to defuse pressure from third-world members to use force to end UDI, a proposal that threatened to cause the breakup of the Commonwealth (Hayes 1982, 164–6). Canada's sanctions against Rhodesia, then, must be seen in the context of its opposition to the use of force and its continuing commitment to the preservation of the Commonwealth rather than as any precedent for sanctions against South Africa.

The Trudeau government's major foreign-policy white paper, *Foreign Policy for Canadians* (Canada 1970), was to articulate a subtle, but important shift in Canada's policy towards Pretoria. Up to this point, its South African policy had adhered to the liberal position that social justice and economic growth were essentially complementary priorities. The white paper, however, framed the issue in terms of the need to strike a "careful balance" between these two important priorities. Nevertheless, in practice the Trudeau government's policy towards Pretoria continued to be heavily weighted towards the imperative of economic growth. The British Preferential Tariff continued to be the basis of trade relations, and the benefits of all government trade promotion programs and activities were still extended to Canadian traders in South Africa. The goal of social justice was pursued in a number of indirect ways: by increasing aid to neighbouring frontline states; by extending a small program of humanitarian assistance to black victims of minority regimes in the region; and by divesting the minority holding that Polymer, a Canadian crown corporation, had in a South African government-controlled company (Redekop 1984–85, 86–97). By 1972 Canada's traditionally favourable trade balance with South Africa had become (and has remained) a deficit. The deep resistance of the Canadian government to economic and other sanctions, however, persisted.

Despite Pierre Trudeau's initial scepticism about the usefulness of the Commonwealth and his disparagement of Canada's post-war role as international "helpful fixer," he was to fall easily into the diplomatic footsteps of Diefenbaker and Pearson. He played a key mediatory role in the 1971 Commonwealth meetings in Singapore by forging an accommodation over the dispute about Britain's decision to resume arms sales to South Africa. Canada's opposition to the resumption of British arms sales was partly shaped by its own continued opposition to such sales, as signalled by the recent extension of its own embargo to include spare parts. But the commitment to preserve the Commonwealth "as a viable multiracial organization" (Redekop 1982, 176) again loomed as a more significant factor in its policy stance.

During the first half of the 1970s, the government's refusal to back up its stated priority of promoting social justice in South Africa with more practical economic, social, and political measures drew increasing domestic criticism, particularly from the relatively small, but active and vociferous "Southern African constituency," based in various nongovernmental organizations, churches, and universities (Legge, Pratt, et al. 1970, 1–2). While Canada took no concrete political or economic actions against apartheid in South Africa through most of the 1970s, some initiatives were undertaken by the Fitness and Amateur Sport Branch. In response to threats by anti-apartheid sport organizations and black African nations to boycott the 1974 Commonwealth Games if athletes from white Commonwealth countries participated in the South African Games in 1973, Lou Lefaive, director of Sport Canada, sent a letter in December 1972 to all national sport organizations. In this letter, Lefaive stated that, although the decision to take part in the South African Games ultimately rested with the sport governing bodies and individual athletes, the federal government would no longer provide financial assistance for this or any other sporting events hosted by South Africa. Despite this announcement, some fourteen Canadian athletes attended the South African Games at their own expense (Burrows 1978, 115).

The government strengthened its position somewhat in 1974, when it announced that it would no longer give either moral or financial support to Canadian sport bodies travelling to competitions in South Africa or to events staged in Canada at which South African athletes competed (Campagnolo 1977, 1). In March 1975 it announced that, in compliance with the rules of the International Olympic Committee (IOC), South Africa would not be invited to the pre-Olympic trials in Montreal (Burrows 1978, 116).

The government was called upon to enforce its new sport policy on a number of occasions in the next few years. For example, in the summer of 1975 it withdrew its $24,000 contribution to the Canadian Masters' Association when it learned that this organization had invited South African and Rhodesian athletes to compete in an international track and field meet, to be held in Canada (ibid.). The next summer, in a similar situation, the government withdrew funds amounting to some $500,000 from the Committee for the Olympiad for the Disabled because it had invited a racially integrated team from South Africa to compete in an international competition in Etobicoke (HC Debates, 11 May 1976, 13427). Meet organizer Roger Jackson had insisted that South Africans should be allowed to participate in the Olympiad, but the Canadian Olympic Association and James Worrall, a member of the IOC from Canada, refused to lend him their support. One country, Kenya, had threatened to boycott the Olympiad if South Africa competed. Such a boycott might well have had repercussions for the Montreal Olympics.[2] In both of these cases, the offending organization protested that it had not been informed of the policy (Burrows 1978, 116–7).

The resolve of the Canadian government to take a tougher stand on sporting contacts with South Africa was doubtless reinforced by actions taken at the UN. The UN General Assembly had adopted a series of resolutions (in 1971, 1975, and 1976), which were supported by the Canadian government, that called on member states to assist in the campaign to eliminate racially discriminatory practices from sport. As well, in 1976 the UN's Special Committee Against Apartheid passed a resolution that called for sanctions to be imposed on national teams competing with South Africa (Lapchick 1976a, 73).

The Soweto "disturbances" of 1976, which led to the deaths of 176 people and unleashed a wave of unrest that swept across South Africa, dramatically increased the pressure, both at home and abroad, for Canada to take stronger and more substantive measures against South Africa. These events were a contributing factor to the last-minute boycott of the 1976 Montreal Olympics by African nations. In January 1977 Canada began a two-year term on the UN Security Council at a time when international pressure for stronger action against apartheid was becoming increasingly irresistible. This position gave Canada's South African policies a higher international profile (Blouin 1978, 159). These, then, were the larger political, economic, and social determinants that were to set the parameters for Canada's diplomatic efforts to avert a boycott of the 1978 Edmonton Commonwealth Games.

SOUTH AFRICA AND INTERNATIONAL SPORT

The underlying cause for concern over a black African nation boycott of the 1978 Commonwealth Games lay in the long history of racism in sport in South Africa. Sporting contacts with South Africa had been a vexatious issue for sport organizations and governments for many years. As far back as 1934, the British Empire Games, which had originally been awarded to South Africa at the conclusion of the 1930 Games in Hamilton, were relocated to London, England, because of concern raised by South African officials about the "colour question" (Hoy 1979, iv).

Although racism had been practised in South Africa since the arrival of white settlers, it was not until the election of the National Party in 1948 that laws were introduced confirming existing segregation practices and apartheid became formalized. Because sport was not perceived as a threat to apartheid and because it was largely organized on racial lines anyway, it was initially little affected by these new laws. Gradually, however, the government began to take control of sport policy making. In 1956 it released a comprehensive policy about sport, which decreed that sport must be organized along the lines of the "separate development" which applied to other aspects of social life in South Africa (Guelke 1986, 119–20).

By the early 1960s any pretense of independent sport bodies had been dropped, and all meaningful decisions regarding apartheid in sport or South Africa's international sport relations were controlled by the government (Lapchick 1975, 203–4). Because the endorsement of the South African Olympic and National Games Association (SAONGA) was a prerequisite to participation in the Commonwealth and Olympic Games, coloured and black athletes were prevented from participating in these games. SAONGA was "white-only" and upheld the government's position on segregated sport. Many outstanding non-white athletes were forced to move to other countries in order to compete in such events. Some of these athletes and some sport officials found their way to England.

In 1958, in order to mount a protest over racial injustices in sport, a number of these non-white athletes and officials formed the South African Sports Association (SASA) in London, England (ibid., xi). In May 1959 this group was able to bring the matter of racial discrimination in South African sport to the attention of the IOC. At a 1960 executive board meeting, the IOC heard a deposition from a SAONGA delegation, in which certain promises were made about changes in its racial policies with regard to sport (Lyberg, 1988–89b, 54). This matter was discussed later that year at a meeting between the IOC and the National Olympic Committees in Rome in connection with the 1960 Olympics (Quick 1990, 22). But the IOC was evidently satisfied with the explanations of Reginald Honey, an IOC member from South Africa, about race policies in that country and took no action on the SASA protest.[3]

The issue was again brought to the attention of the IOC, this time by a member from the Soviet Union, Constantin Andrianov (Ramsamy 1984, 45), at its executive board meeting in 1962, when SAONGA was asked to give an explanation of the racial policies in sport in its country.[4] The first formal attempt to expel South Africa came later that year, at the IOC's general assembly meeting in Moscow. However, an expulsion motion put forward by the Soviet Union received only five votes (Quick 1990, 23). But the IOC did threaten to suspend South Africa unless SAONGA could give assurances that sport discrimination would be ended.

In October 1962 the South African Non-Racial Olympic Committee (SAN-ROC) was formed at the instigation of SASA, with the ultimate objective of replacing SAONGA as the legitimate Olympic committee of South Africa (Guelke 1986, 123). Shortly after SASA itself was dissolved. The South African government, however, took immediate steps to suppress SAN-ROC by placing banning orders on all its officers. Refusal to co-operate with apartheid sport policies meant withdrawal of sport facilities and travel documents, which, of course, prevented these officers and athletes from competing in international sport events (Lapchick 1975, 205–6). In addition, the South African government commenced to persecute the SAN-ROC officials. Indeed, the president of SAN-ROC, Dennis Brutus, was shot and injured by South African special police in September 1963 (Quick 1990, 24). Eventually SAN-ROC was forced into exile and reconvened in London in 1966 (Lapchick 1976a, 57–8).

But international pressure over South Africa's apartheid sport policies was building. At a meeting in Baden-Baden in October 1963, the IOC made two demands of SAONGA as pre-conditions for participation in the 1964 Tokyo Olympics: first, that it declare that it would abide by the IOC rule banning racial discrimination; and, second, that it obtain from its government a change in racial policies in sport. As a result, changes were made in the way that Olympic representatives were selected so that a few black athletes were declared to be members of the South African 1964 Olympic team. The IOC was so encouraged by this move that it dropped its second condition, that is, that the government change its policy, but still insisted that SAONGA publicly denounce the policy of segregated sport (Guelke 1986, 124–5). The South African government, however, rejected this demand and at the same time announced that it was not going to allow mixed teams to represent South Africa in international sport competitions.[5] Consequently, at its meeting in conjunction with the 1964 Winter Olympics in Innsbruck, the IOC banned South Africa from the Tokyo Olympics.

But SAONGA continued to lobby its many friends on the IOC for recognition at the 1968 Mexico City Games. In the mean time, in December 1966, thirty-two African nations banded together to form the Supreme Council for Sport in Africa (SCSA). The following year, SCSA was formally recognized by the Organization for African Unity (OAU). SCSA was committed to end racial discrimination in South Africa and along with its associated member, SAN-ROC, was to be a driving force for the eventual expulsion of both South Africa and Rhodesia from the Olympic movement (Hain 1982, 242). SCSA's first step was to inform the IOC that its members would not participate in the 1968 Mexico City Olympics if South Africa participated while segregated sport still existed in that country (Ramsamy 1991, 541).

International anti-apartheid sport organizations and black African nations were confident that the IOC would exclude South Africa at its executive board meeting in Tehran in May 1967. But they were surprised to find that some of the IOC membership was still trying to find some compromise on this issue. The new South African prime minister, John Vorster, had made a speech in the House of Assembly in April

1967 that appeared to represent a marked departure from previous policy towards segregation in sport. South Africa, said Vorster, would select a mixed team for the Mexico City Olympics so that the country could play "its rightful role in world affairs" (Guelke 1986, 127). As a result of this speech and further supplication from the SAONGA delegation at the Tehran meeting, the IOC decided to send a fact-finding team to South Africa the following September (ibid., 132).

This committee was led by Lord Killanin, who was to be the next president of the IOC. Its report conceded that South Africa was not abiding by the IOC's code on racial discrimination, but, according to Killanin's (1983, 37) account, it made no recommendations about South African participation at Mexico. Other sources, however, suggest that the committee did recommend that South Africa be permitted to send a team to Mexico because that would allow a small number of blacks from South Africa to participate in the Olympics (see Guelke 1986, 132). Be that as it may, the report apparently was enough to carry the day for the pro–South African members of the IOC, and in a mail ballot in February 1968, by a count of 36 to 25, the IOC sanctioned South Africa's participation in the Mexico Games (Lyberg 1988–89b, 144).

An international controversy ensued. At the end of February, SCSA gave approval to a boycott of the Mexico City Games, and SCSA and SAN-ROC mounted a campaign to gain support for such a boycott. This was to be the first of many successful uses of the boycott by the international anti-apartheid sport movement. As a result, some fifty countries, including many Asian nations, as well as black members of the United States Olympic team, announced that they would withdraw from the Games if South Africa was allowed to participate. In addition, Mexican officials made it clear that it was opposed to South African participation and would not extend an invitation to that country (Guelke 1986, 132). Mexican Olympic and Organizing Committee members flew to Chicago to meet with IOC president Avery Brundage. At first, Brundage refused to back down and was quoted as saying that the Games would be held even if only he and South Africa attended (Quick 1990, 27; see this source for an insight into the role that Brundage's racist views played in this struggle). But the pressure brought to bear on him was too great, and Brundage was forced to call a meeting of the IOC executive in April 1968. The executive voted unanimously to withdraw the invitation to South Africa and this vote was sustained in a mail ballot of the entire membership by a count of 46 to 14 (Guelke 1986, 132).

The anti-apartheid sport organizations and the black African nations continued their efforts to have South Africa expelled from the IOC.

Brundage and other South African supporters were able to resist this pressure at the IOC meetings in Warsaw in 1969. But the following year in Amsterdam the inevitable happened, and the IOC voted 35 to 28 (with 3 abstentions) to expel South Africa (Lyberg 1988–89b, 163). At this meeting, South Africa evidently made no attempt to defend its position; rather, it insisted that the IOC not interfere with its domestic affairs (Ramsamy 1984, 48).

The Commonwealth Games Federation (CGF) had a much easier time than did the IOC in banning South Africa from its Games. When that country withdrew from the Commonwealth and declared itself a republic in 1961, the federation was able to bar it from the 1962 Games in Perth, Australia, on the grounds that it was no longer a member of the Commonwealth. But expelling South Africa from the Olympics and the Commonwealth Games was not to end the efforts of the international anti-apartheid sport organizations and their allies to use sport to fight apartheid in South Africa. These organizations turned their efforts towards ending all sport contacts with South Africa and their endeavours were ultimately to cause more grief for organizers of the Commonwealth Games than for the Olympics.

The most important of South Africa's sporting contacts were with those white Commonwealth nations that shared a common heritage and a passion for the same games as South Africa. Rugby and cricket were white South Africa's most popular sports, with golf and tennis next in line. In rugby and cricket, South Africa had a long history of test matches with Britain, Australia, and New Zealand. These ties were to prove very difficult to break, in part because these sports were not part of the Olympics or the Commonwealth Games, and thus their international sport organizations could not be coerced into putting pressure on offending countries. Another reason was that the governments of some of these white Commonwealth nations were very reluctant to interfere with the "rights" of sport organizations or individuals to travel abroad and compete as they wished. Finally, there was a belief (and still is in some quarters in Britain) that "bridge building" was a more effective way of breaking down apartheid in South Africa than isolation. This belief carried over into sport (Lapchick 1979, 164).

The two leading international anti-apartheid sport organizations, SCSA and SAN-ROC, were to turn to secondary boycotts to stop these sporting contacts with South Africa, and the Commonwealth Games were to become an important battleground in the fight to end apartheid in sport (Kidd 1983, 8). If nations such as Britain, New Zealand, and Australia did not stop their sporting contacts with South Africa, either they were to be banned from competition or the black African nations would boycott the event. In 1970, for instance, a proposed cricket tour of Britain by South Africa met with massive resistance from the "Stop the Seventy Tour Committee." This organization had used protests and demonstrations against the 1969–70 South African rugby tour of Britain as a show of strength. SCSA, headed by Abraham Ordia, had threatened to boycott the 1970 Commonwealth Games in Edinburgh if the rugby tour went ahead as planned (Lapchick 1976a, 68–70). The British Sports Council, the Race Relations Board, and the Organizing Committee for the 1970 Commonwealth Games all exerted pressure to cancel the 1970 cricket tour. In a debate in the British House of Commons on 14 May 1970, members from both sides of the House called for government intervention in cancelling the tour (Parliamentary Debates, 1969–70, 1461–1523). When the Marylebone Cricket Club (MCC) refused, British Home Secretary James Callaghan intervened. In asking the MCC to withdraw its invitation to the South African team, Callaghan stated: "We have particularly in mind the possible impact on relations with other Commonwealth countries, race relations in this country, and the divisive effect on the community. Another matter for concern is the effect on the Commonwealth Games" (*Guardian* [Manchester], 22 May 1970; quoted in Lapchick 1976a, 69–70). Shortly after, the MCC backed down and cancelled the tour.

In 1971 the South African rugby tour of Australia met with such violent demonstrations that the federal government there refused to back a proposed cricket tour by South Africa later that year. As a result, the Australian Board of Cricket Control was forced to cancel it (Lapchick 1976b, 39). The following year, protests over the proposed 1973 South African rugby tour of New Zealand and threats by SCSA to boycott the 1974 Commonwealth Games scheduled for New Zealand prompted the New Zealand prime minister, Norman Kirk, to withdraw government support and eventually to cancel the tour (Lapchick 1975, 213). This strategy of secondary boycotts by SCSA and SAN-ROC was a most effective one – one that was to cause major disruptions of future Olympic and Commonwealth Games and to become an issue with which the Canadian government would have to wrestle for years to come.

THE 1976 MONTREAL
OLYMPICS BOYCOTT

The black African nation boycott of the 1976 Montreal Olympics evidently came as a complete surprise to both Department of External Affairs and Canadian Olympic officials.[6] Attention had been focused on the Taiwan issue, which had occupied External Affairs and Olympic

Games organizers right up to the commencement of the Games. But there had been plenty of warnings about the impending boycott. As early as 1973, Dennis Brutus, the founder of SAN-ROC, had informed External Affairs that his organization intended to launch a protest movement against South African and Rhodesian participation in the Montreal Olympics.[7]

The immediate cause of the Montreal boycott was the 1976 tour by the New Zealand All-Blacks (ironically, the name of that country's mostly white national rugby team) of South Africa. New Zealand rugby contacts with South Africa had been a major point of contention for some time with those fighting apartheid. In 1971 Prime Minister Vorster's "outward policy" had softened South Africa's restrictions on the colour of touring athletes from the countries with which it had traditional sporting ties (Lapchick 1976b, 37–8). This change meant that New Zealand could use Maori (non-white) players on its touring rugby teams. Despite this concession, New Zealand's Labour government continued to express its disapproval of sporting contacts with South Africa (Thompson 1978, 128). But the majority of New Zealanders were anxious to renew their traditional rugby rivalry with South Africa. Robert Muldoon, the leader of the National Party, took advantage of these sentiments in the general election campaign of 1975 by promising that he would revive sporting contacts with South Africa. When his party won the election, it brought about a return in government policy on sport exchanges to that of non-interference and a prime minister who was, at least initially, quite outspoken about this policy (ibid.).

In January 1976, after South Africa had accepted New Zealand's invitation to participate in the World Softball Championships, Abraham Ordia, the president of Supreme Council for Sport in Africa (SCSA), called for a world-wide boycott of these championships. When the softball championships came off as scheduled, there were further threats to boycott the 1976 Olympics (Hoy 1979, 78–9). At the same time, Canada's policies also came under criticism from Ordia because a Canadian team participated in these championships.[8] Tensions increased in April, when the New Zealand prime minister rejected demands by SCSA to end all sporting contacts with South Africa and, in particular, to cancel a proposed tour of South Africa by the New Zealand All-Blacks rugby team (Newnham 1978, 32). This action precipitated a unanimous vote by SCSA to boycott the Montreal Olympics if the rugby tour went ahead as scheduled. The All-Blacks' departure for South Africa coincided with the Soweto massacre and further infuriated anti-apartheid organizations (ibid.). At its meetings in Mauritius, the OAU, SCSA's parent body, passed a motion calling on all African nations to boycott the Montreal Olympics to protest New Zealand's presence at the Games.[9]

But none of the other parties in the dispute was willing to take any action. The New Zealand government refused to withdraw its team from the Montreal Olympics or to change its sport policies, citing the autonomy of New Zealand sport organizations and the absence of rugby from the Olympic program as justifications for its position (Strenk 1978, 25). The Canadian government maintained that the boycott threat was a problem that needed to be resolved by the parties directly involved, that is, SCSA, New Zealand, and the IOC.[10] The matter was serious enough to precipitate the first sign of Commonwealth involvement. Commonwealth secretary-general Sonny Ramphal visited New Zealand in May 1976 and warned that its government must do more than merely express verbal opposition to apartheid (Payne 1991, 419). Given the IOC's traditional position that politics had no place in the Olympic movement, it is not surprising that its president, Lord Killanin, denounced the boycott threat, expressing the view that the African nations would go through various motions to draw attention to their opposition to apartheid in sport, but in the end would not impose a boycott (ibid.).

Most of the teams from black African nations did, indeed, arrive in Montreal early in July in preparation for the Games. However, this was a strategy that the anti-apartheid sport organizations had used successfully in 1972 in order to get the IOC to back down at the last minute and ban Rhodesia from the Munich Games. On that occasion, both the Rhodesian and most of the black African nations' teams were already in residence in the Olympic village. But on that occasion the target was Rhodesia, a country that had been forced from the Commonwealth and had few allies championing its cause. In fact, the UN's Committee of Twenty-Four had passed a resolution on 30 April 1971 urging the IOC to suspend the membership of the Rhodesian National Olympic Committee and asking the Munich Organizing Committee to annul its invitation to Rhodesia.[11] In the case of the Montreal Olympics, New Zealand was a Commonwealth member in good standing, with allies both in the Commonwealth and among other nations around the world. Barring New Zealand from the Montreal Games was beyond the reach of any political pressure that the black African nations could bring to bear on the IOC. In addition, as noted before, the international controversy about the Canadian stand on Taiwan's participation in the Montreal Games made it impossible for the black African nations to focus world attention on their cause.

Early in July, sixteen of the black African nations sent a letter to IOC president Lord Killanin protesting the New Zealand rugby tour and calling on the IOC to bar New Zealand from the Games. Failing this, the "respective National Olympic Committees of Africa reserve the right to reconsider their participation in the Games of the XXIst Olympiad"

(IOC, July 1976b, 70). The protest was considered at the IOC general assembly meetings in Montreal immediately preceding the Games. Following a brief discussion, it was decided to take no action on the matter. Lord Killanin wrote to the president of SCSA stating, "Rugby is a sport over which the IOC has no control whatsoever ... the full IOC Session ... unanimously agree that this is not a matter within its competence" (ibid., 71). As a result, on the weekend before the Montreal Games were to commence, black African nations began to drop out and return home. By opening day, twenty-two nations had withdrawn (IOC, October 1976, 45). The boycott precipitated immediate action in the international sport scene. International sport organizations in athletics, football, and swimming took immediate steps to expel South Africa from their respective associations (Ramsamy 1984, 50).

DIPLOMACY AND
THE COMMONWEALTH GAMES

If Canadian government officials had been unaware of the potential of a black African boycott of the Montreal Olympics, they were certainly cognizant of the possibility of a similar occurrence at the 1978 Edmonton Commonwealth Games. Over the summer of 1976, SCSA secretary-general Jean-Claude Ganga announced to the press on several occasions that the black African nations would boycott the 1978 Commonwealth Games if New Zealand did not change its policy on sporting contacts with South Africa (Hoy 1979, 83, 85). These pronouncements placed Canada in an extremely awkward position. New Zealand could not be barred from the Commonwealth Games because of its membership in the Commonwealth, but if it did not change its policy on sporting contacts with South Africa, most non-white Commonwealth countries would likely boycott the Edmonton Games.[12] Such a boycott would not only put the Games in financial jeopardy (the federal government had committed some $12 million to the capital costs of these Games and goods and services estimated to be at a similar level [Baka and Hoy 1978, 7–8]), but it would be damaging to the future of the Commonwealth Games as an institution and to the harmony of the Commonwealth as a whole.

Canada's reputation as a progressive force within the Commonwealth and as a friend to third-world countries (Matthews and Pratt 1978, 74) would also suffer. Prime Minister Trudeau had managed to win the confidence of third-world leaders and to reinforce the image of Canada as a bridge between developed and developing countries (Radwanski 1978, 353–4). The government was determined to maintain this image. On the domestic front, there was concern that a failure of the Edmonton Commonwealth Games would create further political problems for the government in western Canada.[13] There was also, as noted earlier, growing pressure on the government from advocacy groups in Canada for some concrete action against apartheid. In sum, it would have been politically impossible for Canada to host an (almost) all-white Games in Edmonton (Payne 1991, 419). It is not surprising, then, that Canada took a much stronger position towards apartheid in South Africa in the two years leading up to the 1978 Commonwealth Games than had previously been the case.

Deep divisions in attitudes toward getting South Africa to change its position on apartheid existed within the Commonwealth (Matthews and Pratt 1978, 170), so Canada found itself trying to mediate among these differences. Much of the Canadian efforts over the next two years, therefore, would be directed toward bringing New Zealand and the African countries together in order to reconcile their differences. To this end, a series of *démarches* ensued. Numerous meetings were held during the fall of 1976, in which Canada expressed its concerns over the boycott threats and explored ways in which New Zealand prime minister Robert Muldoon's position could be changed in order to increase the chances of African participation in the Edmonton Commonwealth Games (Hoy 1979, 86–92). Canadian secretary of state for external affairs Allan MacEachen met with Muldoon and members of his cabinet (*Edmonton Journal*, 1 September 1976, 55), as well as with a number of ministers in Malaysia, Indonesia, and Australia (Wederell, 25 September 1976).

MacEachen's successor, Donald Jamieson, conferred with Sir Keith Holyoake, minister of state and chairperson of the New Zealand delegation to the UN General Assembly, to inquire whether there was any possibility of New Zealand moving towards a sport policy that would be more in line with that of Canada.[14] Jamieson also sought the assistance of Anthony Crosland, the British foreign affairs minister, in relaying the message to New Zealand that it had to start acting on its pledges (Calamai, 7 December 1976, 6).

Trudeau also joined in the diplomatic efforts to save the 1978 Commonwealth Games by seeking the assistance of Michael Manley, the Jamaican prime minister, to intervene with third-world Commonwealth nations in the impasse over New Zealand's sporting contacts with South Africa (*Edmonton Journal*, 29 October 1976, 8). By mid-December 1976, government officials had prepared a list of recommendations for Trudeau aimed at defusing the boycott threat. These included urging the New Zealand high commissioner to impress upon his government the necessity of meeting with SCSA president Ordia, requesting the personal assistance of leaders of key Commonwealth countries, and sending a special emissary to appropriate countries to seek a solution to the problem.[15]

By January 1977 Commonwealth Games officials were optimistic enough about the prospects for the Edmonton Games to send out the official invitations (Powers, 13 January 1977, 25). They had delayed sending them out earlier because of the uncertainty about the boycott. Indeed, there had been a few bright signs. During October 1976 New Zealand's minister of foreign affairs, B.E. Talboys, had released a statement asking all New Zealand sport bodies to consider UN resolutions on apartheid in sport when deciding whether or not to maintain sporting relations with South Africa, and the minister of state, Sir Keith Holyoake, had announced that the New Zealand government would discourage sporting bodies from going to South Africa (*Globe and Mail,* 19 October 1976). A public opinion poll released that same month had indicated that the majority of New Zealanders disapproved of sporting contacts with South Africa (*Globe and Mail,* 10 November 1976). Sir Alexander Ross, chair of the CGF, had patched up a quarrel between himself and SCSA president Ordia at a meeting in November, which, at the time of the confrontation, had prompted Ordia to call a press conference to renew boycott threats by denouncing the federation and New Zealand.[16] Ross responded by asking Commonwealth countries to give serious consideration to the matter of sporting contacts with nations that practised racial discrimination (*Edmonton Journal,* 18 November 1976, 1).

In December 1976 the New Zealand Rugby Union had refused an invitation for the Maori team to tour South Africa. Prime Minister Muldoon had congratulated them on this decision but still denied that his government had changed its non-interference policy (Ingram, 26 January 1977). However, there were signs that he was beginning to adopt a more conciliatory position. He had indicated that all New Zealand sport federations had been advised to consider the wider implications of any sporting contacts with South Africa (*Edmonton Journal,* 10 December 1976, 6). Muldoon also responded to a personal letter from SCSA secretary-general Jean-Claude Ganga, indicating that his government supported the campaign against apartheid and deploring the selection of any sports team on the basis of racial discrimination. Furthermore, he stated that he believed significant contacts with racially selected teams from South Africa would no longer take place (Ingram, 26 January 1977).

This growing optimism of Commonwealth Games officials seemed well founded when, at the end of January, the SCSA executive announced that it had decided against a boycott of the Edmonton Games. But these hopes were dashed shortly after, when the OAU announced that it would advocate a boycott unless New Zealand severed all sporting contacts with South Africa (Nichols, 1 April 1977, 7). This measure by its parent body forced SCSA to back down on its previous statement, and by early March there were reports from SCSA that black African nations would come to Edmonton only if New Zealand were barred (Hoy 1979, 93–4).

While these events were taking place, SCSA raised the question of New Zealand's visa practices. This turn of events put Canada in an embarrassing situation because its position on visas for South Africans was a weak one. In order to try to defuse this issue, Canadian officials took the position that the central problem was New Zealand's sport contacts with South Africa and not the hypothetical application of local immigration laws. But Muldoon's reply to Ordia essentially put all countries not refusing visas to South Africans in the same boat as New Zealand.[17]

The wide differences that remained between New Zealand and the black African nations of the Commonwealth on the issue of sporting contacts with South Africa made it clear that the issue was not going to be resolved in bilateral negotiations between New Zealand and other nations and organizations. It was a matter that would have to be settled collectively by the leaders of the Commonwealth nations – a multilateral "end run" around the New Zealand – African stalemate.

THE GLENEAGLES DECLARATION

By the middle of March 1977 a consensus was developing among officials from Britain, Canada, and Australia and Commonwealth secretary-general Ramphal that a solution would have to be found before the upcoming Commonwealth meetings in June. If the impasse was not resolved by that time, the possibility remained that the Commonwealth heads of government might request that the CGF cancel or postpone the Edmonton Games. If the federation ignored this request, the Canadian government would face the awkward decision of intervening itself, with the brouhaha that would ensue, particularly in western Canada.[18]

Any agreement would have to meet the requirements of Africans, be acceptable to New Zealand, and confirm British, Australian, and Canadian opposition to sport contacts with South Africa. Canada supported the suggestion of British sport minister Dennis Howell that a statement of principles acceptable to Commonwealth heads be developed by the three countries. Because there was not enough time to consult ministers, Canadian officials informed the British government of Canada's endorsement of Howell's proposal and asked Britain to draft a statement for Canadian and Australian review.[19]

The task of developing this statement, however, was to fall largely on Ramphal, who agreed to produce a draft communiqué and to do some of the preliminary diplomatic work with the various Commonwealth governments. Following a meeting between Trudeau and Ramphal in Ottawa at the end of March, the work of selling the idea to all Commonwealth governments began in earnest. Canadian officials circulated a first draft of the statement. Most Commonwealth countries reacted cautiously, waiting to see how the document would be received by New Zealand (Morse 1978; quoted in Hoy 1979, 96–7). After his consultations in Canada, Ramphal worked with three third-world Commonwealth leaders, Michael Manley of Jamaica, Julius Nyerere of Tanzania, and Kenneth Kaunda of Zambia, to develop the document further to meet the demands of third-world countries.[20]

During the month of April, the Department of External Affairs, in conjunction with Fitness and Amateur Sport, prepared an option document for the Prime Minister's Office. The options included: first, refusing to grant visas to visiting South African athletes as suggested in Article 6 of the UN resolution on sporting contacts with South Africa; second, withholding all funds for a period of time from national sport organizations that invited South African athletes to Canada; and third, open criticism of sport contacts with South Africa (Burrows 1978, 125). The first two options were rejected in favour of the third, and as a result, fitness and amateur sport minister Iona Campagnolo drafted a statement reiterating Canada's position on sporting contacts with South Africa and deploring all such contacts. In order to bolster this rather insipid statement, Campagnolo asserted that "the Government will in the future strongly discourage and, if necessary, take a very critical attitude in public towards any proposed sporting contact between Canadians and South Africans, whether federal funding is involved or not" (ibid., 121).

At this point, Campagnolo had been lobbying within the cabinet for parallel "compensatory" action against South Africa on the economic side. In particular, she called for the closing of all trade offices in South Africa to balance the contribution being made by sport in opposing apartheid. But any type of economic sanction had been consistently opposed by private interest groups doing business in South Africa. These groups had the support of the Department of Industry, Trade, and Commerce, which used its influence with the Department of External Affairs to apply pressure within the cabinet and the Liberal Party caucus to oppose economic sanctions. This lobby group, according to Campagnolo, was equally, if not more, effective as those groups calling for increased sanctions against South Africa.[21] Allan Gotlieb, who was under-secretary of state for external affairs, says the dominant view in Industry, Trade, and Commerce at this time was that Canada should trade with everyone; if you imposed sanctions, then you open the way for others to do the same to you in different circumstances, that is, use trade for political purposes.[22] Despite this "trade" lobby within the government, Campagnolo was able to get assurances that the issue of closing down trade offices in South Africa would have a "high priority" at the forthcoming meetings of the Commonwealth heads of government.[23]

The policy statement deploring sporting contacts with South Africa was sent in early May under Campagnolo's name to all national sport governing bodies, as well as to all Commonwealth governments, every African nation, and to the UN (Morse 1978 cited in Hoy 1979, 98, 100). There was very little in the way of new policy in this statement, but it contained a great deal of rhetoric that served to give a high profile to what little action Canada had taken about sport contacts with South Africa, and it was timed to make an appropriate impression for the upcoming Commonwealth heads-of-government meetings in London. Apparently Campagnolo's statement had no appreciable effect on Prime Minister Muldoon.

The heads-of-government meetings convened in London in early June 1977, with the possibility of a boycott of the Edmonton Games still paramount in the minds of Canadian officials. Prime Minister Trudeau had said in the House of Commons shortly before leaving for the London meetings that "of the Commonwealth Games there has been a great deal of preparatory work by myself, by the Minister of External Affairs and our officials. On many occasions we have tried to solve this question. If it is not solved before the London Conference next week, then we must find some way of solving it there" (HC *Debates*, 31 May 1977, 6110; quoted in Olafson 1988, 21). Discussions about apartheid commenced on the third day of the formal meetings. But it was not until the prime ministers retired by themselves on their traditional retreat from these meetings to Gleneagles, Scotland, that serious negotiations about a Commonwealth accord on sporting contacts with South Africa got under way. Trudeau was always a dominant figure at these Commonwealth meetings. He loved the informal atmosphere – the give and take of debate – and shone at them,[24] and these attributes stood him in good stead in the private negotiations that followed. Manley was designated by the others to secure Muldoon's co-operation, presumably because he was seen as someone who could provide a link between the developed and third-world nations in the Commonwealth.[25] Thus Manley provided the leadership for discussions among

Muldoon, Ramphal, Trudeau, Brigadier Shehu Yar'Adual (the Nigerian military chief of staff), Lee Kuan Yew (the prime minister of Singapore), and Aboud Jumbe (the vice-president of Tanzania). The outcome of these negotiations was a draft that followed closely the one that had been prepared earlier by Ramphal (Payne 1991, 420).

This document was presented to the Commonwealth leaders when the meetings reconvened in London the following week and was accepted by all the heads of government. The Commonwealth Statement on Apartheid in Sport, which became known as the Gleneagles Declaration, was deliberately set in the broader context of the Declaration of Commonwealth Principles, a document that had been adopted by the Commonwealth heads of government in Singapore in 1971. The Singapore declaration had pointed to the diverse racial nature of the Commonwealth, noting that sporting contacts with countries practising apartheid served to "condone this abhorrent policy" (ibid., 421). The Gleneagles Declaration itself called on each Commonwealth government, as its "urgent duty," to take every practical step to discourage sporting contacts with South Africa (see Appendix B for the complete text of this accord). However, it was drafted in such broad terms that it allowed discretion by individual governments in fulfilling this obligation in accordance with their own laws. As such, it allowed New Zealand to sign and thus break the impasse between that country and the black African Commonwealth nations over sporting contacts with South Africa. Trudeau was credited with having played a central role in bringing this agreement to fruition (see, for instance, Kidd 1988, 655; Macfarlane and Herd 1986, 110).

The next step was to convince the OAU that the Gleneagles Declaration represented a significant step in the fight against apartheid in sport. To this end, Trudeau wrote to several of his francophone African colleagues to solicit their support at the upcoming OAU meetings. Apparently francophone Africans tended to suspect any Commonwealth activity of being "just another colonial ploy."[26] Despite these sentiments, these efforts were apparently effective because the Gleneagles Declaration was approved by the OAU in Gabon at the end of June.

In July the New Zealand parliament gave its approval to a resolution supporting the Gleneagles Declaration, and Prime Minister Muldoon issued a statement defining government sport policy calling on all national sport bodies to adhere to the accord. These measures made Canadian officials much more optimistic that a major boycott of the Edmonton Commonwealth Games would be avoided. Indeed, there was a belief that the question of sporting contacts with South Africa had been placed "on a more rational footing."[27]

CONSOLIDATING THE GAINS

Despite the successful negotiations in London, there was still much to do to ensure that the Gleneagles Declaration did not come apart and jeopardize the success of the 1978 Commonwealth Games. External Affairs and Commonwealth Games officials set about wooing leaders of African Commonwealth nations to ensure their attendance in Edmonton the following summer. Canadian missions in Africa proved to be important in these endeavours. In the first instance, they served as channels of communication between African nations and New Zealand. New Zealand had no diplomatic missions in Africa; nor did most African nations in New Zealand (Burrows 1978, 120). In the spring of 1977, Iona Campagnolo had met with the Canadian ambassador to Italy and was able to confirm that he would mobilize support for the Edmonton Games in the six Commonwealth African nations that were also part of his ambassadorial responsibilities.[28]

Canadian missions were also to provide invaluable services for the African tour by the president of the Edmonton Commonwealth Foundation, Maury Van Vliet, in the fall of 1977. This promotional and goodwill tour of African Commonwealth nations proved to be an important diplomatic endeavour in saving the 1978 Commonwealth Games. Government officials made arrangements through the Canadian missions in Africa for Van Vliet to meet with representatives from all Commonwealth countries. The tour provided him with the opportunity to discuss the New Zealand problem and to promote the Gleneagles Declaration as "something more than a piece of paper" (Morse 1978; quoted in Hoy 1979, 108–10).

The trip also allowed Van Vliet a chance to publicize Canada's offer to all African team members and officials of air transportation at reduced rates from Algiers to Edmonton at the close of the Pan-African Games (which were being held two weeks before the Commonwealth Games) and then return them to London after the Commonwealth Games (*Edmonton Journal,* 24 October 1977, 15). This offer fulfilled the Edmonton Organizing Committee's promise to provide travel costs that would not exceed those to the site of the rival host, Leeds, England, as well as overcoming the logistical problems created for African Commonwealth nations by the juxtaposition of the Pan-African and Commonwealth Games.[29] These incentives were well received by African officials, and Van Vliet returned home expressing optimism that "there would be no African boycott of the 1978 Commonwealth Games in Edmonton despite continuing controversy over New Zealand's sporting links with South Africa" (*Edmonton Journal,* 14 October 1977, A6).

One negative reaction to Van Vliet's trip came from scsa president Abraham Ordia, who accused Canada of not doing enough to force New Zealand to conform to the Gleneagles Declaration.[30] In early November 1977 Ordia was still insisting that Africans would not participate in the Edmonton Games (*Globe and Mail*, 15 November 1977). With the issue of the boycott on the agenda of the scsa meetings later that month in mind, Iona Campagnolo wrote a letter of appreciation to all the African authorities who had met with Van Vliet.[31] Canada's efforts paid off when scsa adopted a resolution in mid-November urging all African Commonwealth nations to attend the Games in Edmonton (Powers, 31 December 1977).

In December, during the first debate about foreign affairs in the House of Commons in seven years, external affairs minister Donald Jamieson announced a package of measures designed to demonstrate Canada's disapproval of apartheid. These included the phasing out of all government-sponsored commercial-support activities in South Africa, the withdrawal of all Export Development Corporation support from any transactions relating to South Africa, a commitment to publish a code of conduct and ethics for Canadian companies operating in South Africa (issued on 28 April 1978), and the requirement of non-immigrant visas from all residents of South Africa coming to Canada. Previously South African residents had been able to enter Canada on the presentation of their passports, the normal requirement for Commonwealth citizens (HC *Debates*, 19 December 1977, 2000). Several factors led to this symbolically significant, if substantively minimal, break with previous Canadian policy not to interfere with normal social and commercial intercourse with South Africa: the international impact of the 1976 Soweto "disturbances"; Canada's accession to a temporary seat on the UN Security Council, where the South African issue was considered urgent; and growing domestic pressure from interest groups opposed to apartheid (Keenleyside 1983). However, these measures were no doubt also designed to strengthen Canada's anti-apartheid credentials with other Commonwealth countries in the run-up to the Edmonton Games.

These steps were also precipitated by complaints from Iona Campagnolo that sport had been shouldering all the responsibility for Canada's inaction over apartheid in South Africa and that it was time for Canada to take a stronger economic position. Trudeau had supported Campagnolo's argument in cabinet for fairness in distributing more broadly sectoral responsibility for opposing apartheid. She fought particularly hard, over opposition from Industry, Trade, and Commerce and some factions in External Affairs, for the closing of Canadian trade offices in Capetown and Durban as a "significant signal."[32] It was not that Campagnolo was opposed to using sport sanctions: she was strongly committed to the struggle against apartheid but wanted the government to take stronger action on all fronts.[33]

The new Canada Immigration Act, requiring non-immigrant visas for all South Africans visiting Canada, was implemented on 10 April 1978. At about the same time, Trudeau decided not to take to cabinet the recommendation that entry visas be denied to South African sportspersons, "in view of the domestic political situation."[34] Evidently there was concern that any revision of the existing South African sport policy deny entry visas might not increase its effectiveness, given the difficulty of detecting all South African sportspersons trying to enter the country. Also, there were fears that with the Commonwealth Games so close, institution of a new sport policy "might create a worse controversy at home than retention of the present policy with its admitted weaknesses."[35] Indeed, tennis and golf lobbies were opposed to any restrictions on visas for South African sportspersons because some of those players were feature attractions at Canadian professional golf and tennis tournaments. This tennis and golf – and, indeed, sailing – lobby was particularly strong at this time.[36]

Although Uganda had accepted its invitation to the Games in February 1978, it officially withdrew during May 1978 because of alleged Canadian hostility towards that country. Its withdrawal was precipitated by media speculation about the possible attendance at the Games of Ugandan president Idi Amin as coach of the boxing team (Jackson, 22 April 1978). In the House of Commons, Conservative MP John Diefenbaker demanded that the government refuse Amin entry to Canada because of his "diabolical murderous conduct," asserting, "We need no coaches for murder and terrorism in this country" (Jackson, 1 May 1978, A8). Consequently, Uganda withdrew from the Games, making the accusation that "Canada has used Uganda's intention to participate in the Games to mount a vicious and entirely unwarranted anti-Ugandan campaign" (Powers, 19 May 1978, B4).

As a last-minute effort to co-ordinate departmental activity on the Edmonton Games and ensure maximum participation by African nations, External Affairs created a special Task Force for Commonwealth Games in May 1978, and Eric Bergbusch was appointed special co-ordinator for Commonwealth Games.[37] The department also made the necessary diplomatic arrangements for Ivor Dent and a group of business persons from Edmonton to undertake a goodwill tour of African Commonwealth nations in late June and early July (Hoy 1979, 121). Dent had been the mayor of Edmonton from 1968 to 1974 and during his tenure of office, had been instrumental in gaining African support for the city's successful bid for the Commonwealth Games. To this end, he had himself made a tour of African Commonwealth nations in the spring of 1972.[38] The Dent trip, according to Campagnolo, was a "triumph," and much credit went to Horst Schmidt, Alberta minister of culture, youth, and recreation, who integrated the resources available in Alberta with contacts around the world in order to provide Dent with the best possible chance for success.[39]

By the end of June 1978, eleven of the thirteen African Commonwealth nations had accepted their invitations to the Games (Hoy 1979, vi). But diplomatic efforts were still being undertaken to ensure maximum participation at Edmonton. During July 1978 Prime Minister Trudeau sent a message of greeting to all Commonwealth teams through their respective heads of government. At the same time, Commonwealth secretary-general Ramphal informed all Commonwealth heads of government that, in his opinion, all Commonwealth governments had abided by the Gleneagles Declaration (Morse 1978; cited in Hoy 1979, 122–3).

Despite the Canadian government's misgivings a few months earlier, Campagnolo announced on 14 July that it had established specific criteria for withholding Canadian visas from South African sportspersons (Minister of State for Fitness and Amateur Sport, 14 July 1978). This initiative was evidently precipitated by a memo sent in late June to the prime minister and the secretary of state for external affairs that advocated denying entry visas to South African sportspersons who represented their country. This memo had come from an ad hoc committee, with representatives from the Games Task Force, External Affairs, and the Privy Council, established to discuss the danger of a boycott and to determine what further steps might be needed to ensure the success of the Games.[40] To this end, Campagnolo had applied constant pressure to overcome the opposition in cabinet to this measure, using the importance of a successful Edmonton Games to advantage to finally win her point.[41]

The new criteria disallowed visas for all South African athletes and sports representatives wishing to enter Canada to participate in sport competitions or associated congresses. Campagnolo felt that this new policy would take an "unfair burden" off individual sport governing bodies, by meeting the request of many Canadian sportspersons "that the government take full responsibility for administration of the South Africa Sport Policy" (Minister of State, Fitness and Amateur Sport, 14 July 1978). When questioned, Campagnolo stated that this policy was a follow-up to the Gleneagles Declaration and was designed "to ensure the success of the Commonwealth Games" by demonstrating Canada's "good faith" to the other Commonwealth countries (Powers, 15 July 1978, A1).

Certainly this decision, one that effectively reversed the government's earlier position, must be seen as a final tactical step taken to ensure the attendance of African countries at the Commonwealth Games. Indeed, Commonwealth secretary-general Ramphal noted that Canada's refusal to permit visas for South African athletes and sport officials was "very greatly appreciated within the Commonwealth" (Powers, 2 August 1978, C1). In Pretoria the measure was certainly connected with the Commonwealth Games. One report there quoted Campagnolo as saying, "We could not take any chances that there might be some South African representatives coming to the Games who could precipitate some unpleasantness."[42] At home, however, this new policy met with strong criticism from some segments of the Canadian public. Letters to the *Globe and Mail* and the *Toronto Star* queried why Canada was adopting such a strong position with South Africa, while taking a "wishy-washy" approach to the Soviet Union.

Success seemed close at hand when the CGF received word on 23 July from the executive committee of SCSA that it had authorized African Commonwealth members to participate in the Edmonton Games (*Edmonton Journal*, 26 July 1978a, A1, 3). However, on 26 July optimism was supplanted by disappointment and shock when Nigeria's newly appointed sports minister, Sylvanus Williams, announced that his country (the largest and most powerful nation in black Africa) would boycott the Commonwealth Games (*Edmonton Journal*, 26 July 1978b, A1). Described as "a very high political decision" (Powers, 31 July 1978a, B1), the withdrawal of Nigeria from the Commonwealth Games may well have been influenced by the Nigerian president of SCSA, Abraham Ordia. Ordia, who was regarded as having a strong influence on decisions made by the Nigerian government, maintained that New Zealand had not severed its sport ties with South Africa (Powers, 20 April 1978a). At a news conference on his visit to Edmonton in April, he had indicated that he did not believe that the spirit and letter of the Gleneagles Declaration was being carried forward, citing the example of five New Zealand rugby players who had accepted an invitation to compete on an international team in South Africa in August 1977 (Powers, 20 April 1978b). Ordia had been brought to Edmonton by the Department of External Affairs, along with the secretary-general of SCSA, Jean-Claude Ganga, to visit the Games sites and talk with officials because Ganga had been unable to meet with Maury Van Vliet on his African trip.[43]

To exacerbate the situation, Ordia was incensed by inflammatory telegrams he had received from some New Zealanders (Powers, 20 April 1978a), and by provocative statements made by officials of the CGF (*Edmonton Journal*, 18 November 1976, 1, 3). Furthermore, he had crossed swords with the New Zealand prime minister, Robert Muldoon, in an acrimonious meeting prior to the boycott of the 1976 Olympics; the antipathy between these two men probably helped to keep the boycott threat alive (Ferrabee, 12 October 1977). However, Ordia still accepted the External Affairs invitation to fly him to the Edmonton Games, and while there, confided to Eric Morse that Nigeria's last-minute decision to boycott the Games was taken "in the barracks" (i.e., by the military) and without consultation with him.[44] Indeed, he advised Campagnolo, at the time of the Nigerian withdrawal, that she should let Nigeria go its own way, but seek to stop other Commonwealth nations from following suit.[45] Evidently, there was both an "official" and a "personal" side to Ordia.

Because news of the Nigerian boycott was so unexpected and so late "there was very little one could do to secure its reversal," according to Commonwealth secretary-general Ramphal (*Edmonton Journal,* 3 August 1978, A1). Nevertheless, diplomatic efforts were made to dissuade other African Commonwealth countries from following Nigeria's lead. These included telephone calls by Donald Jamieson to key African leaders.[46] Sierra Leone was a particularly doubtful participant and Iona Campagnolo made a personal telephone call to its president.[47] Prior to the announcement of Nigeria's withdrawal, that country had launched a campaign to recruit support for a wider, last-minute boycott of the Edmonton Games if New Zealand insisted on competing.[48]

Nigeria was to have one last attempt at disrupting the Games. After making his boycott announcement, Nigerian sports minister Sylvanus Williams flew with other government officials to Algeria, where the Pan-African Games were concluding. He was able to convince Algerian Games officials to postpone the closing ceremonies by one day, hoping in this way to disrupt Canada's plans to fly the competing athletes directly to Edmonton and at the same time giving him time to dissuade other African nations from attending the Games. However, Eric Bergbusch, the newly appointed games co-ordinator, and Iona Campagnolo were able to make arrangements with Air Canada to delay its regular flight, despite considerable disruption to its overseas schedule. One day late, African athletes were on board and Nigeria's last effort had failed.[49]

By the time of the opening ceremonies of the XI Commonwealth Games on 3 August 1978, the only African Commonwealth nations not in attendance were Nigeria, Uganda, and Botswana. During July, Botswana had indicated that it would be unable to attend because of other priorities in its national sport program (Powers, 31 July 1978b). Following the "diligent two-year efforts of the external affairs department" (*Edmonton Journal*, 1 August 1978, D4), 1,900 athletes from forty-six Commonwealth countries entered Commonwealth Games Stadium in Edmonton to participate in the Games (Hoy 1979, 128). Not only had Canada's diplomatic efforts during the previous two years been successful, but the country was to go on to have its most successful ever Commonwealth Games, besting both its traditional rivals, England and Australia, in the unofficial medal count for the first time in the history of the Games. They were skillfully televised by the CBC and attracted an unprecedentedly large Canadian audience for such a non-Olympic event. In this way, they vindicated the federal government's support of high-performance sport in the 1970s and contributed to the realization of Pierre Trudeau's vision of sport as an instrument of national unity (see Macintosh, Bedecki, and Franks 1987, chap. 10). The Games also illustrated the role sport could play in projecting a positive image of Canada to the rest of the Commonwealth.

CONCLUSIONS

Certainly, Canada was successful in its efforts to avert a boycott of the 1978 Commonwealth Games. Its prodigious diplomatic endeavours, particularly in the development of the Gleneagles Declaration and the last-minute policy of denying visas to South African sportspersons, were key factors in these efforts. This was in spite of scepticism among African nations about New Zealand's sincerity in living up to the Gleneagles Declaration and despite apparent violations by that country. The commitment by the other white Commonwealth nations to stand behind this agreement was a major step in gaining the confidence of the international anti-apartheid organizations and the black African Commonwealth nations. The Gleneagles Declaration was also to become the basis for further, more stringent agreements about sporting contacts with South Africa in the years to come. It was certainly a diplomatic triumph for Canada and was to help to set the stage for future Canadian leadership in the Commonwealth in the fight against apartheid in South Africa.

At the same time, these diplomatic measures served to maintain Canada's reputation and good relations with third-world countries in the Commonwealth and the UN, and to focus and stabilize international views regarding Canadian attitudes toward apartheid (Olafson and Brown-John 1988, 15–16). Sport had become an area in which there was a convergence of views between Western industrialized nations, who objected to South Africa's violation of the principle of equality in sport, and black African and other third-world countries, who saw sport as an instrument that could be used effectively to break down apartheid in South Africa (Guelke 1986, 144).

These efforts by Canada were made easier by the more aggressive stand that the UN took following the 1976 Montreal Olympic boycott and the Soweto riots. The UN reacted to these events with a series of aggressive resolutions aimed at combatting South Africa's apartheid policies. The sport resolution adopted at the thirty-first session in November 1976 urged states to refuse any official sponsorship, assistance, or encouragement to sport contacts with South Africa; to refuse visas to South African sportspersons; and to deny facilities to teams or sportspersons for visits to South Africa. The most aggressive recommendation, to support projects aimed at the development of non-racial sports in South Africa, suggested that South Africans did not have the sovereign right to develop their own inter-racial sport structure (Hunter 1980, 22–3); thus it went beyond the international norm of non-interference in the domestic affairs of a sovereign state.

Canada's role in the UN on sport and apartheid is instructive because it points to the country's traditional disposition towards consensus seeking in international affairs rather than taking a lead in implementing measures it believed to be desirable. During one of the UN sessions about sport and apartheid in South Africa, a recommendation came forward that a working group be formed to draw up a convention against sporting contacts with South Africa. This proposal had been originally suggested to the Special Committee against Apartheid by the Jamaican prime minister, Michael Manley, in a message sent to the International Seminar on the Eradication of Apartheid.[50] Such a working group was appointed by the president of the General Assembly and consisted of the existing members of the Special Committee against Apartheid and seven other member states, including Canada (Brutus 1978, 1). Of the twenty-four members of the newly formed Ad Hoc Committee on the Drafting of an International Convention against Apartheid in Sports (ibid., 1–2), Canada was the only Western nation. The Jamaicans had been anxious that Canada seek a place on the committee, in order to ensure a fair degree of Western support.[51] On the other hand, Canadian officials had hoped that such membership would establish more firmly Canada's credentials as an opponent of apartheid before the 1978 Commonwealth Games.[52]

During the ensuing deliberations, Canada worked hard to stave off the drafting of a convention, instead advocating a legally weaker "declaration," because it felt that many progressive Western countries would find the precise and enforceable language in a convention difficult, if not impossible, to accede to.[53] Canada stressed that a declaration might form a consensus upon which more binding resolutions could be developed (Burrows 1978, 119). Subsequently the UN General Assembly adopted the International Declaration against Apartheid in Sports in December 1977 and instructed the ad hoc committee to continue its work by preparing an International Convention against Apartheid in Sports (Brutus 1978, 1). The declaration contained eighteen articles that elucidated the ways in which states and sport organizations could isolate South Africa from international sport (Hunter 1980, 23), including, in Article 6, denial of visas to representatives of sport bodies, members of teams, or individual sportspersons from any country practising apartheid.[54]

While the technique of refusing entry visas had been employed internationally on twenty known occasions between 1969 and 1978 (ibid., 25), there was still residual resistance among some member states to endorse the withholding of visas or passports, and this point had caused difficulties and disagreements during the preparation of the declaration (Brutus 1978, 2). Even though Canada had opposed the creation of a binding international convention and had refused to deny entry visas to South African sportspersons earlier in 1978, this very measure became official policy during July 1978. The adoption of the UN declaration in late 1977 gave an "aura of legitimacy" (Hunter 1980, 28) to this practice at a time when Canada felt it needed to adopt some tangible measure that would increase its diplomatic credibility with the anti-apartheid sport movement and black African nations in order to avert a last-minute boycott of the 1978 Commonwealth Games. This change of position points to another feature of Canadian foreign policy, that of buttressing policy departures by reference to the actions of international organizations (in this case, the UN).

It is hard to avoid the conclusion that sport carried the lion's share of Canada's more aggressive stance towards apartheid in South Africa. Indeed, this is the position that the fitness and amateur sport minister, Iona Campagnolo, had taken in cabinet. As a result, she played a significant role in the introduction of the economic measures against South Africa that external affairs minister Donald Jamieson introduced in parliament in December 1977 (Burrows 1978, 130–3). But these economic sanctions had a minimal effect on economic activity between Canada and South Africa (Olafson and Brown-John 1988, 6–7). The symbolic shift in policy from one of promoting economic relations to one of passivity toward such interchanges fell far short of active government discouragement of Canadian trade and investment in South Africa that many groups had been advocating (Langdon 1978, 15). However, effective economic measures against South Africa would certainly have run into opposition from the private sector because they would have hurt Canada's trade with that country. In addition, they would have run counter to deeply held opposition by government officials to trade sanctions of any kind. This opposition was based on the view that, as a trade-dependent state, Canada's overriding national interest lay in ensuring that the liberal international trading system should be as free as possible from politically motivated disturbances.

However, even the minor trade concession that Campagnolo had been able to win was not sustainable after the Games were over. She recalls that the Canadian trade offices in Durban and Capetown were quietly reopened, much to her disappointment.[55] In fact, what the Canadian government did was to hire a South African as a commercial counsellor at its Pretoria embassy (Redekop 1984–85, 98), a measure not quite so hypocritical. Moreover, other realities would produce further disappointment for Campagnolo. When Prime Minister Trudeau returned from the Group of Seven (G7) economic summit in West Germany, he made drastic cuts in the federal budget (including to Fitness and Amateur Sport) without any consultation with his minister of fitness and amateur sport. Sport officials in both the government and the national sport organizations reacted bitterly to this measure, seeing it as a betrayal of Canadian sport in the face of the best performance ever at the Commonwealth Games.[56]

Campagnolo may take some solace in the fact that the sport boycotts imposed on South Africa were a particular irritant to South Africans, given their strong traditional sport ties with white Commonwealth countries in cricket, rugby, tennis, and golf. In contacts with South Africans while serving on the External Affairs Southern African Task Force in the early 1980s, one Canadian official noted that they considered the sport boycotts by far the most irksome of all the sanctions imposed on them.[57]

It is no surprise that, while the Canadian government continued to maintain a low profile on economic sanctions during the 1976–78 period, it pursued a leadership role in the Commonwealth on sport sanctions. This role was far easier for Canada to play than for Britain, Australia, and New Zealand because Canada had no significant sporting ties with South Africa in that country's most important sports: rugby and cricket. These games had little indigenous following in Canada, and thus the government did not face the opposition to sport sanctions from strong national sport organizations that was characteristic of those in the other three Commonwealth nations. One can only conclude, then, that sport was a convenient vehicle with which Canada could show its resolve against apartheid without either doing harm to the economy or running into any significant opposition from special-interest groups. At the same time, the government was able to play a leadership role in the Commonwealth and point to some concrete measures against apartheid, albeit limited to sport, to placate the small, but vociferous domestic groups that wanted much stronger anti-apartheid measures.

Many observers have noted that sport boycotts have been far more effective than have other types of measures, particularly economic ones, designed to isolate South Africa and its apartheid policies (see, for instance, Hain 1982; Kidd 1988; Lapchick 1976a). Kidd (1988, 644) has pointed out that the success of sport boycotts lies partly in the fact that there exists in modern sport a "hierarchical governance." Thus, in contrast to business or other voluntary organizations, sport governing bodies are able to impose the discipline of "powerful and monopolistic associations" (ibid.) on athletes in a way that is not possible in other spheres of activity in modern society. This characteristic of sport has made it easier for international anti-apartheid sport organizations to isolate South Africa from the international sport scene, because when they have been called upon to make good their threats of boycotts, they have been able to keep black African athletes away from prestigious international events. Our story of the 1978 Edmonton Commonwealth Games illustrates clearly that these "transnational" sport organizations had, by this time, come to influence the actions of Commonwealth governments and their intergovernmental organization, the Commonwealth heads of government. These transnational sport organizations were to change their strategies and become even more influential in the Commonwealth and on the international sport scene in the 1980s, as we shall see in chapter 5. But first we turn to Canada's role in the struggle between the IOC and the United States over the latter's frantic efforts to impose a world-wide boycott on the 1980 Summer Olympics in Moscow.

CHAPTER FIVE

The Moscow Olympics Boycott

The Canadian government's decision to support the United States–led boycott of the 1980 Summer Olympic Games in Moscow in protest over the Soviet invasion of Afghanistan in December 1979 was the most traumatic event in the annals of Canadian international sport. For most people associated with high-performance sport, it was the first time that they had felt the impact of government policy on Canada's participation in international sport events. According to a Department of External Affairs official responsible for co-ordinating Canada's response to the proposed boycott, this "question dominated the Canadian public foreign policy debate (during the period, January to April 1980) to the virtual exclusion of all other topics" (Morse 1987b, 9). The boycott mystified and angered many sport officials and most athletes; at the same time, they were unable to take any effective steps to counter the political machinations that led up to the final decision to boycott the Moscow Games. In retrospect, many politicians and most sport officials condemned the boycott.

As we argued in chapter 1, the vagaries of international politics limit and often dictate the behaviour of states. In order to make sense of the 1980 Moscow boycott, then, we first situate it in the wider perspective of a return to the Cold War atmosphere that existed between East and West at the end of the 1970s. During that period improved relations between East and West began to deteriorate. Finally, with the invasion of Afghanistan, *détente* was off. These international tensions coincided with some impelling internal political realities, both in Canada and the United States, that go far in helping us understand the motives of both US president Jimmy Carter and Canadian prime minister Joe Clark in pressing for sanctions against the Soviet Union. These domestic political concerns, along with the events that surrounded the decision to impose boycotts and sanctions against the Soviet Union are discussed next.

INTERNATIONAL POLITICAL
BACKGROUND

The Soviet invasion of Afghanistan in December 1979 was preceded by a decade of official *détente* and actual Soviet expansionist policies, which culminated in a series of foreign-policy successes in the second half of that decade. By the end of the 1960s, the Soviet Union had attained approximate nuclear parity with the United States. This was followed by a tacit recognition by the United States of Soviet superpower equity; at least, this was how the Soviets interpreted the "Basic Principles of Mutual Relations" document signed by President Richard Nixon on his visit to Moscow in May 1972. From this new-found position of strength, the Soviets, under the leadership of Leonid Brezhnev, were able to pursue a more aggressive foreign policy than had been possible in the two decades immediately following World War II. A number of successful "interventions" in third-world countries followed, events which made the Soviets more confident of their "equal" status with the United States.

The Soviet Union's successful intervention in Angola in 1975 was followed by strategic initiatives in countries around the Horn of Africa, first in Ethiopia and then in Somalia and the People's Democratic Republic of Yemen, all at the invitation of governments friendly to the Soviet Union. The ensuing conflict between Ethiopia and Somalia forced the Soviets to choose sides; as a result, they were expelled from Somalia. Despite this later setback, these initiatives strengthened the Soviet military and political presence in Africa and in the strategic entrance to the Red Sea, a development that was seen to be a threat to the security of Western nations' oil supply. This was to be a factor in the West's response to the Soviet invasion of Afghanistan. At the same time, the Soviet Union pressed forward with arms sales and undertook to sign treaties and extend some limited foreign aid to other third-world countries. These initiatives were undertaken with little financial commitment by the Soviets, but they extended the Soviet Union's interests and afforded strategic military access in key areas in Asia and Africa. Political events in certain Arab nations also resulted in a more friendly attitude towards the Soviet Union in this strategic area.

Of more direct relevance for our story, however, was the takeover in Afghanistan in April 1978 by the People's Democratic Party of Afghanistan (PDPA), a regime seen as one that would develop even closer ties with the Soviet Union than had been the case with the previous government. Factional disputes broke out within the PDPA; initially, the radical Khalq gained control, an event that had the potential to strengthen Soviet influence in the country even further. But the Khalqs proved to be too radical for other factions of the party, and an opposition along a number of political lines developed. Although quite disparate, together these factions threatened the stability of the PDPA government. The Soviet Union was faced with the question of what to do. The hegemony of the United States was on the decline, no small part of which could be attributed to its humiliating capitulation in Vietnam. By the late 1970s American military pre-eminence had come under considerable doubt and, perhaps as important, the domestic political will for US world leadership had all but vanished (for a sample of the enormous literature on the US decline, see Kennedy 1988; Pfaff 1989; for a dissenting view, see Nye 1990). Inspired, perhaps, by its recent international political and military success and by an apparently increasingly vulnerable and chastened United States, the Soviets decided to invade Afghanistan in support of the Khalq regime in December 1979. (The political events that have been highlighted here are drawn from a more detailed account by Page 1988.)

INTERNAL POLITICAL REALITIES

The initial reaction to the Soviet invasion of Afghanistan, both in the United States and in Canada, was a mild one. News of the invasion did not command the front pages of newspapers; editorials condemned it, but did not see any dire threats to the stability of the Middle East. Flora MacDonald, secretary of state for external affairs in the Clark Conservative government, issued a statement on 28 December that expressed "deep regret" over the invasion, but gave no notice of sanctions nor expressed any fears of further Soviet advances in the Persian Gulf or the Indian Ocean (Bayer 1988, 2–3). Perhaps one reason for this apparently mild response was the fact that it was the holiday season; most senior public servants and politicians were not in Ottawa.

But the rhetoric was to change dramatically. The first sign was to come the day after MacDonald issued her statement. US president Jimmy Carter called for an emergency meeting of NATO nations to consider stronger measures than mere protest. Three motives were apparently behind this change of heart by Carter. The first was his precarious political position. At the time of the Soviet invasion of Afghanistan, Carter found himself well behind his political opponents; his popularity had fallen so far that he was trailing fellow Democrat Ted Kennedy in voter-preference polls and was facing the unprecedented possibility, as an incumbent president, of losing the 1980 Democratic presidential nomination. In Canada, Joe Clark's Conservative government was far behind the Liberals in the popularity polls. Both these leaders were searching desperately for ways to improve their political fortunes (ibid.,

5–6) or at least to divert attention from their perceived weaknesses on domestic matters. A strong position on Afghanistan would suggest leadership, something both seemed to lack.

The second reason for Carter's intensification of pressure on the Soviets was ostensibly a reassessment of Soviet motives by officials in Washington. The invasion was now being seen as a precursor to further Soviet moves in the Persian Gulf and the Indian Ocean. In fact, this act was seen by hard-liners in Washington (and elsewhere) as the end of *détente* (see Howard 1980; Kaiser 1980; Questor 1980). The NATO meetings, called at Carter's behest, were held in London and Brussels on 31 December 1979 and 1 January 1980. Canada was one of six nations in attendance. Although a number of measures were discussed, including a proposal by West Germany to boycott the Moscow Olympics, no consensus was reached and the meetings disbanded without any concrete proposals (Bayer 1988, 5–7).

But a final, important motive was personal. When Carter came to the presidency in 1976, he had taken a "dovish" position on the Cold War. Indeed, in a convocation address he delivered at Notre Dame University on 22 May 1977, Carter had declared that the Cold War was essentially over. This was not a popular view in government or military circles at that time, and he was under much pressure to revise his stance on the issue. The Soviet invasion of Afghanistan vindicated the views of the hard-liners in his government. Carter felt betrayed, and his reaction was a particularly vindictive one.[1]

In Canada Clark was facing the prospect of opposition parties focusing on the government's waffling over the Afghanistan crisis; both the NDP and the Liberals had been capitalizing on the public's perception of Clark as a weak and vacillating leader. His about-face on his election campaign promise to move the Canadian embassy in Israel from Tel Aviv to Jerusalem had already caused considerable political damage. His political fortunes were at a low ebb. Clark could not afford to be seen to be weak and indecisive on the Afghanistan issue. A flurry of editorials in Canada's major newspapers after the turn of year called for stronger responses on the part of his government.

It was in this atmosphere that Clark unilaterally announced early in January 1980 that Canada would not recognize the new Afghan government, that development-aid programs to Afghanistan would be suspended, that Canada would press the UN Security Council for action, and that he would write a letter of protest to President Leonid Brezhnev. Not strong action, especially in light of the fact that Canada had already decided to terminate its aid to Afghanistan at the conclusion of the current projects, but it was enough to satisfy public opinion at this stage (Bayer 1988, 7–10).

This first statement by Clark, however, made no mention of a boycott of the Moscow Games. In fact, at a news conference on 4 January, Clark stated that Canada was unlikely to withdraw from the Games because it would have "no practical effects" on the Soviet invasion of Afghanistan. The president of the Canadian Olympic Association (COA), Richard Pound, was quoted as saying at this time that his organization would defy any government call for a boycott and reminded the government that the COA "acts independently from government" (Kereliuk 1986, 156). This statement by Pound, apparently made without consultation with his executive or membership, was to get him in trouble with the press and many of the members of the COA.

Immediately after Clark's news conference, Carter stepped up his attack. He announced a number of retaliatory measures, including curtailed Soviet fishing and air landing rights in the United States, a restriction on US credit to the Soviet Union, and a ban on the further sale of grain to the Soviet Union. Carter also served notice that the United States would consider a boycott of the Olympic Games in Moscow if the Soviets did not pull out of Afghanistan. These announcements caught both European allies and Canada off guard. Nevertheless, Clark immediately announced that Canada would not make up the shortfall of grain caused by the United States ban by increasing its exports. This was a hollow promise because the country was not in a position to increase significantly its wheat shipments to the Soviets (Bayer 1988, 7–11).

Meanwhile, a cabinet review of further protest measures by Canada revealed that it had few options at its disposal to inflict any economic damage on the Soviet Union and very little precedent for doing so. Trade between the two countries, when Canadian wheat exports were excluded, was at an inconsequential level. Any wheat embargo would hurt Canada more than the Soviets. Bans on Soviet fishing off the Grand Banks and suspension of Aeroflot landing rights at Gander would harm the economy of Newfoundland far more than that of the Soviet Union. Despite public opinion in Canada, which was decidedly in favour of harsher sanctions against the Soviets, no segment of the population was willing to shoulder the economic consequences of sanctions; certainly, most people were in favour of measures that would not affect them. In facing an impending federal election, Clark found himself in the unenviable position of losing critical Conservative votes on the prairies if he imposed a wheat embargo, losing support in Atlantic Canada if he curtailed Soviet landing and fishing rights, but facing the loss of votes across the country if he chose to take no action. Canadian public opinion, as reflected in the newspapers, was deeply divided on the question of boycotting the Moscow Olympics (ibid., 11–16).

In these circumstances, Clark was forced to walk a fine line in imposing any further sanctions. Still, on 11 January he announced further
sanctions, including restricting wheat sales to traditional levels, sus-
pending talks on long-term credit agreements with the Soviet Union,
and severing of scientific and cultural exchanges with the USSR.
Although sounding harsh, these measures would have little impact on
Canadian trade. Included in this round of retaliations, however, was
the announcement that Canada would urge the IOC to move the 1980
Summer Olympics to a city outside the Soviet Union. To this end, a governmental committee was struck to examine the feasibility of holding
the Games in Montreal, a site that Clark also offered in announcing
Canada's opposition to the Moscow venue. Subsequently, the Canadian
government approached some one hundred countries and the IOC in
order to gauge support for an alternative site for the 1980 Summer
Games (Bayer 1988, 18–23) and to find out whether any other recent
hosts of the Olympics would be prepared to take on the 1980 Games.
Clark was still not committed to a boycott of the Moscow Olympics,
saying that "this is not being contemplated" (Trueman, 12 January
1980, 1).

The boycott issue escalated further on 20 January, when Carter
issued an ultimatum that the United States would not participate in the
Moscow Games unless the Soviet Union pulled all of its troops out of
Afghanistan in one month (Kereliuk 1986, 155). Ironically, he made
no mention of the large contingent of Soviet athletes already in the
United States in preparation for the 1980 Winter Olympics to be held
in Lake Placid, N.Y., in February. A week later, Clark reversed his position completely; he announced that his government would press for
a boycott of the Moscow Olympics if the Soviets did not pull out of
Afghanistan. Sandra Kereliuk suggests that this decision was precipi-
tated by a personal message from Carter to Clark, urging that Clark
support the boycott (ibid., 156–7). However, opposition leader Pierre
Trudeau claimed, in a public address he gave in Toronto late in
January 1980, that Clark had changed his mind because the Toronto
Progressive Conservative caucus had urged him to support the boycott.
Trudeau capitalized on this about-face by announcing, "Every time Joe
Clark talks to his Toronto candidates [members of parliament],
Canadian foreign policy is set back 20 years" (Library of Parliament,
29 October 1990, 9).

The Conservative government had been defeated on a non-
confidence motion in the House of Commons in mid-December 1979.
With the election looming in mid-February, further action on the boycott by the Clark government was curtailed. But Clark's counterpart in
the United States stepped up his attack on the Moscow Olympics.

President Carter assigned the task of convincing the IOC to his secretary of state, Cyrus Vance. Vance took advantage of the host country's prerogative to address the IOC meetings held in conjunction with the Winter Olympics in Lake Placid to urge the general assembly to cancel or change the site of the 1980 Summer Games. He justified the United States position by stating that to "hold the Olympics in any nation that is warring on another is to lend the Olympic mantle to another nation's actions" (Nafziger 1980, 71). United States Olympic Committee (USOC) president Robert Kane added that the Soviet invasion of Afghanistan had made Moscow "an unsuitable place for a sports festival" (*The Journal*, 13 February 1980). These efforts were in vain. According to Lord Killanin, "Vance's speech was greeted in absolute silence by everybody" (Killanin 1983, 184). In his zeal, Vance had forgotten to carry out the one task he was supposed to: open the IOC meetings (Wilson 1982, 59). All seventy-three IOC members present, including the two from the United States, voted to keep the Games in Moscow (Hoberman 1986, 66–7).

Reactions in Canada to the IOC decision were mixed. The external affairs minister, Flora MacDonald, considered it to be "fairly predictable," while Clark maintained that "the IOC clearly was wrong." Both remained committed to supporting a boycott if Soviet troops did not withdraw from Afghanistan.[2] But opposition leader Pierre Trudeau saw the decision as indicating that any boycott would not be unanimous and that international solidarity was required to effectively display moral condemnation of the Soviet Union. If the Western nations and the third world were divided on the issue, Trudeau maintained that Canada should not support a boycott (Simpson, 30 January 1980, 1 February 1980).

The US proposal for an alternative site to Moscow was a "non-starter" from the very beginning and probably cost Carter credibility with his European allies. Besides being politically unacceptable to the IOC, which had a binding contract with the Soviet Union, it was unrealistic to expect that an alternative site could be found on such short notice. Even Montreal, the most often mentioned alternative to Moscow, lacked suitable accommodation for Olympic athletes. The Olympic Village built for the 1976 Games had been converted into a private housing project. Indeed, Lord Killanin had been informed by both Richard Pound and Mayor Jean Drapeau that it would not be feasible to hold the Olympics in Montreal in 1980.[3] In addition, Quebec taxpayers were just beginning to realize the magnitude of the debt that had been left in the wake of the 1976 Games and would not likely have been in the mood to host another such potential financial disaster. It is not surprising, then, that Killanin maintained that the site for the 1980 Summer Games would be either Moscow or nowhere.

When his IOC initiative failed, Carter put pressure on both the USOC and his NATO allies in Europe to support his proposal to boycott the Moscow Games. Only Margaret Thatcher expressed enthusiasm, but even she was to be thwarted by a recalcitrant British Olympic Association (BOA). This cool reception on the part of his European allies seemed only to spur Carter on. He alternately courted and threatened the USOC and the country's Olympic athletes, guided resolutions in favour of the boycott through both the Senate and the House of Representatives, put pressure on corporate sponsors to withdraw their financial support from the USOC, and threatened to remove its tax-exempt status (Morrison 1982, 12–14; Pound 1984, chaps. 9–10). He ordered a halt to any further US technical support and supplies for the Moscow Games and arbitrarily cancelled the final $20 million owed by NBC to the USSR for the broadcast rights to the Games (Kanin 1981, 121). He even resorted to threatening to revoke the passports of any American athletes who might try to attend the Games in Moscow (Macfarlane 1986, 221).

Ultimately, on 12 April the USOC caved in to these pressures and voted 1,604 to 797 in favour of boycotting the Moscow Games (Kereliuk 1986, 155–6). In this case, Vice-President Walter Mondale had been assigned the task of appearing before the USOC's house of delegates to argue Carter's case (Kanin 1981, 121). Carter's efforts were greatly aided by the press and American public opinion, which was decidedly in favour of the boycott (Hoberman 1986, 66). According to a poll cited in *Le Devoir*, 75 per cent of the American public favoured an Olympic boycott (*Le Devoir*, 12 February 1980). As a sop to the USOC, the White House announced in early May that it would propose an amendment to the 1980 budget that would provide the USOC with one dollar of federal funds for every two dollars that it could raise from the public, to a maximum of $11 million (Morrison 1982, 14). Some newspaper reports claimed that this was part of the deal that Carter had struck with the USOC for its support of the boycott (ibid.).

In Canada the press and public opinion were more divided (Bayer 1988, 16–17). Still, similar, although less ubiquitous, political pressure was facing the COA. But the final turn of the screw was to await the return to office of the Trudeau government.

THE CANADIAN OLYMPIC BOYCOTT

The Liberals under Pierre Trudeau were returned to power in the federal election of 18 February 1980. But there was a period of respite for the COA because Parliament was not recalled until 14 April, and the new government could take no formal action until then. No one knew what to expect from this government. Trudeau had taken an independent stance in his foreign-policy initiatives in the 1970s and had opposed the United States on a number of important issues, particularly in his recognition of the People's Republic of China and with respect to trade with Cuba. His defiance of the IOC over the conditions under which Taiwanese athletes could compete in the 1976 Montreal Olympics was an extension of his one-China policy. On the other hand, Trudeau was on record as supporting the Moscow boycott *if* there were unanimity around the world. Still, there was some optimism in Canadian sport circles that his attitude of independence would prevail and that he would reverse the stand of the Clark government on the Olympic boycott. James Worrall, a Canadian member of the IOC, was certainly of this view.[4] Steve Paproski, minister of state for fitness and amateur sport in the Clark government, also expressed doubts that Trudeau would support the US–led boycott (*Toronto Sun*, 21 February 1980).

On 3 March 1980 the newly appointed minister of fitness and amateur sport, Gerald Regan, announced that his government would arrive at a decision on the boycott issue in due course, after consulting with allies and Canadian sport federations. In the meantime, Australian officials, who had previously announced that they would support a Moscow boycott, were putting pressure on the Canadian government for an early indication of its position.[5]

The president of the COA, Richard Pound, was himself strongly opposed to any boycott of the Moscow Games. However, he had no illusions about the precarious position of his organization in the face of pressure, both from the United States and in Canada, for such a measure. But he struggled to resist this pressure. On 30 March he was instrumental in getting the board of directors of the COA to vote in favour of attending the Moscow Games. This vote, secured despite considerable opposition, was carried by a 5-to-1 margin (Pound 1984, chap. 14). It precipitated a meeting three days later between new cabinet ministers Gerald Regan and Mark MacGuigan (External Affairs) and Pound and his COA colleague and fellow IOC member James Worrall, at which Pound and Worrall sought to find out the new government's position on the boycott. But the government was evidently not yet willing to commit itself. The only public outcome of that meeting was a statement by Pound that after the government made its stance public, the COA would consider its request, but would make its own decision.[6]

A crushing blow had been dealt to Pound's hopes a day after the COA executive vote, when Wally Halder, the executive director of the Olympic Trust of Canada, an organization set up in the early 1970s to raise money for the COA, announced that the trust would withhold funds from the COA if it persisted with plans to send its athletes to the Moscow Olympics. Ironically, one of the original motives for setting up the Olympic Trust was to maintain some independence from government (see Macintosh, Bedecki, and Franks 1987, 82). Some have suggested that this measure was taken because of pressure from head offices in the United States of Canadian subsidiary companies who were major contributors to the trust. Pound's view, however, was that these Canadian corporations took the decision on their own (Pound 1984, 346). Nevertheless, the COA found itself in the position of having both its major sources of funding cut off. The Clark government had already announced that it would not provide monies to support the Canadian Olympic team's participation in the Moscow Games. Unless the Trudeau government reversed this decision, the COA would be left without the means to send its team to Moscow.

In April, Trudeau wrote to a number of Commonwealth and francophone heads of government asking for their views on the Olympic boycott. He stated that he had been hesitant to announce a boycott of the Moscow Games because he hoped that other means would be found to unite international opinion on the withdrawal of Soviet troops and the restoration of Afghan independence. However, there had been no significant Soviet response to international pressure. Trudeau reiterated his position that if a boycott was to be part of the Canadian response to the invasion of Afghanistan, it would be more effective if it was widely supported.[7]

It soon became apparent that the Liberals were not going to change the sanctions that had been imposed on the Soviet Union by the Clark government. The Olympic boycott was to be no exception. The cabinet met on the matter shortly after Parliament convened, and Mark MacGuigan announced in the House of Commons on 22 April that the government had decided to boycott the Games in retaliation for the Soviet invasion of Afghanistan. He defended the government's decision by arguing that Trudeau's consultations with leaders in the Western alliance and third-world nations, coupled with his own conversations with foreign ministers attending independence celebrations in Zimbabwe, had convinced it that the criteria for an effective boycott were present (Secretary of State for External Affairs, 22 April 1980).

Taking a markedly different approach to that of the United States government, MacGuigan stated that his government would impose no overt measures, such as seizing passports or interfering with foreign travel. Canadian athletes, he said, would be free to participate in the Moscow Games, although without the "moral and financial support of the government of Canada" (ibid., 4). But this statement had a hollow, moralistic ring about it in the face of the weight of government decision on the Canadian public and the withdrawal of funds by both the government and the Olympic Trust. The palliative offered by the Canadian government was an amendment to the Grains Compensation Bill to provide financial compensation to the COA to the amount of $1.2 million (HC *Debates*, 19 June 1980, 10796–7). MacGuigan and Regan evidently pushed this measure through cabinet over strenuous opposition from the Finance Department, who argued that the government should not apologize for its action.[8] The government would also announce on 5 June that $1.5 million would be added to the Sport Canada budget to allow the country's high-performance athletes to participate in alternative sport events to the 1980 Summer Olympics (HC *Debates*, 9 June 1980, 1876).

The cabinet decision to support a boycott was evidently not taken easily. The recommendation that came up from the Department of External Affairs offered, as was customary, a number of alternatives, but according to several sources, leaned strongly towards supporting the boycott of the Moscow Games. Indeed, James Taylor, the deputy under-secretary of state for external affairs responsible for the response on the boycott, took the position that it was inevitable that Canada support its ally (the United States) in this matter.[9] According to Gerald Regan, Mark MacGuigan was strongly influenced by the department's position. But Regan himself argued strenuously in cabinet against the boycott.[10] MacGuigan also had a reputation for being decidedly pro-American and much influenced by Alexander Haig, the US national security advisor.

Trudeau personally was uncomfortable with a boycott of the Moscow Games. According to Allan Gotlieb, under-secretary of state for external affairs at the time, Trudeau believed in the spheres-of-influence school of thought, that is, that Canada should not interfere with the Soviet's sphere of influence. The problem with this view in External Affairs was that, although Afghanistan had a pro-Soviet premier, it was still seen as a neutral nation.[11] Eric Morse claims that Trudeau was influenced by the Canadian ambassador to the Soviet Union, Robert Ford, who had returned to Ottawa for a briefing. Ford believed that a boycott would convey a strong message to Moscow about Canada's opposition to the Soviet invasion of Afghanistan.[12] Indeed, he recalls that he had suggested a boycott of the Olympics to Tom Watson, the American ambassador in Moscow, on the day following the invasion (Ford 1989, 320).

Richard Pound believes that the urgings of government ministers from the "golden horseshoe" of southern Ontario had an important impact on the cabinet. According to him, these ministers did not want to alienate the large ethnic population living in the greater metropol-

itan Toronto area who had emigrated from Eastern European countries and who held strong anti-Soviet views. Certainly, the ethnic
question played a role. Steve Paproski, who had not only been the fitness and amateur sport minister in the Clark cabinet, but had also held
the multiculturalism portfolio, had come under increasing pressure in
the summer of 1979 from both his multicultural advisors and the ethnic community to boycott the Moscow Games because of alleged violations of human rights in the Soviet Union.[13] Pound saw Trudeau and
his fellow francophone cabinet colleagues as being largely indifferent
about the boycott (Pound 1984, 342).

The determining factor in the Canadian government's decision,
however, appears to have been that a break with the United States by
Canada on this issue would have had a serious impact on US efforts to
gain world-wide support for the boycott and, indeed, might have
caused a collapse of these efforts.[14] This undoubtedly would have had
a very negative impact on Canada–US relations.

At any rate, Pound was now faced with the unenviable task of chair-
ing a meeting of the full COA, knowing that pressure was growing to
support a boycott of the Olympics, but being himself still opposed to
such a step. A delegation of twenty-four Olympic athletes who had been
invited to Montreal to make a presentation had voted, just previous to
the meeting, 13 to 7 in favour of going to the Games (Kereliuk 1986,
158). But the opinion of the Olympic athletes evidently had little effect
on the outcome of the meeting. Gerald Regan started off the debate on
26 April by urging, on behalf of the Trudeau government, that the COA
support the government's protest of the Soviet invasion of Afghanistan
by declaring a Canadian team boycott of the Moscow Games. Given his
own view on the boycott, this was the most difficult task that he ever had
to undertake as minister of state for fitness and amateur sport.[15] As the
meeting wore on, it became apparent that the government's position
was to prevail. Although a small faction of the COA membership with
a strong sense of Olympic idealism supported Pound's position, the
rest, made up largely of the representatives of national sport organizations and Olympic Trust members and others from the business community, voted in favour of the boycott (Cantelon 1984, 149). The final
vote was 137 to 35 in favour, a margin even greater than that which had
been secured by the United States government at the USOC meeting
some two weeks earlier.

The votes of Olympic committees in Canada, the United States, and
certain other countries in favour of the boycott were seen by the IOC
as being unfairly dominated by persons who did not properly represent
Olympic sport. As a result, the IOC changed the rules so that a majority
of the voting membership of national Olympic committees had to be

representatives of national sport governing bodies and/or Olympic sport organizations.[16] At any rate, Pound was left with the distasteful task of facing the press to announce the COA's decision.

AFTERMATH

In retrospect, the Western nations' sanctions and boycott were seen by most, including many of those who had supported them at the time, as being ineffective and more damaging to the West than to the Soviets. Soviet troops were to remain in force in Afghanistan until 1989. The decision to withdraw them was the result of growing Soviet public opinion against the "Vietnam-like" war in Afghanistan and of Gorbachev's new policies of *perestroika*, rather than any response to pressures brought to bear by the Western alliance boycott and sanctions. In fact, one year after the imposition of the sanctions, most had either been lifted or ignored. Wheat sales to the Soviets were never seriously affected. Suspension of credit lines to the USSR hurt Canadian manufacturers, who lost equipment orders to other countries (see McMillan 1988 for a full assessment of the economic impact of the boycott).

Some have argued that the sanctions were a factor in turning the Soviet Union away from an invasion of Poland in December 1981 in response to the internal political upheaval in that country (Page 1988, 23–4). Indeed, Jimmy Carter was to justify his actions in retrospect on these grounds. His diary in mid-December 1981 records, "I was convinced that the Soviets would already have moved into Poland if they had not been bogged down in Afghanistan and condemned by most nations in the world for it" (Carter 1982, 585). We are not likely to know the truth about this claim unless *glasnost* is extended beyond the expectations of even the most optimistic of Soviet political analysts.

Ultimately, it was Canada's high-performance athletes who paid the greatest price for Canada's stance against the invasion of Afghanistan. These athletes saw years of training and sacrifice go for naught. In many cases, they had to forego their dreams of ever competing in the Olympic Games. Four years later, most would either be too old to compete or would have turned their attention to their future careers.

But there is more to any analysis of the 1980 Moscow boycott than its impact on Canadian athletes. What were its effects on international sport? Carter's efforts to gain support for his boycott were only moderately successful. Certainly Trudeau's criterion of unanimity among Western and third-world nations was not met. Although close to 50 nations joined the US boycott of the Moscow Games (Carter's count was 55), some 81 nations and 5,326 competitors did attend. At the 1972 Munich Olympics, the last Summer Games until Seoul to be boycott-free, some 6,085 competitors from 122 countries took part (Mac-farlane 1986, 227). The Soviets made every attempt to go on with the Games as if nothing was amiss. The Games themselves were seen by most neutral observers as being a success. Lord Killanin, then president of the IOC, was quoted as saying that "the Olympic world has stood up magnificently to the power of the United States and its fawning political friends" (ibid., 227–8). Of course, Killanin cannot be counted in the ranks of neutral observers. He was extremely resentful of the United States attempts to interfere in what he saw as a "non-political" matter.

But despite efforts by the Soviet Union to conduct the Games "as usual," it is impossible to overlook the fact that the Soviet Union missed what was perhaps its greatest opportunity to parade before its own people its athletic superiority over the United States. The American team would have had great difficulty in holding off the German Democratic Republic (GDR) to maintain its traditional second-place position in the unofficial standings, much less mount any serious challenge to the Soviet Union. Certainly, the USSR retaliated by boycotting the 1984 Los Angeles Games. This boycott was less successful in that only the Soviet Union, its Eastern bloc allies (with the exception of Romania), and a handful of other countries stayed away from Los Angeles in support of the Soviet protest. Indeed, a then record number of some 140 nations and 7,078 competitors took part (ibid., 238).

But it can be argued that the Soviet boycott of the Los Angeles Games ultimately turned out to the advantage of the United States. The US was able to celebrate an overwhelming superiority in these Games by flaunting its victories all around the world. Most of the hundreds of millions of television viewers world-wide, including many Americans, were either able to ignore the fact or did not realize that the presence of teams from the Soviet Union and its Warsaw Pact allies would most likely have relegated the United States to a third-place position, behind not only the Soviet Union but also the GDR. That is, in fact, what happened in Seoul in 1988. Thus, in the world of international sport politics, Jimmy Carter's boycott paid off handsomely for the United States, albeit not in the way that he had anticipated.

What of the impact of the boycott on the Olympic movement itself? Certainly the Olympics, already shaken by the massacre of eleven Israeli athletes by Arab terrorists at Munich in 1972 and the black African nations' boycott of the 1976 Montreal Olympics, were further weakened by the 1980 and 1984 boycotts. In fact, many observers predicted that a major boycott or political disturbance at the 1988 Seoul Games would spell the end of the Olympic movement (see, for instance, Christie 1986; Macfarlane 1986, chap. 12; Shaikin 1988, chap.

4). Indeed, Juan Antonio Samaranch, who succeeded Lord Killanin as president of the IOC in 1980, took it as his central mission to ensure that such a disaster did not occur.

LESSONS TO BE LEARNED

Can those concerned with high-performance sport in Canada learn any lessons from the 1980 Moscow Olympic boycott? What about the experiences of other countries? Obviously the political pressure and public opinion brought to bear in the United States on the USOC was too great to resist. But in that country, anti-Soviet sentiment was far greater than in most Western countries. In Britain, despite Margaret Thatcher's enthusiastic support of the Olympic boycott and despite considerable pressure by her government on the British Olympic Association (BOA), it decided that each sport and each individual should make the decision as to whether to go to Moscow. In the end, the majority of British athletes attended the Games (Macfarlane 1986, chap. 2). Indeed, a number of other national Olympic committees voted to defy their governments and sent teams to Moscow. This number included Australia, Belgium, Costa Rica, Ireland, Italy, Luxembourg, the Netherlands, New Zealand, Portugal, and Spain.[17]

One difference in Britain was that the BOA had maintained a far greater independence from government than was the case in Canada. In part, this was due to its financial independence; BOA funds were raised to a great extent from donations by a large number of individuals. Another reason advanced is the greater value placed in Britain on the right of individuals to make political decisions on their own. In his retrospective view of his efforts to avert the boycott in Canada, Richard Pound wished that he had made more of the point that individuals should be given the right to make their own decision (Pound 1984, chap. 16). Indeed, there were no *legal* barriers to any Canadian athlete going to Moscow and competing in the Games. Although IOC rules require that all participating athletes must first be endorsed by their respective national Olympic committees, in the case of the Moscow Olympics the IOC was prepared to make exceptions to this rule.

Kim Nossal concludes his paper "Knowing when to fold: The termination trap in international sanctions" (1988a) by making two recommendations: first, that sanctions be used only as retributive punishments; and second, that such punishments for acts of wrongdoing be highly specific, involving a hurtful, but limited "price" that can be "paid" in a limited period of time. Although he is referring to economic sanctions, sport boycotts fit his requirements quite nicely. First, they can easily be applied as retributive punishments; in fact, this was what Jimmy Carter was hoping for when he called for an all-nations boycott of the Moscow Games. Certainly, if he could have gained the support of all his Western allies, his boycott would have been even more successful. Second, boycotts of sport events certainly meet Nossal's requirement that sanctions involve a hurtful, but limited price that can be paid in a specific time frame.

Indeed, there has been a great deal of debate in the political science literature over the effectiveness of sanctions. As Nossal notes, "the view that these measures are an ineffective tool of Statecraft has become almost axiomatic"; nevertheless, "policy makers do not seem to have been deterred by any academic conventional wisdom" (Nossal 1989b, 301). Perhaps this fact has much to do with the symbolic value of sanctions and boycotts.

But if we look to the Canada Cup hockey series involving Canada and the Soviet Union that was being planned during the critical period in January 1980 when the Clark government was deciding on its options, we can see that there are domestic factors which also come into play when governments weigh one sanction option against another. This series was to take place in Canada in September 1980. Certainly, any move by the Clark government to cancel the Canada Cup would have gained far more publicity than the measures that it did take. In fact, the external affairs minister, Flora MacDonald, was quoted as saying that "the government might consider barring Soviet hockey teams from playing in Canada to protest the Soviet invasion of Afghanistan" (*Toronto Star*, 15 January 1980, A2). But the great popularity of this hockey series with the Soviets and the slavish addiction that the average Canadian has to hockey mitigated against any cancellation of the series as part of the government's sanctions against the Soviet Union. The government, however, was resourceful in rationalizing its decision not to prohibit hockey contacts with the Soviet Union. Although Steve Paproski announced on 12 February that all relations between Canadian and Soviet athletes under the existing bilateral Canada-Soviet sport exchange agreement were being terminated (*Toronto Sun*, 12 February 1980), the government argued that the arrangement between Hockey Canada and the Soviet Union was not a bilateral event.

The Canada Cup series with the Soviet Union was eventually postponed for one year, but not through any efforts by the federal government. When Canada's Olympic athletes found that they would not be able to compete in the Moscow Games, they complained that they should not have to bear the entire burden of Canada's protest over the Soviet invasion of Afghanistan. To this end, they appealed to the NHL Players' Association to show solidarity with them (*Winnipeg Free Press*,

28 April 1980). The players' association responded by refusing to compete in the upcoming Canada Cup. Bobby Clarke, a former president of the association, commented that politics and sport do intersect and that professional athletes cannot be hypocritical *vis-à-vis* Olympic athletes (*Globe and Mail*, 1 May 1980).

Olympic sport has a lower profile and less fan support than do Canada's international hockey fortunes. Still, the Olympic Games elicit a great deal of idealistic sentiment and contain much symbolic power. In many sports and countries, they also appeal to baser jingoistic instincts. These characteristics make them an excellent weapon in the political wars among nations. Indeed, Juan Samaranch was quoted just before the Los Angeles Games as saying: "To boycott the Olympic Games has become extremely spectacular. The rulers doing so know it very well. They secure, for months on end and with little risk, the headlines of all the information media. They capture world attention. The Games are a formidable sound box" (cited in Shaikin 1988, 87).

Pound's point about emphasizing the rights of individuals in order to counter any future use of boycotts of the Olympic Games is one that does not appear to hold out much promise. The right of individuals to act according to their own political convictions is not an idea that is much in fashion in North America today. More relevant is the fact that the COA remained politically impotent during the crisis. There is no record in Pound's memoirs or elsewhere of attempts to rally the political support of cabinet ministers or members of Parliament or to influence the course of the debate in the news media. Certainly, an election period was not a propitious time for such political action. Not only were MPs preoccupied with their respective riding campaigns, but the election featured much anti-Soviet rhetoric by both major political parties. But once the Liberal Party won its majority, concerted political action to get the Trudeau government to reverse the Conservative position on the boycott might well have been successful.

We have lamented elsewhere the fractious nature of the Canadian sport community and its inability to mount any kind of an united front in times of crisis (Macintosh 1988, 128–9). In the past, these shortcomings have manifested themselves largely in the relationships between the federal government and the sport community in the making of internal sport policy. In the case of the 1980 Olympic boycott, the Canadian sport community was unable to mount a challenge to the pressures brought by government and the business community and, ultimately, to avert not only what it saw as an unfair measure, but one that, in retrospect, was seen by almost everyone as ineffective as well. In the present circumstances, where the federal government is pledged to make greater use of sport in meeting its foreign-policy goals, it is imperative for Canada's sport community to organize itself so that it can take united and effective political action in times of crisis. It could learn much from other, more successful examples of the articulation of special interest in Canada.

CHAPTER SIX

Sport, South Africa, and the Commonwealth: The First Half of the 1980s

Once its position on the Moscow boycott was resolved, Canada's international sport diplomacy focused once again on the Commonwealth and relations with South Africa. As was the case in the 1970s, the international anti-apartheid movement would continue to bring pressure to bear to isolate South Africa from international sport. This was to cause considerable discord and debate within the Commonwealth. We deal first with these issues during the Liberal government's term of office under Pierre Trudeau (1980–84).

THE LIBERAL YEARS

Trudeau's Liberal Party returned to power in 1980, following the short-lived Clark Conservative minority government of 1979–80. Although sporting contacts with South Africa and their effect on Commonwealth relations were to remain vexatious issues throughout the 1980s, South and southern Africa were not high priorities with the new Liberal government. Domestic issues and North American irritants – the Quebec referendum, the patriation of the constitution, the National Energy Program, and the Foreign Investment Review Agency – would preoccupy the Trudeau government in its last term of office. In addition, the deep recession of 1981 and 1982 had a profound influence on both the domestic and the foreign policies of the Trudeau government (Granatstein and Bothwell 1990, 311–35). These difficult economic times undoubtedly strengthened the hands of those in the bureaucracy and the government who had long argued against any interference with "trade in peaceful goods with all countries and territories regardless of political consideration" – including South Africa (Redekop 1984–85, 84).

The Canadian sport community regarded the boycott of the Moscow Olympics in 1980 as a failure and used this view to argue against the imposition of further sport sanctions against South Africa, claiming that these measures would hurt Canadian athletes while doing little to end apartheid. Indeed, Abby Hoffman, former international track and field athlete and sport activist, who was appointed director-general of Sport Canada in 1981, and Eric Morse, head of International Sport Relations in the Department of External Affairs,[1] attended a meeting of the Athletes Advisory Council of the Canadian Olympic Association (COA) in April 1983. There they presented the case for the new Sport Canada sanctions against South Africa that had been introduced in 1982 (these are discussed shortly). This advisory council had been established because of protests from Canada's high-performance athletes, who felt they had not been sufficiently consulted when the COA voted to join the US–led Moscow boycott. There was little support for these new sport sanctions against South Africa, with athletes expressing considerable reservation over their "cut and dried" nature. They were particularly concerned that this policy would prohibit them from participating in major international competitions, especially World Championships, and as a consequence, threaten their world rankings. The irony of this situation was quickly pointed out to Hoffman; the loss of world rankings would put athletes in jeopardy in Sport Canada's Athlete Assistance Program, which is itself based on such rankings (Canadian Olympic Association 1983, 3, 5).

Even the largely symbolic measures announced by the previous Trudeau government in 1977, designed to end the use of "taxpayers' money to promote economic relations with South Africa," were subsequently interpreted and implemented very narrowly and had had little impact on the growth of Canadian–South African economic relations (Redekop 1984–85, 98–101). Indeed, by 1983 one critic concluded that government policies intended to register Canada's opposition to apartheid were weaker than they had been in 1977 (Pratt 1983, 522). While the rhetoric condemning apartheid continued unabated, the traditional Canadian policy of maintaining normal diplomatic and economic relations with Pretoria remained essentially unchanged.

This policy approach was once again reinforced by the situation in international diplomatic circles in the early 1980s. Within the Commonwealth, so often the main stimulus for Canadian action on southern Africa, "a smug self-satisfaction took hold of all concerned" following the organization's success in helping to guide Zimbabwe to independence during 1979 and 1980 (Chan 1990, 98). No important new initiatives on southern Africa were put forward, in spite of communiqués from the Melbourne (1981) and New Delhi (1983) meetings that dealt at some length with the region (Commonwealth Secretariat 1987, 224–6, 250–2). The southern Africa issue had been put on the back burner and would not return until the Nassau Commonwealth heads-of-government meetings in 1985 (Chan 1990, 98). At the United Nations, the Western "contact group" (Britain, Canada, France, the United States, and West Germany), which since 1977 had been attempting to negotiate an internationally acceptable agreement for Namibian independence from South Africa's illegal rule, was increasingly marginalized by the United States. The new Reagan administration had decided to conduct its diplomacy with Pretoria on a largely unilateral and relatively friendly basis. In the mean time, however, the Canadian government continued to argue that it should do nothing (mainly in terms of sanctions against South Africa) to jeopardize its ability to take an active, mediatory part in efforts to achieve a negotiated settlement in Namibia (Pratt 1983, 522).

As had been the case in the 1970s, rugby and cricket sporting contacts with South Africa by British and New Zealand teams were to be a major cause of conflict within the Commonwealth, threatening the Commonwealth Games and causing discord among its leaders. By the early 1980s, South Africa had been expelled by many international sport federations (see Kidd 1988, 643). The International Cricket Conference had banned South Africa in 1970 because that country's prime minister had said that a tour of South Africa by an English cricket team (the Marylebone cricket club) was "unacceptable because of its selection of a South African coloured player, Basil d'Oliveira" (Macfarlane 1986, 127). But the cricket conference did not put South Africa off limits to individual athletes, and so star Australian and British cricketers and rugby players were often offered lucrative sums of money to go to South Africa to play in exhibition matches and off-season leagues.[2] In the case of professional cricket players, these monies sometimes exceeded their total yearly salaries back home (see, for instance, Mays, 3 August 1989, 14). Indeed, the South African government itself expended substantial sums of money to finance sport tours by Commonwealth countries. In 1985, for instance, the Australian rebel cricket tour of South Africa was supported by $3 million (Australian) in secret government funds (Forbes, 18–24 July 1986).

As sport organizations and governments in Britain, New Zealand, and Australia began to clamp down in the 1980s on sporting contacts with South Africa, rebel cricket and rugby tours of South Africa were to become a major bone of contention with the anti-apartheid forces. These tours usually consisted of players who were at the end of their careers and therefore had little to fear from suspensions by their national sport governing bodies back home. In addition, South Africa was still a member of the (international) Rugby Football Board, a federation dominated by members from white nations that had little concern that sporting contacts with South Africa were causing disruptions in the Commonwealth (Macfarlane 1986, 141). Unlike many other international sport federations, the Rugby Football Board had no inclination to discipline national sport governing bodies in countries that maintained contacts with South Africa. Moreover, neither rugby nor cricket was on the Commonwealth Games program, making it harder for governments and Commonwealth Games associations to put pressure on the Rugby Football Board or the International Cricket Conference.

Three tours involving South Africa were the specific incidents that threatened the 1982 Brisbane Commonwealth Games: those of the British Lions rugby team to South Africa in 1980, the South African representative rugby team – the Springboks – to New Zealand in 1981, and the party of English "rebel" cricketers to South Africa in the spring of 1982 (ibid., 115). But it was the Springbok tour of New Zealand that became the focus of attention, because black African nations were not convinced that New Zealand prime minister Robert Muldoon was sincere about his proclaimed commitment to the Gleneagles Declaration. This tour was met with massive demonstrations by anti-apartheid groups and caused deep divisions within the country itself (Guelke 1986, 139). The demonstrations became so violent that rugby officials had to impose a blackout on information about the sites of provincial matches (Macfarlane 1986, 115). Muldoon took the position that once he had asked the New Zealand Rugby Union to cancel the tour, his responsibilities under the Gleneagles Declaration were fulfilled. Any further measures on his part would interfere with the Rugby Union's right to invite whomever it wished (ibid., 116). This explanation, however, was not acceptable to black African Commonwealth nations, and the tour was to have significant international repercussions.

In the first instance, the 1981 Commonwealth finance ministers' conference, which had been scheduled for Auckland, was moved to Bermuda (Ramphal, 5 August 1981). At the Commonwealth heads-of-government meetings held later that year in Melbourne, however, the rugby tour, according to a Canadian official, was discussed in a "non-provocative" manner, and it was agreed that the withdrawal of the finance ministers' meetings was a sufficient statement of protest.[3] The heads of government were content to fall back on a re-endorsement of the Gleneagles Declaration, and the meetings were described by an experienced Commonwealth journalist as being "probably the most harmonious [ones] in two decades" (Ingham, as quoted in Payne 1991, 425).

Despite this attempt by Commonwealth heads of government to demonstrate accord, the tour provoked threats from black African member nations to boycott the 1982 Commonwealth Games in Brisbane. By this time, however, differences in strategic approaches to using sport to fight apartheid in South Africa were beginning to emerge among black African nations. Successive black African nations' boycotts of the 1976 Montreal and 1980 Moscow Olympics were seen in some quarters as having isolated Africa from some of the most important athletic events of the second half of the 1970s and denied international competition to black African athletes, as well as not allowing them a chance to gain honours at these Games (Monnington 1986, 169). Some black African sport officials claimed that these boycotts had also been a contributing factor in the decline in performance levels of their athletes in the late 1970s. On the other hand, the 1976 Montreal Olympics boycott and the threat of a 1978 Commonwealth Games boycott had been most successful in attracting world-wide attention to the anti-apartheid cause. Indeed, shortly after the Montreal boycott, Lord Killanin, the president of the International Olympic Committee (IOC), had publicly condemned a French rugby tour of South Africa. In contrast, when, before these Games, the black African nations protested to the IOC about New Zealand's participation despite that country's continued sporting contacts with South Africa, Killanin claimed that this was not a proper matter for IOC consideration.

It was time for a new approach to the anti-apartheid sport campaign. As a result, the strategy adopted in the early 1980s by the Supreme Council for Sport in Africa (SCSA) and the Association of National Olympic Committees of Africa was to isolate South Africa, rather than black African nations, from international sport (ibid., 170) and to punish athletes and countries who persisted in sporting contacts with South Africa. Sam Kamau, an influential sport official from Kenya, who was also the vice-chair of the Commonwealth Games Federation (CGF), was one of the leaders of this more moderate group in the black African anti-apartheid sport movement.[4] The success of this strategy could be seen in the changing role of the black African anti-apartheid sport movement in international sport organizations. In 1976 the movement stood outside the sport establishment (in this case, the IOC) in boycotting the Montreal Games. By 1978 it, for the most part, was working in co-operation with the Commonwealth towards a successful Edmonton Commonwealth Games. By 1982 (as we will see) the support of the black African anti-apartheid caucus in the CGF had become essential for the success of future Commonwealth Games.[5]

This new strategy became apparent at an extraordinary CGF general assembly meeting in London in May 1982. The 1981 Springbok tour of New Zealand was "unanimously" condemned, and Tanzania put forward a resolution to bar New Zealand from the 1982 Brisbane Games. This resolution did not receive much support, and in the end it was announced that there would be full attendance at Brisbane. At the same time, however, it was resolved that the CGF's constitution would be amended to provide for a Code of Conduct to strengthen its position in regard to the Gleneagles Declaration (Commonwealth Games Federation, 5 May 1982). This new Code of Conduct was adopted at the 1982 meetings of the CGF, held in conjunction with the Brisbane Games. The code defined a "breach of the Gleneagles Declaration," something that was not attempted in the 1977 agreement (see Appendix C for the text of the Code of Conduct). Commonwealth sportspersons were prohibited from competing in a country that practised apartheid or elsewhere in a sport event when an individual from such a country was "competing in a representative capacity for his country or sport body" (Commonwealth Games Federation 1988, 52).

The status of professional athletes under the Code of Conduct was to become a bone of contention (as we shall see). One interpretation was that the code covered all athletes who needed the sanction of their sport governing bodies to compete abroad (Kidd 1983, 9). The code also made it the responsibility of each national Commonwealth Games association to enforce the Gleneagles Declaration; hitherto, this had been the province of the respective governments. Thus the national associations were charged with taking action to prevent sporting contacts with South Africa, even in non-Commonwealth sports (Kidd 1988, 656). Finally, the code provided for the suspension from the CGF of national associations in violation of the Gleneagles Declaration. The Commonwealth nations voted overwhelmingly in favour of the new code, with Britain and New Zealand (and Nigeria, according to Kidd 1983, 9) abstaining (Guelke 1986, 139).

The code, however, did not have a smooth passage. Some of the older Commonwealth countries not only had serious reservations about its contents, but were resentful that many black African nations were represented at these meetings by their respective ministers of sport or by anti-apartheid leaders such as Sam Ramsamy, rather than the normal non-governmental members. Reservations about the code were not surprising because it exceeded, by some measure, the sport sanctions that most white Commonwealth nations, including Canada, had adopted. Sir Arthur Gold, president of the English Commonwealth Games Council, stated that while his council could accept responsibility for implementing it in those sports over which it had jurisdiction, he was not empowered to go beyond that mandate: in other words, to try to impose it in sports that were not on the

Commonwealth agenda (Commonwealth Games Federation, 6 October 1962, 9–10). The belief in some white Commonwealth nations in the autonomy of sport from politics made sport officials such as Gold horrified at the prospect of policing other "independent" sport organizations in their countries.[6] On the other hand, L.O. Adegbite of Nigeria complained that modifications to the code agreed upon at an earlier meeting had watered down some of its measures (Commonwealth Games Federation, 6 October 1962, 10). The Canadian government's position was that it welcomed the code to the extent that it supported Canada's position, but that the document went far beyond what the country could practically enforce.[7] In light of the objections raised by Gold to some of the provisions of the code, it was anticipated that England would challenge the constitutionality of this measure at the federation's general assembly meetings, to be held in conjunction with the Los Angeles Summer Olympics in 1984.

The threat of boycotts, however, still remained in the black African nations' repertoire. South African sport officials arranged that the 1981 Springbok rugby tour of New Zealand be extended to play matches in California, presumably to draw attention to South Africa's efforts to be reinstated by the IOC in time for the Los Angeles Olympics. There was a rumour circulating at this time that the IOC was considering sending a fact-finding team to South Africa to review that country's status in the Olympic movement. Indeed, the IOC decided in 1980 that incoming president Juan Antonio Samaranch should take up South Africa's status (Lyberg 1988–89b, 289). The IOC general assembly referred the matter of sending a fact-finding team to South Africa to the executive board in 1982 (ibid., 297), but nothing came of the matter. Leading anti-apartheid activist Dennis Brutus (now residing in the United States) and anti-apartheid groups got wind of this rumour and raised a protest in the media. The Springbok tour and the possibility of South African participation in these Olympics also drew an angry response from SCSA. The president of SCSA, Abraham Ordia, appealed to the IOC executive board to move the 1984 Summer Games from Los Angeles; otherwise, he threatened that the African nations would boycott the Games. Samaranch replied that although the IOC had denounced the Springbok tour, it was powerless to do anything to prevent it.[8]

In 1984 another series of sporting incidents were building up that would cause confrontations over the 1986 Edinburgh Commonwealth Games. One of these incidents involved a young South African by the name of Zola Budd. Budd catapulted on to the world athletics scene in January 1984, when she broke the world record in the 5,000-metre run by some six seconds (Macfarlane 1986, 152). But international sport bans meant that she would not be able to compete as a South African in the 1984 Olympics. A few months after her record-breaking performance, however, Budd arrived in Britain and was granted British citizenship within a few weeks of her arrival.

The rapidity with which Budd's application for citizenship was processed caused a stir inside Britain, and the issue was picked up by the anti-apartheid sport movement (Guelke 1986, 140). Her subsequent appearance at the 1984 Los Angeles Olympics as a British citizen caused much controversy. On the one hand, she was championed by South Africa as a sport heroine; on the other, she became the target for anti-apartheid protests. Black African nations kept up the pressure even after Budd's disastrous encounter with American track star Mary Decker in the 3,000-metre Olympic finals. Eventually, after a long and acrimonious debate, in which black African nations threatened to withdraw from the 1986 Edinburgh Games if Budd competed, the CGF declared her ineligible shortly before the Games on the grounds that she had not met the residence requirement to participate as a British citizen. Evidently, Budd had spent much of the previous eighteen months living and training in South Africa. This action was taken despite the fact that the English Commonwealth Games Council had earlier deemed her to be eligible and led to charges in England that the CGF had succumbed to blackmail (Bateman and Douglas 1986, 69).

During this same period, another potential storm was brewing in England. The English Commonwealth Games Council evidently took no action in the spring of 1984 to dissuade the English Rugby Football Union from stopping a British Lions tour of South Africa in May that year. This, combined with dismay over the Budd affair, caused black African and other third-world countries to call for the suspension of England from the 1986 Commonwealth Games in Edinburgh (Freeman and Penrose, 13 May 1984). In April 1984 Abraham Ordia, who was also the secretary-general of the Nigerian Olympic Committee and one of the most influential black African sport officials, wrote to the CGF secretary expressing consternation over the English Commonwealth Games Council's inactivity in the matter of the British Lions tour of South Africa and requesting that this violation of the Code of Conduct be placed on the agenda at the CGF general assembly meetings in Los Angeles.[9] This was further evidence of the shift in strategy by the black African anti-apartheid sport lobby.

The confrontation between the English Commonwealth Games Council and black African and other third-world Commonwealth countries at the CGF's Los Angeles meetings in the summer of 1984 was evidently clouded with confusion. The distraction of the Olympic Games, the fact that many black African members of the federation were also members of the IOC, and the logistical problems associated with delegates being spread out between two separate and distanced Olympic villages meant that communications among black African and other third-world Commonwealth countries were extremely poor. According to Sam Ramsamy, the president of the South African Non-Racial Olympic Committee, he was unable to caucus with the African delegates until two days after the federation's general assembly and was unable to meet with the Caribbean and South Pacific delegates at all.[10] At any rate, efforts to suspend the English Games Council from the CGF were unsuccessful, but a resolution of reprimand was endorsed (Commonwealth Games Federation, 26 July 1984). This resolution upset the English delegation greatly, but did much to appease the African nations.[11] According to Eric Morse, Ivor Dent, one of the Canadian delegates, played a major role in diffusing the tensions and preventing them from blowing up in the press by manœuvring the passage of a motion to establish a committee that would recommend a course of action against the English council.[12] It was this group that later in the day brought forth the resolution of reprimand against the English council. The English council's motion to amend the article in the Code of Conduct that provided for suspensions of member nations for violations received only two affirmative votes: England and the Isle of Man (Commonwealth Games Federation, 26 July 1984).

Two further proposed rugby tours of South Africa threatened the 1986 Edinburgh Commonwealth Games: those of the New Zealand All-Blacks in July 1985 and the British Lions the following year. In response to these announced tours, five African nations – Gambia, Ghana, Nigeria, Tanzania, and Zimbabwe – announced at the CGF advisory committee meeting in Edinburgh in June 1985 that they would "reserve their right to take appropriate action which could include the Commonwealth Games in Edinburgh in 1986, and in the long term, the 1990 Games if Auckland still remains the venue for the Commonwealth Games" (Commonwealth Games Federation, 4 June 1985). This meeting was the most acrimonious of any that Ivor Dent had ever attended. The New Zealand representative, Roy Dutton, who had been a vigorous anti-apartheid leader in that country, was subjected to an angry personal attack by Abraham Ordia and other African representatives.[13]

Both these tours, however, were called off. In the case of the All-Blacks tour, the New Zealand Rugby Union had defied internal political pressure to cancel it. But a temporary injunction against the tour was granted by the New Zealand High Court in July 1985, just a few days before the players were to depart for South Africa. The court ruled that it would violate the rugby union's constitutional responsibility to promote and foster the game and further noted "that the tour was contrary to clear Government direction, the unanimous expression of Parliament, and against the spirit of the Gleneagles Agreement" (Macfarlane 1986, 149). Subsequently, the South African tour was cancelled (Guelke 1986, 139–40). The election in July 1984 of a Labour government under David Lange, which took a strong stand against sporting contacts with South Africa, was also a welcome sign to Commonwealth leaders.[14] The British Lions tour was also cancelled five months later, on this occasion because the South African Rugby League wished to keep its relations with the four rugby unions in the British Isles "intact" (Macfarlane 1986, 149–50). According to Kidd, the reason behind this decision was the real possibility that English athletes would be barred, under the terms of the Code of Conduct, from participating in the 1986 Edinburgh Games (Kidd 1988, 657). The cancellation of these two tours made the Edinburgh Games organizers breathe much easier (Bateman and Douglas 1986, 68).

THE MULRONEY GOVERNMENT

In the mean time, the Conservative Party under Brian Mulroney had won a huge majority in the federal election of September 1984. There had been nothing in the election campaign or in statements immediately after the election suggesting that the new government had any real interest in southern Africa or that it would interfere with normal business relationships between Canada and South Africa (Redekop 1986, 3; Nossal 1988b, 12–15). Its early foreign-policy statements had been anti-Soviet, pro-American, and supportive of Canada's traditional allies (i.e., Britain, France, Israel, and the United States). On the economic side, the new Conservative government's predilections were towards privatization, deregulation, and free trade. Thus, despite what had been termed as a "massive insurrection" in South Africa in September 1984 (Saul 1988, 2), its green paper on foreign policy, *Competitiveness and Security: Directions for Canada's International Relations*, published in May 1985, devoted only one paragraph, "detached" in tone, to southern Africa (Redekop 1986, 3).

This initial impression, however, was to prove to be very misleading. By June 1985 the government had decided that it would take a radically new approach to Canada's South African policy (Nossal 1988b, 16). While the extent of this transformation was probably overestimated by most observers at the time, the shift was a real and significant one, and it marked the start of a period during which southern Africa was to become a higher foreign-policy priority than it had ever been previously.

This shift in Canadian policy was signalled in a speech by external affairs minister Joe Clark in Baie Comeau on 6 July 1985. He announced that his government intended to take twelve substantive measures to "either put pressure on Pretoria or to punish the South African government" (ibid.). Later that month, in the face of mounting unrest, the South African government imposed draconian measures under a state of emergency. On 15 August, in a speech that was widely expected to announce significant new reforms, South African president P.W. Botha instead vigorously defended white control and denounced "internal agitators and foreign intervention" (Redekop 1986, 6). As a result, Clark announced a smaller package of additional sanctions measures in the House of Commons on 13 September. He also intensified the government's rhetoric considerably when he stated that while "as a general principle, we believe that diplomatic and economic relations should exist even though governments might disagree," the Canadian government was prepared to "invoke full [diplomatic and economic] sanctions" if lesser measures were ineffective in inducing meaningful change (HC *Debates*, 13 September 1985, 6587–9). This threat was to be reiterated by Prime Minister Mulroney in a speech at the United Nations in October (Mulroney, 23 October 1985, 25–7) and was subsequently to haunt the Conservative government.

A number of factors were important in the Conservative government's departure from the traditional Canadian policy on South Africa. First, following an international media blitz that highlighted the dramatic resurgence of resistance within South Africa, the South African government had introduced a campaign aimed at destabilizing neighbouring frontline states, several of which were Canada's Commonwealth partners (Anglin and Godfrey 1987, 2–3). These developments strengthened the hand of the anti-apartheid constituency in Canada, which had long argued that traditional government policy was inadequate and morally unacceptable and that much stronger measures were called for (Redekop 1986, 4). Second, the loss of business confidence and the political embarrassment over these developments caused a large-scale flight of international banks and other companies from the southern African region (North-South Institute 1987, 7). This made it much easier for the Canadian government to contemplate substantive economic and political sanctions. It also reinforced the "enlightened capitalist" view, probably shared by Mulroney, that if South Africa was to be "saved for capitalism," apartheid had to be abolished before a full-scale revolution developed (Saul 1988, 3). Finally, and perhaps most importantly, a number of the key figures in the new Conservative government, including the prime minister, the external affairs minister, United Nations ambassador Stephen Lewis, and the high commissioner to Britain, Roy McMurtry, all manifested a high degree of personal interest in, and commitment to, the southern African issue. At times, the prime minister himself "demonstrated an almost visceral and intense anger at the institutionalized racism of apartheid" (Nossal 1988b, 28). It was an issue that seemed to strike a very strong personal chord in Mulroney.

It was in this atmosphere (and in conjunction with the other measures that Joe Clark had announced in Baie Comeau on 6 July) that he and the minister of state for fitness and amateur sport, Otto Jelinek, issued a statement that "reaffirmed Canada's support for the Commonwealth policy limiting sporting contacts with South Africa" and at the same time produced guidelines to assist Canadian sport organizations in interpreting the policy (Canada, 8 July 1985). Initially, it was intended that this new policy would prevent contacts with "nationally-representative South African sport" (ibid.), not only in Canada and South Africa, but in other countries as well. Indeed, the South African sport policy statement released by Fitness and Amateur Sport in 1982 had "actively discouraged in the strongest possible terms" sporting contacts with South African athletes under any conditions (Fitness and Amateur Sport 1982, 1). Even if athletes or teams did not know of the presence of South African athletes in a competition in a third country before they left Canada, they were required to withdraw from the event or face the loss of government funding (ibid., 2).

While this policy had been enforced by Sport Canada for national sport organizations since 1982, it was one with which the Department of External Affairs was uncomfortable.[15] During the early 1980s Sport Canada director-general Abby Hoffman had a good deal of freedom and was able to take such initiatives without extensive consultation.[16] She herself held strong personal beliefs about apartheid and would continue to advocate stronger sport sanctions against South Africa, even though her scope for action would become more limited as the Department of External Affairs became increasingly involved in Canadian sport policies vis-à-vis South Africa.

The blanket provision against all competition with South African athletes was included in a draft of the proposed policy that the external affairs minister, Allan MacEachen, had sent to Senator Raymond Perrault, minister for fitness and amateur sport, on 25 July 1983. But this initiative was never acted upon. By the time the government had changed and the policy was officially announced two years later by Clark and Jelinek, it had been revised to allow athletes to compete against South African athletes in a third country as long as the presence of these athletes was not known to Canadian officials at the time of departure. Under these conditions, however, Canadian sport officials were required to request that the host nation ban the South African competitors and, failing this, were required to participate under official protest (Canada, 8 July 1985).

The most vexatious problem for the government, however, was the participation of South African golfers and tennis players at international professional tournaments, particularly those held in Canada. The fitness and amateur sport minister, Gerald Regan, had put forward the Liberal government's position on this matter in a letter to Bruce Kidd in 1981, when he stated that to deny any professional athlete the right to enter Canada to "earn a living is an abominable affront to one's civil liberties and should not be condoned."[17] As long as competitions were not organized along national lines, Regan continued, his government would not interfere with the rights of any South African to travel to this country.

Anti-apartheid activists and the press kept pointing to this apparent anomaly in the government's position on sporting contacts with South Africa. For instance, the *Globe and Mail* noted that Carling Bassett had played South African Roz Riach at the 1982 Wimbledon Championships.[18] Regan made this contradiction even more apparent when later in July, he notified the World (professional) Boxing Association that South African officials would not be granted visas to attend meetings in Halifax.[19] In the same month, however, South Africans had competed in the Labatt's International Golf Tournament in Ridgeway, Ontario, the Peter Jackson Golf Classic in Toronto, and the Canadian Open Golf Tournament in Oakville.[20] South African athletes were also to compete in both the men's and the women's Canadian Open Tennis Championships in the summer of 1983. Senator Raymond Perrault (one of a series of Liberal fitness and amateur sport ministers who succeeded Gerald Regan), however, said that Canada was not likely to do anything about professional sportspersons until other signatories of the Gleneagles Declaration pursued a similar approach.[21] This position was reiterated by Eric Morse in 1984, when he explained that professional soccer players employed by Canadian clubs were not considered to be representing South Africa; rather, this was a private commercial arrangement.[22]

The July 1985 policy statement from Clark and Jelinek did nothing to change this position because one of its criteria was that the ban on sporting contacts with South Africa applied only to those events that were organized on the basis of national representation. Canada was required to support this position again in December when it abstained from voting on the United Nations International Convention against Apartheid in Sport. The explanation offered by External Affairs was that there were "legal and policy impediments which preclude the Canadian government from ratifying the proposed convention at this time."[23] In this same month Eric Morse was to explain to Guy Wright, who represented the Canadians Concerned about South Africa, that the government's sport embargo was "directed against institutions that put themselves at the disposal of the apartheid system, not against individuals who may indeed be opposed to apartheid."[24]

This matter of South African tennis and golf professionals, however, was not one that was going to disappear. The Canadian Tennis Association (CTA) was particularly vulnerable to criticism because it received fairly substantial government grants from Sport Canada. In contrast, contributions to the Royal Canadian Golf Association (RCGA) were relatively small. For instance, in the budget year 1984–85, the CTA received approximately $350,000 from Sport Canada compared with only about $64,000 for the RCGA (Fitness and Amateur Sport 1985, 32). In February 1985 Bruce Kidd had written to external affairs minister Joe Clark pointing out that South African Kevin Curren had competed in a professional tennis tournament in Toronto earlier in the month and that because it was in violation of government policy, the CTA should be required to forfeit the monies it received annually from Sport Canada.[25] Nora McCabe, a feature columnist in the Toronto *Globe and Mail*, picked up this theme in August, when she asked why the CTA was not required to abide by government rules regarding sporting contacts with South Africa like all other sport governing bodies that received grants from the federal government. Klaus Bindhardt, president of the CTA, was quoted by McCabe as saying that he was not worried because the government had ruled that professional tennis players of any nationality were independent business people, not athletes. As to the CTA initiating a move to have South Africa expelled from the International Tennis Federation, Bindhardt said, "I don't see why Tennis Canada [the CTA] should try to adjudicate what is an internationally disputed matter" (McCabe, 10 August 1985, S7).

The question matter of South African professional athletes competing in Canada was eventually to bring acute embarrassment to the Conservative government and cause it to take measures in 1988 to plug part of this loophole in its sport sanctions against South Africa. We return to this story in the next chapter. But first we turn to the events leading up to the massive boycott of the 1986 Edinburgh Commonwealth Games. Ironically, this boycott did not come about, as anticipated, because of sporting contacts with South Africa. The efforts in Commonwealth sporting circles to prevent such contacts, as noted earlier, had been reasonably successful, and the organizers were looking forward to a boycott-free Games. Instead, it was to arise over wider differences in the Commonwealth concerning economic sanctions against South Africa.

By the summer of 1985, the Commonwealth Secretariat had decided that new initiatives should be launched against South Africa (Chan 1990, 99). In anticipation of the pending Commonwealth meetings in

Nassau that October, Prime Minister Mulroney signalled his commitment to the southern Africa issue by sending his personal emissary, the director of the North-South Institute, Bernard Wood, to meet with leaders of the frontline southern African states (Nossal 1988b, 31; Wood 1990, 286–7). At the Nassau meetings, a major split began to develop between Britain's prime minister, Margaret Thatcher, who was deeply resistant to full-scale economic sanctions, and the frontline states and other third-world members, who were calling for comprehensive sanctions. Mulroney and India's prime minister, Rajiv Gandhi, were reported to have played key mediatory roles in working out the compromise agreement with Thatcher that eventually emerged from these meetings (Wood 1990, 287).

This agreement, the Commonwealth Accord on Southern Africa, included a mild package of sanctions, most of which had already been implemented by the Canadian government. More significantly, the accord called for the establishment of a "group of eminent Commonwealth persons to encourage through all practicable ways ... [a] process of political dialogue" aimed at ending apartheid in South Africa (Commonwealth Secretariat 1987, 268). It also made provision for a meeting of seven Commonwealth heads of government (including Canada's) in six months' time to review the progress of this "eminent persons" group, holding out the threat of further sanctions if adequate progress was not made.

The eminent persons group aborted its mission when, on the day the members returned to South Africa for a second round of meetings, the South African military struck targets in the capital cities of Commonwealth frontline states Botswana, Zambia, and Zimbabwe. On 11 June 1986, the group issued its report, which called for economic sanctions as probably "the last opportunity to avert what could be the worst bloodbath since the Second World War" (Commonwealth Group of Eminent Persons 1986, 141). The next day, South Africa reimposed the state of emergency, and the Canadian government announced several additional sanctions. These developments set the stage for the review that had been called for at the Nassau meetings.

This "mini-summit" was held in London from 3 to 5 August and involved the prime ministers of Australia, the Bahamas, Britain, Canada, India, Zambia, and Zimbabwe. Prime Minister Mulroney had met with Margaret Thatcher at Mirabel Airport in Montreal on 12 July 1986 in an effort to head off a confrontation in London between Thatcher and African leaders (*Ottawa Letter*, 1985–86, 666). But his efforts were evidently unsuccessful. To the consternation of the other prime ministers and Commonwealth officials, Thatcher remained recalcitrant at the

London meeting, turning her misgivings about sanctions into a matter of firm principle (Chan 1990, 102; Wood 1990, 288). As a result, the six other Commonwealth nations endorsed eleven new measures against South Africa, eight of which had been foreshadowed in the Commonwealth Accord on Southern Africa. These included bans on the importation of agricultural products, coal, iron, and steel, a voluntary ban on new investments and reinvestment of profits earned in South Africa, and the withdrawal of all consular facilities in South Africa, except those serving one's own nationals. Mulroney's role in these negotiations resulted in heady talk in the Canadian press of the leadership of the Commonwealth passing to Canada (Fraser, 6 August 1986).

As a result of Margaret Thatcher's refusal to go along with these new initiatives, black African and other third-world Commonwealth countries called for a complete boycott of the Edinburgh Games. Despite disappointment over her opposition to stronger economic sanctions against South Africa, however, Canada was not prepared to support the boycott and face the political storm that would surely develop on the domestic front. Or so it appeared when, shortly before the Games, Mulroney announced that the Canadian team would compete in Edinburgh (Morse 1987b, 15). Indeed, the team, the fitness and amateur sport minister, Otto Jelinek, and the director-general of Sport Canada, Abby Hoffman, all arrived shortly after in Edinburgh.

Despite Mulroney's announcement, a joint Privy Council – DEA task force was still giving serious consideration to some kind of a boycott (ibid.). Several Canadian high commissioners in Africa had urged the government to take some action, such as withdrawing its own officials from Edinburgh (Kidd 1987, 3). Indeed, the Department of External Affairs received word from its Nairobi counsel that the *Daily Natoria*, Kenya's most widely read newspaper, had carried a front-page headline to the effect that there was a real possibility Canada might pull out from the Games because Mulroney supported sanctions.[26] The Canadian acting high commissioner in London had received a message from Archbishop Trevor Huddleston, head of the British anti-apartheid movement, telling him that "under the circumstances, it would be inappropriate for the United Kingdom to host the forthcoming Games in Edinburgh."[27]

As a result of this last-minute debate back home, instructions were sent to Jelinek that he was not to attend a pre-Games press conference or to comment on Canada's position on the boycott. A few days earlier in Edinburgh, he had stated that those nations that used the Commonwealth Games as a forum to fight apartheid should be punished financially (*Globe and Mail*, 24 July 1986). The Games organizers did eventually bill (with no success) the thirty-two boycotting nations to a total of £2.7 million sterling (Bateman and Douglas 1986, 113).

Jelinek's embarrassment over being muzzled was not made easier when Ivor Dent, the Canadian team's *chef de mission*, announced at this press conference that the team would not withdraw from the Games, despite any instructions to the contrary from its government. Dent, a seasoned politician who had spent six years as mayor of Edmonton, had asked, on behalf of the executive of the Commonwealth Games Association of Canada (CGAC), that the team's general manager, Jim Daly, canvass the managers of all his various teams. This poll had confirmed that a preponderance of Canada's athletes would defy any boycott order; thus Dent was able to convey the CGAC position at the pre-Games press conference.[28] The position of the Canadian team was of some interest to the three major political parties back home. At the request of the NDP national office, Dent relayed this information to party leader Ed Broadbent, and he passed it on to Liberal leader John Turner's office. Otto Jelinek, who was in constant touch with his government back home throughout this incident, also communicated this information.[29] Evidently, there were members of parliament from all three major parties who were in favour of a Canadian boycott of the Games.[30]

New Zealand took advantage of the opposition to the black African boycott by proposing to the CGF general assembly, shortly before the opening of the Games, that non-Commonwealth countries, as well as Canadian provincial and Australian state teams, be invited to compete in the Commonwealth Games so that the influence of black African countries would be diminished. Ivor Dent was quoted as seeing some merit in this proposal because it would bolster enthusiasm among Canada's provinces and ensure successful competition in many events in the case of future boycotts (Martin, 27 July 1986). This was an impromptu proposal at an emotional time, one that seemed out of touch with the political realities of the Commonwealth.

Canada's final position on the boycott, however, revolved around a number of considerations. First, the government had to take into consideration the sport community, which was almost unanimously opposed to the boycott and had the support of much of the Canadian public. Jelinek's opposition to any type of a boycott and the strong advocacy role he took with the cabinet for his position, albeit from Edinburgh, played an important role in the final decision.[31] The Canadian government also did not want to risk further alienating British prime minister Margaret Thatcher, which it certainly would have done if it had supported a boycott of these Games.

Another factor in the final decision had to do with "what kind of company Canada would be keeping." If, in addition to the black African nations, most of the other third-world countries were to withdraw from the Games, then Canada would be "left on the burning bridge" with England.[32] India's position, as a leader in the Commonwealth, was particularly important, and when that country withdrew at the last minute, Canada's dilemma was magnified. Sir Shridath Ramphal, the Commonwealth secretary-general, evidently played an important role in Canada's final decision when he gave the go-ahead for non-black-African countries to participate in the Games. The fact that many of these nations decided to participate – most of the Caribbean countries, however, eventually supported the boycott – also played a role in the decision. Canada's good standing with the black African nations, given the very strong stand against apartheid that it had taken at the Commonwealth heads-of-government meetings in the Bahamas the previous spring, was a final important factor in the cabinet's last-minute decision not to mount any type of protest over these Games.[33] This decision evidently was taken despite a strong predilection in some sectors in External Affairs and, in particular, with the southern African task force, to make some kind of a protest at the Edinburgh Games.[34]

The day after he had been barred from speaking about Canada's position on the boycott, Otto Jelinek convened an impromptu press conference in Edinburgh, at which he announced that the Canadian team would participate in the Games and that the Canadian government was fully behind its athletes.[35] He was also able to air his views about sport boycotts shortly after the Edinburgh Games in a keynote address he gave in New York at the International Sport Summit later in August. In this speech, entitled "Sport Should 'Build Bridges between Nations and People,'" Jelinek condemned sport boycotts, pointing to the senselessness of the black African boycott of the Montreal Olympics over New Zealand's having "played a rugby match, which isn't even an Olympic sport, against South Africa" (Jelinek 1986, 53). On the topic of the 1980 Moscow Olympics boycott, he pointed to the fact that the Soviets were still in Afghanistan. "If there would be some form of achievement from boycotts, then maybe we should consider them, but nothing is ever achieved" (ibid.). This, as we pointed out at the beginning of the chapter, was a view that was widely held in the sport community in Canada at this time.

The Edinburgh boycott, however, was one of the most effective ever staged at a major international sport event, what with about one-half of the some fifty-eight competing nations withdrawing (these figures vary, depending on the source; see for instance, the *Globe and Mail,* 24 July

1986, in contrast to Macfarlane 1986), and it had a disastrous impact on the Games. It reduced some feature events, particularly boxing and middle-distance running, to mediocrity (Wilson, 25 July 1986). The Games, which were already in a precarious financial position and would eventually suffer unprecedented losses (that is, for Commonwealth Games; see Bateman and Douglas 1986, chap. 9), were further damaged by the boycott. Attendance and television audiences sagged badly. Margaret Thatcher had to endure the abuse of large crowds of Scots protesting her position on South African sanctions when she arrived in Edinburgh to open the Games (Stead, 2 August 1986). She had also to bow out of visiting the Commonwealth Games Arts Festival because of pressure from the Labour-controlled district council, who protested against her "unconsidered remarks" over not imposing full economic sanctions against South Africa (Goodbody, 31 July 1986). Even her tour of the athletes' village was marred when most athletes remained in their quarters in protest.[36] This was exactly the magnitude of boycott that the Canadian government had striven (successfully) to avoid in Edmonton in 1978.

CHAPTER SEVEN

An Expanded Role for Sport in Canadian Diplomacy

The announcement at the end of October 1987 by external affairs minister Joe Clark and fitness and amateur sport minister Otto Jelinek (Canada, 28 October 1987) that a Cabinet record of decision had called for sport and Canada's athletes in promoting the country's image abroad and for a strengthening of Canada's influence in the international sport movement marked the first time that the Department of External Affairs had committed itself to the notion that sport could play a positive role in meeting the country's diplomatic goals. Previously External Affairs had assumed "a defensive and reactive posture *vis-à-vis* sport in international relations" (Morse 1987b, 18). The origin of this initiative was a recommendation in the report of the Health and Sports Study Team (Canada 1986) to the Nielsen Task Force on Program Review that the government "should consider directing Sport Canada and External Affairs to complete a thorough evaluation of the role of sport in the area of foreign policy." Such a study "should result in a realistic proposal that would determine the future direction of international sport relations" (ibid., 273). Bryce Taylor, a prominent physical educator at York University and a former president of the Canadian Gymnastics Federation, was appointed to chair this study team. The appointment was also a political one; Taylor had been active in the Progressive Conservative Party and had been unsuccessful in winning a nomination to run as a Conservative candidate in the 1984 federal election.

An International Sports Relations desk had been created in External Affairs on a part-time basis in 1972 to deal with the diplomatic exigencies of the first Canada Cup hockey series with the Soviet Union. This post was filled by a permanent officer when a Cultural Policy Division within External Affairs was established by cabinet in 1974. But the sports relations desk had remained a one-person operation with minimal funding right up until the time of the cabinet decision in 1987. According to the briefing documents for the Health and Sports Study Team established by the Nielsen task force, its budget in 1984–85 amounted to some $169,000 (Canada 1986, 271). We first trace the forces and events that led up to the 1987 cabinet record of decision to expand the role played by sport in international relations.

CABINET RECORD OF DECISION

Shortly after the release of the report of the Health and Sports Study Team, Jelinek and Clark commenced to manœuvre for the primary position in any such new international sport enterprises (Morse 1987b, 17–18). In the fall of 1986 Jelinek embarked on a "path to develop a strategic overview and the origins of a policy aimed at enhancing Canada's role in international sport relations" (Jelinek, 26 October 1987). He was the first minister of state for fitness and amateur sport to have been an international athlete; he and his sister won the gold medal in the pairs competition at the 1962 World Skating Championships in Prague. Jelinek had spent his childhood in Czechoslovakia, immigrating to Canada in 1951. These experiences left him with a strong conviction that sport could be a powerful tool in international relations because it "transcends political and ideological differences."[1] He was to be the driving force behind the creation of an international sport arm in Fitness and Amateur Sport, and according to Lane MacAdam, Jelinek's executive assistant, his strong feelings on this matter certainly filtered down to Bryce Taylor and were likely instrumental in shaping Taylor's recommendations about international sport in the Health and Sports Study Team's report.[2] Jelinek had also been very impressed during his travels abroad with the capacities and functioning of international sport units in many of the sport ministries of European nations and was increasingly frustrated by not having this expertise in Fitness and Amateur Sport. These feelings also played an important part in his drive to create an international sport division within his department.[3]

Early in the negotiations over an expanded role for sport in international relations, Jelinek suggested to External Affairs officials that Fitness and Amateur Sport go ahead and prepare a single memorandum to cabinet on the issue. But External Affairs balked at this suggestion for two reasons. First, the October 1987 cabinet record of decision asked the secretary of state for external affairs, in consultation with the minister of state for fitness and amateur sport, to review the role of sport in foreign policy. Second, a cabinet record of decision on international cultural relations, issued in June 1986, had placed responsibility for leadership in that area clearly with the Department of External Affairs. This document discussed international cultural relations, under three headings: the arts, academic relations, and sport. Although sport had been "a tag-on," its inclusion did raise the question within External Affairs as to whether sport might be put to more use as an instrument to promote Canadian interests abroad. For both of these reasons, External Affairs officials were reluctant to allow Fitness and Amateur Sport to develop a single memorandum to cabinet.[4]

Consequently Fitness and Amateur Sport and External Affairs went about their own ways to develop two separate memoranda to cabinet on international sport relations. Early in September 1986 Jelinek contracted with Richard Pound, former president of the Canadian Olympic Association and an executive vice-president of the International Olympic Committee, to prepare a report on how an international sport relations mandate might best be met. Pound's final report, *Development of an International Sport Policy* (Pound 1987), was submitted in January 1987, but preliminary drafts were circulating in Fitness and Amateur Sport and External Affairs in the fall of 1986.[5]

Anne Hillmer, who had taken over as head of International Sports Relations from Eric Morse earlier in the year, began the Department of External Affairs review by consulting fifty-seven of its posts abroad. She felt that they knew best how sport might meet the department's needs.[6] Forty-nine responded, almost all positively, about the importance of sport in Canada's foreign policy, and many offered suggestions as to how sport could be best used in the respective Canadian "missions" abroad. There was general agreement that sport's potential had not yet been realized (Hillmer 1987, 26). This support from Canada's posts, according to Hillmer, was a key factor in convincing External Affairs that it should go ahead and recommend to cabinet that sport play a more important role in the department's activities.[7]

Because there were little in the way of discretionary funds in the International Sports Relations section's budget, an extensive external review was not possible. Instead, SportCom International Inc., a small consulting firm, was hired to tell External Affairs *how* to accomplish the objectives that were implicit in the suggestions from the Canadian posts. This report, *Development Strategy for Canadian Sport Diplomacy* (Sportcom International Inc., December 1986), was used to prepare a draft of External's memorandum to cabinet. Various versions of this memorandum were circulated around the department, and the final draft went up to the cabinet committee on foreign affairs and defence policy in the spring of 1987.[8]

After various drafts of the Fitness and Amateur Sport memorandum to cabinet had been prepared by assistant deputy minister Lyle

Makosky and the director-general of Sport Canada, Abby Hoffman, it was sent to the cabinet committee on social development in late May.[9] This memorandum highlighted the fact that the Canadian international sport profile could be enhanced through better exposure abroad and argued that Canada should take a much stronger leadership role in international sport organizations. Doping, fair play, and women in sport were identified as issues that Canada should promote to exert this leadership role. The Fitness and Amateur Sport memorandum also put some emphasis on Canada's responsibility to provide sport aid to less fortunate countries.[10]

The External Affairs memorandum put its emphasis on the way in which sport could be used to enhance Canada's foreign policy.[11] According to Hillmer, there was little overlap in the two memoranda to cabinet, except on the matter of sports promotion programs. Such programs involved using élite athletes, sport administrators, coaches, and sport scientists to make appearances, conduct demonstrations, or mount technical assistance programs abroad. Whereas Fitness and Amateur Sport wanted to use such programs primarily to enhance its influence in international sport organizations, External Affairs saw them rather as promotion tools to achieve its broader foreign-policy objectives, particularly in third-world countries.[12]

Considerable intrigue and extensive negotiations took place at this stage. Evidently there was much "blood on the floor" and a great deal of bizarre correspondence exchanged between External Affairs and Fitness and Amateur Sport before the cabinet record of decision was announced by Clark and Jelinek.[13] On at least one point, the responsibility for sport promotions abroad, the two departments could not agree. Fitness and Amateur Sport wanted Sport Canada to be the channel for all contacts by External Affairs with Canadian national sport organizations, while External Affairs wanted the right to contact these organizations directly in order to make arrangements for its own sport promotions abroad.[14] Disagreement also surfaced in the matter of technical assistance, or "sport aid," to other countries.[15] This point of difference was never resolved and would continue to be a sore point between External Affairs and Fitness and Amateur Sport. (We return to this issue in chapter 10.)

The Fitness and Amateur Sport memorandum was questioned at the committee level because it included estimates of the additional funds that would be required to mount the proposed new international sport relations activities. On the other hand, the Department of External Affairs document committed funds from its existing budget to support its new initiatives. Consequently the request for additional funds was dropped from the Fitness and Amateur Sport memorandum.[16] Otherwise, the two memoranda went to cabinet from the respective committees as submitted. At the cabinet level, questions were raised as to why there were two memoranda instead of one. At the very least it had been anticipated that each memorandum would be signed by both ministers. But instead the two memoranda went to their respective cabinet committees without the signature of the other minister, with the memorandum from the other department appended for information.[17] This was another example of the tensions between the two departments.

But evidently senior officials in cabinet were convinced that the two documents were complementary and that responsibilities did not overlap.[18] The cabinet record of decision called for External Affairs and Fitness and Amateur Sport to co-operate closely on international sport initiatives. Fitness and Amateur Sport was to be consulted by all government departments on foreign-policy sport initiatives, and new initiatives were to "build on and utilize" existing Fitness and Amateur Sport programs.[19] According to one senior External Affairs official, this language was used to placate Otto Jelinek and to smooth over the disputes between the two departments. It was clear to External Affairs that, although it would not duplicate Fitness and Amateur Sport programs, it would be able to branch out on its own on new initiatives.[20] To the naïve outsider, however, this certainly seemed the time to resolve more clearly the respective responsibilities for international sport relations between External Affairs and Fitness and Amateur Sport.

External Affairs allocated monies from its existing budget to the Cultural Affairs Division (an additional $235,000 in 1987–88, $300,000 in 1988–89, and $500,000 in 1989–90) to enhance its sport initiatives abroad (Morse 1987a, 20). Additional operating expenditures were also forthcoming for the sport section.[21] These monies allowed the international sport section to go ahead with the initiatives that External's memorandum to cabinet had identified:

1 increase Canadian embassies' capacity (through higher-profile information and public-relations campaigns) to exploit the presence of Canadian athletes in their respective countries;
2 employ current or former sport stars to appear abroad as "good-will" ambassadors, thus putting Canadian excellence in sport on view and thematically linking it to excellence in other fields;
3 exploit "blockbuster" events, such as the 1988 Calgary and Seoul Olympics, to present a positive image of the country;
4 arrange for tours by Canadian teams and athletes to geographic areas where they would not normally travel for competitions;
5 attach greater importance to sport technical assistance programs as a part of Canada's foreign-policy initiatives[22] (see also Morse 1987a).

This last initiative was to provide external affairs minister Joe Clark with a platform for a leadership role in the Commonwealth. The additional monies were also to allow for the appointment of a second staff member to the International Sport Relations section in the fall of 1988.

Although the cabinet record of decision authorized Fitness and Amateur Sport to establish an international sports relations arm, the department was required to find the funds from its existing budget. Despite this, Otto Jelinek moved forward to establish such a unit. After some debate within the branch, it was decided that a separate directorate would be created, reporting directly to the assistant deputy minister. Abby Hoffman was opposed to this idea, seeing it unnecessary to create a third separate unit within the federal government bureaucracy with responsibilities for international sport relations. This decision would cause further confusion and rivalry with External Affairs about respective responsibilities and would complicate collaboration between Sport Canada and the national sport organizations.[23] Lyle Makosky, assistant deputy minister of fitness and amateur sport, supported the minister on this issue.[24]

The Pound report on international sport provided support for Jelinek's decision because it had recommended a specialized, independent capacity within Fitness and Amateur Sport to deal with international relations, one that would report directly to the assistant deputy minister (Pound 1987, 108, 110). Jelinek also expanded the mandate of this new unit by proposing that fitness be included in its purview. Fitness had not been mentioned in the cabinet record of discussion, but its inclusion provided additional rationale for an international relations division that could operate on an equal footing with both Fitness Canada and Sport Canada.[25] Certainly, fitness would become an important function in the Fitness and Amateur Sport international sport relations division. The Canadian-Soviet "Fit Trek" competition, which was initiated in 1989 and pitted respective cities in the Soviet Union and in Canada against one another in friendly fitness contests, was one such endeavour.

The advertisement for the new international relations post in Fitness and Amateur Sport was circulated in Canada and abroad in October 1987. The selection committee interviewed a short list of candidates, including a number of Canadians and one non-Canadian applicant. After some debate, it was decided that none of the Canadian candidates had enough international sport relations experience.[26] Consequently, John Scott was appointed as acting director of the Directorate of International Sport Relations in March 1988. He had previously been the head of international affairs with the British Sport Council and as such, had considerable expertise in dealing with European sport ministries.

VISA BAN ON SOUTH AFRICAN
PROFESSIONAL SPORTSPERSONS

In the summer of 1988, the issue of South African professional athletes' participation in tennis and golf tournaments in Canada was finally to come to a head. The specific incident that precipitated this crisis must be put into the perspective of wider foreign-policy initiatives. The Mulroney government had continued its efforts to maintain a leadership role in the Commonwealth in the fight against apartheid in South Africa. By 1987, however, there were indications that the importance of Canada's role in this issue was being overestimated, both within and outside the country (Ross, 24 October 1987, 6 February 1988). In January 1987 Mulroney had undertaken a tour of Zimbabwe – the first Western leader to have done so (Valpy, 31 January 1987). In August he and the external affairs minister, Joe Clark, were among the first Western leaders to meet with African National Congress president Oliver Tambo. These and other events were building towards the Commonwealth heads-of-governments meetings in Vancouver in October.

Chaired by the Canadian prime minister, these meetings produced a stalemate between Britain and the rest of the Commonwealth over the issue of sanctions. Britain excepted itself from several provisions of the Okanagan Statement on Southern Africa and Programme of Action, which emerged from the meetings. Although no new sanctions were adopted, the statement called for efforts to secure the "wider, tighter, and more intensified application" of existing measures. For Canada, this review included its existing South African sport policies.[27] The Okanagan Statement also urged measures to "reach into South Africa" with assistance to the victims and opponents of apartheid, and to promote dialogue and counter South African propaganda and censorship. A Special Commonwealth Fund for Mozambique, the frontline state hardest hit by South Africa's "destabilization" efforts, was also established. Finally, an eight-member Committee of Foreign Ministers on Southern Africa (CFMSA), to be chaired by Canada's external affairs minister, Joe Clark, was struck at this summit (Cruickshank, Sallot, and Valpy, 17 October 1987). Predictably, Britain did not support the establishment of this committee. In fact, the Vancouver Commonwealth meetings apparently featured an "electric" confrontation between fellow Tories Mulroney and Thatcher over South Africa (Valpy 1988, 15). It was a confrontation that went a long way towards cementing the Canadian prime minister's anti-apartheid credentials among the frontline and other Commonwealth states.

The first meeting of the CFMSA was held in Lusaka, Zambia, in February 1988, with Joe Clark in the chair. In fact, his mandate was to chair the four meetings of this committee that were to be held before the October 1989 Commonwealth summit in Kuala Lumpur (*Calgary Herald*, 2 February 1988). At the Lusaka meeting, Clark and the committee reached agreement on a continued Commonwealth anti-apartheid campaign against South Africa (Commonwealth Secretary-General 1989). The following summer (1988), he found himself in the embarrassing position of hosting the second meeting of the CFMSA in Toronto at the same time as the annual Players' International men's tennis tournament was held at York University. There was a strong likelihood that South African players would compete in this tournament. Such participation always drew the attention of the media. The previous summer (1987), David Frost and Nick Price had been top contenders in the Canadian Open Golf Championships in Oakville, Ontario, and the media, in referring to them as South Africans, noted that their presence undermined Canada's commitment to stop sport exchanges between Canada and South Africa.[28]

Clark had responded to a letter from Bruce Kidd[29] by reiterating Canada's position that visitors' visas would be denied to South Africans who wished to come to Canada to participate in sport events as official representatives of their country. However, professional athletes did not represent their country and therefore were not covered by his government's guidelines. He went on to state that his position was consistent with the Gleneagles Declaration, which called for Commonwealth countries to restrict sports contacts "to the extent practical."[30] He made no mention of the fact that the more recent Commonwealth Code of Conduct called for a halt to all sporting contacts with South Africa. The *Calgary Herald* had also brought attention to the fact that South African golfer Hendrik Buhrmann had competed in the Manitoba Open Golf Tournament in Winnipeg that same summer (*Calgary Herald*, 31 July 1987).

Anti-apartheid sport activists also put pressure on York University, the location of the National Tennis Centre and the site for the upcoming Players' International tournament. Bruce Kidd was in touch with the York University Faculty Association and encouraged its president to contact Sam Ramsamy, the executive director of the South African Non-Racial Olympic Committee.[31] As a result, Ramsamy wired the president of York, Harry Arthurs, asking him to use his influence to dissuade the Canadian Tennis Association (CTA) from inviting South African players to this tournament.[32] The CTA responded to Arthurs's subsequent inquiries by stating that it did not invite participants to the Players' International; rather, they were selected on the basis of the world computer rankings. The chairperson of CTA's board of directors, Bob Wright, did tell Arthurs, however, that his association would review this matter at its next board meeting at the end of August.[33] The CTA had supported a resolution at the annual general meetings of the International Tennis Federation in Paris in June 1988 to eliminate sanctioned tournaments in South Africa,[34] but this resolution did not pass.

The probability of adverse publicity over South Africans playing in the Players' International tennis tournament at the same time as the Commonwealth foreign ministers' meetings chaired by Clark was exacerbated by the press having picked up on the story that in early July 1988 a black South African softball player had been denied a visa to attend a tournament in Saskatoon later that month as an observer (*Globe and Mail*, 9 July 1988). This ruling was seen in some circles as hypocritical in light of the laxity of Canadian polices towards admitting South African white professional sportspersons. Indeed, questions were being raised in the House of Commons about South African professionals participating in sport events in Canada (HC *Debates*, 26–7 July 1988, 17959–61, 18058). In response to this adverse publicity on the eve of the CFMSA meetings in Toronto, Clark and the new fitness and amateur sport minister, Jean Charest, announced jointly on 29 July that the government's sport policy would be tightened to close the so-called "Mulroney loophole" by denying visas to all individuals with South African passports seeking to enter Canada to participate in a sports event (Canada, 29 July 1988). The CTA immediately wrote to all South Africans entered in the upcoming tournament asking them to withdraw.[35]

FURTHER RESTRICTIONS?

At the time of his announcement banning visas, Clark promised that there would be a review of the sports directives for dealing with South Africa and that a further statement would be forthcoming before the Seoul Olympics in September (*Calgary Herald*, 15 February 1989). Two issues of concern to anti-apartheid sport activists were still outstanding. One was that the existing regulations allowed for Canadian professional athletes, who were designated by the government as "not being national representatives," to play in international sport contests abroad that involved South African athletes. The second concern was that the South African professional athletes who came to Canadian tournaments on "passports of convenience" were not affected by the new policy (Kidd, 10 February 1989). These two issues were to cause much debate within the government, and anti-apartheid sport activists were to wait for another year before the further policy announcement that had been promised.

Although there was no announcement of stricter sport sanctions against South Africa before the Seoul Olympics, Joe Clark did announce several additional general sanctions, as well as the creation of a "dialogue fund" to supplement an earlier allocation for countering propaganda and censorship in South Africa – a total of $2.4 million for a period of just over a year (Clark, 26 September 1988). These new programs and the expanded programs for humanitarian and educational assistance to South Africans reflected a growing emphasis on "positive measures" in the government's anti-apartheid policies. A small ($2 million) program of "security assistance" for Mozambique, long called for by regional states in southern Africa and by South African activists and scholars concerned with the region (Freeman 1988, 4), was also quietly introduced.

Canada's enthusiasm for new sanctions had waned since the halcyon days of the Vancouver Commonwealth meetings, when its international reputation as an opponent of the South African regime had perhaps reached its high point. The start of this decline and its accompanying troubles may be traced back to the Venice economic summit of the Group of Seven (G7) (Britain, Canada, the Federal Republic of Germany, France, Italy, Japan, and the United States) in June 1987. It had always been recognized by Canadian foreign-policy strategists that Canadian sanctions on their own, or even in conjunction with the country's Commonwealth allies, would have only a minimal impact on South Africa. The key, therefore, was to persuade as many of Pretoria's major economic partners – primarily the largest Western powers, including Japan – to impose sanctions at least to the level of those of the Canadian-Commonwealth consortium. Britain, of course, had rejected this strategy at the Commonwealth "mini-summit" in London in August 1986. When Brian Mulroney attempted to get the G7 to take stronger action against South Africa, he was rebuffed. Although South Africa was noted for the first time in the mini-summit's final communiqué, there was no support for sanctions. At the next G7 summit in Toronto the following summer, Mulroney tried again, with the same result (Nossal 1988c, 15).

As the smallest of the G7 powers, Canada has only a limited amount of influence and has naturally been reluctant to expend too much of it on an apparently hopeless cause. Furthermore, Kim Nossal has argued that "Mulroney's willingness in 1985 to espouse a total break with South Africa as a means of levering Pretoria into accelerating the abandonment of apartheid created the impression among other leaders that Mulroney was diplomatically immature and unrealistic" (ibid.). This view reinforced the hand of the foreign-policy professionals in the Department of External Affairs, many of whom had been uncomfortable from the outset with Mulroney's "adventurism" on South Africa (Nossal 1988b, 34; Smith 1989, 28–9). This failure on the part of

Cánada to persuade the G7 nations to take stronger action against South Africa, along with Joe Clark's predilection towards a more conservative, gradualist approach to sanctions, helps to explain why the government's enthusiasm for additional sanctions had waned significantly since the Vancouver Commonwealth meetings.

This more cautious approach, predictably, was criticized by anti-apartheid forces, both inside and outside Canada (Freeman 1988, 7; Howard, 24 January 1989). Brian Mulroney's commitment at the UN in 1985, "If there is no progress in the dismantling of apartheid, our relations with South Africa may have to be severed absolutely," was to be invoked repeatedly, along with the observation that Pretoria's repression seemed, in fact, to be increasing. At the CFMSA meetings in Toronto that had precipitated the prohibition of professional sportspersons to Canada, Canadian officials had announced that the focus of the meetings was to be on South African censorship and propaganda. This assertion was contradicted by some of the other delegates, who argued that sanctions were the main issue. As well, the Canadian government was roundly criticized by anti-apartheid activists at home (Freeman 1988, 5; *Southern Africa Report* 1988, 9–11).

The fall of 1988 was to mark the start of a long series of interdepartmental negotiations over further restrictions on sporting contacts with South Africa. In the first place, the proposal to deny entry to South African professionals who held passports from other countries was never really on because the employment and immigration minister, Barbara McDougall, was strongly opposed to it. Such a measure, according to the legal advice that she had received, might well be successfully challenged under the provisions of the new Charter of Rights and Freedoms. A successful appeal would have the wider ramification of limiting the discretionary powers that immigration officers now exercised. In fact, McDougall had been opposed to the denial of visas to South African professional athletes on the same grounds,[36] but the political urgency for this measure had evidently allowed Clark to override her objections. Of course, the visa ban placed on South African athletes "representative of their country" just before the Edmonton Commonwealth Games in 1978 was equally vulnerable to a court appeal, but McDougall evidently felt that there was a much greater chance on this occasion of a court challenge on behalf of high-profile South African professional athletes. Finally, it should be noted that to bar South African athletes who held passports from third countries would have violated a long-standing and strongly held international convention that mitigated against challenging passports issued by another nation. To run in the face of this convention was not something the Canadian government was likely to do.

Attention in the government also focused on the possibility of denying entry to Canada to South African athletes who held immigration visas, or "green cards," from the United States and who could gain entry to Canada by presenting these instead of their South African passports. Such athletes were, in fact, the major cause of grief at Canadian tournaments because most South African golf and tennis professionals held these US green cards. Once again, this debate pitted Employment and Immigration against Fitness and Amateur Sport and the Department of External Affairs. The debate extended over many months and was one cause of the continued delay of the new policy announcement. Employment and Immigration objected to the provision for a number of reasons. The first was its concerns, previously mentioned, about the legality of such a measure. Second, it was worried that the United States would object to such a distinction among its permanent residents and that such a measure would open up the whole issue of reciprocity of access across the Canadian–US border. Finally, Employment and Immigration argued that this measure would be extremely difficult to enforce. Large numbers of people came across the Canadian border daily on green cards, and to sort out South African professional athletes from among these would be a formidable task.[37] If such a regulation was put in place, it was entirely likely that a South African professional with a green card would turn up at a major tournament before being discovered by immigration officials, with the embarrassing brouhaha that would ensue.[38] Both Clark and Charest were willing to take these risks and pressed for the implementation of a ban on South African athletes using green cards,[39] but in the end Employment and Immigration won out again and this proposal was dropped.

As far as preventing Canadian professional athletes from competing in third countries against South African athletes, External Affairs was reluctant to take this step because the department felt that it would simply penalize Canadian professionals. Given the lack of international stature of Canadian professional golfers and tennis players, their absence from prestigious international tournaments would have had little impact on the apartheid issue. The CTA argued that the technique which worked so well with so-called amateur sport organizations in Canada, that of threatening to withdraw funds if they violated Canada's policies about sporting contacts with South Africa, simply would not work in tennis and golf. Unlike other national sport organizations, the CTA and the Royal Canadian Golf Association (RCGA) neither provided financial support to players nor controlled entries to their tournaments, and Canadian professionals would certainly ignore any attempts on the part of these organizations to ban them from international tournaments. Attention in the press focused more often on the

CTA (see, for instance, McCabe, 10 August 1985; Ormsby, 13 August 1989), perhaps because Sport Canada contributions to the CTA were substantially higher than those to the RCGA.

Still, there was plenty of media attention focused on golf as well. The *Toronto Star* made note of the fact that Nick Price, a South African travelling on a British passport, was to compete in the Canadian Open Golf Championships in June 1989 (McKee, 21 June 1989). The fitness and amateur sport minister, Jean Charest, was quoted as saying that the federal government was powerless to prevent South African nationals with third-country passports from competing in professional tournaments, but that he would ask the RCGA to remove Price from the Canadian Open (ibid.). Keith Rever, the RCGA president, said that although his association banned South Africans from amateur golf tournaments, it had no authority to stop professionals. "We have a contractual agreement with the (US) Professional Golfers' Association and the contract says we cannot ban anyone (because) he has either played in South Africa or is from South Africa" (Beltrame, 21 June 1989, B1). Later that week, the International Campaign Against Apartheid Sport (Canada) condemned the presence of fourteen golfers on the UN Register of Sporting Contacts with South Africa in the Canadian Golf Championships at Glen Abbey, in Oakville. The organization stated that the "participation of these players also exposes weaknesses of the current Canadian policy ... it (government) takes no action against 'boycott breakers,'" despite prohibiting South African sportspersons from entering the country and condemning all contact with South Africa"(International Campaign Against Apartheid Sport, 25 June 1989).

Sport Canada was strongly opposed to softening the existing regulations, which allowed Canadian athletes to participate against South African athletes in a third country only if such an entry became known after they had departed from Canada. This proviso was little used because the vast majority of Canadian high-performance athletes competed abroad in events from which South Africans had been banned by the respective international organizations or in events where the entry of South African athletes was known well in advance. In addition, any violations by individual athletes had been dealt with by suspensions from their parent sport organizations. These regulations had worked extremely effectively, and Sport Canada was unwilling to create loopholes in the regulations for the sake of professional athletes. It argued that high-profile professional athletes in tennis or golf represented Canada in the same way as did the country's top high-performance athletes and therefore should be treated in the same way with respect to sporting contacts with South Africans.[40]

Despite these strong objections from Sport Canada, External Affairs (and evidently fitness and amateur sport minister Jean Charest eventually as well) bought the arguments of the CTA that professionals should be allowed to compete against South Africans abroad on the condition that both the CTA and the RCGA agreed to lobby their respective international organizations to stiffen their regulations about South Africans competing in international tournaments. There was evidently, at one time, agreement within the government that the CTA be given a two-year grace period before it would have to comply with a total ban on third-country contacts with South African players,[41] but this proposal was dropped when it was decided not to ban professionals from playing in third countries against South Africans.

In responding to an inquiry from Bruce Kidd, external affairs minister Joe Clark said that the government was trying to tighten the measures against sporting contacts with South Africans by urging the national sport organizations to exclude South Africans who did not require a visa (i.e., those on third-country passports) from competing in sport events in Canada; by applying pressure on their international federations to expel South Africa; and by encouraging their athletes to protest participation of South African athletes in sports events in a third country.[42] In December 1988, John Scott wrote to Bruce Kidd stating that the government had not yet developed a strategy for barring those foreign athletes who had defied the international campaign and competed in South Africa, but that a policy statement would be forthcoming in January.[43]

But no such statement was forthcoming, and in February Kidd was quoted in the *Calgary Herald* as saying the tennis lobby had been so strong that it had met Clark and persuaded him to drop the third-country provision. "It's obvious that there is something going on behind the scenes. Besides the strength of the tennis lobby, there is also the feeling within External that they don't want to get too far ahead of the other countries" (*Calgary Herald*, 15 February 1989, D2). Fitness and Amateur Sport files do indeed confirm that Clark had been in touch with Robert Wright, chairperson of the CTA's board of directors, on this matter[44] and that External Affairs officials held meetings with golf and tennis officials without even informing Fitness and Amateur Sport.[45]

Shortly after Kidd's remarks in the *Calgary Herald*, Bob Moffatt wrote on behalf of the CTA to the International Tennis Federation (ITF), requesting that further action be taken against South Africa at its annual general meetings, to be held in September.[46] The complexities of international tennis meant, however, that such measures were unlikely to have any effect on the *status quo.* Unlike most international sport federations, the ITF had little control over the major "sanctioned" tennis tournaments around the world and, indeed, those that were still scheduled in South Africa. Key decisions about these tournaments were in the hands of the Men's Tennis Council (MTC) and the Women's International Tennis Association (WITA). But the Association of Tennis Professionals (ATP), made up of the players' representatives and tournament directors, was contesting the right of the MTC to control the international professional men's tennis circuit.[47] It was not a propitious time for the ITF to press for the expulsion of South Africa when it was itself fighting to maintain some influence over professional tennis. The ITF was represented on the MTC, but not on the ATP.[48]

To show further "good faith," the CTA had commenced, in April 1989, the process of removing the names of four Canadian tennis players from the UN Register of Sport Contacts with South Africa. This was a semi-annual list that had been kept following the UN Declaration against Apartheid in Sport in 1977, which included all the sportspersons who had defied the UN ban on participating in South Africa. Those wishing to get their names off the list had to certify that they would not defy the ban in future (United Nations 1989). The CTA was successful in getting the names of three Canadian tennis players off the list; the fourth was a person unknown to the association.[49]

In fact, the use of this UN "banned list" to exclude athletes who had participated in South Africa from competing in sport events in Canada was also considered in interdepartmental meetings.[50] This was certainly a measure that anti-apartheid sport activists such as Bruce Kidd had been advocating for some time,[51] and one that may have represented an acceptable compromise on the issue. But it was another possibility that was eventually rejected. Lane MacAdam was quoted some time later as saying that the government had dropped the measure because there were too many errors on the list (Christie, 12 December 1989). In rejecting his explanation, Bruce Kidd stated that it would be easy to have the list verified by the Canadian embassy in Johannesburg. In any case, athletes whose names appeared on it in error could have them removed simply by declaring that they would respect the international boycott.[52] However, the use of the UN banned list to bar players from Canada would have raised strong objections from Canadian sport organizations in tennis, golf, and squash because it would have prevented many outstanding professional athletes from participating in tournaments in Canada. For instance, both Boris Becker and Pat Cash, two of the top players on the men's tennis circuit, had played in tournaments in South Africa.[53] The use of the UN banned list would also have caused embarrassment to the government because Canada was not a signatory to the 1977 UN Declaration against Apartheid in Sport, the resolution from which the banned list evolved.

A NEW POLICY STATEMENT

The new policy statement on sport contacts that was finally forthcoming at the end of June 1989 (Canada, 28 June 1989) did little to placate the anti-apartheid lobby in Canada. There was no mention of restrictions on South Africans who held passports of convenience or green cards from the United States, nor did the new policy impose a total ban on sporting contacts with South Africans in third countries. Instead, it stipulated that all Canadian athletes, including professionals, competing against South Africans in a third country must decline invitations, withdraw, or lodge a formal protest. This provision actually represented a step back from the 1985 policy for high-performance athletes (or non-professional athletes), which stated that when the presence of South African athletes was known before departure from Canada, the team or individual athlete had no option but to withdraw.

One new thrust in the June 1989 policy was that the government urged national sport organizations in Canada to take all action possible, including calling for the suspension of South Africa from their respective international organizations, to tighten restrictions against contacts with South Africa. This directive was aimed largely at the CTA and the RCGA, but as noted above, was not likely to have any effect on tennis or golf, because their respective international federations had little influence over decisions about the top international professional tournaments. However, the CTA did respond to the new government policy position in a special report that announced its intention to implement these "guidelines in a reasonable and practical manner, consistent with the Government's policy, while recognizing the fundamental rights of players, officials, coaches and administrators" (Canadian Tennis Association, January 1990, 4).

The new policy also committed the government to strengthen and extend the international boycott against South Africa and to work towards breaking down racial barriers in South Africa (Canada, 28 June 1989), although how this was to be accomplished was not made clear. In early drafts of the new policy, reference had been made to specific measures that Fitness and Amateur Sport wanted the Department of External Affairs to undertake to put pressure on governments whose position on preventing sporting contacts with South Africans was weak.[54] The final draft made no reference to these measures. They were dropped, presumably because External Affairs did not want to undertake the unpleasant task of ruffling feathers in the foreign offices of other countries, and thus the job was left to Fitness and Amateur Sport and the national sport organizations themselves.

Finally, the new policy included the commitment by Canada of financial support to international anti-apartheid sport organizations to tighten the ban on sporting contacts with South Africa and simultaneously to encourage the development of non-racial sport in South Africa (ibid.). Breaking down racial barriers in South Africa itself was a goal that the international anti-apartheid sport movement was moving towards (Kidd 1988). Indeed, at a meeting in Harare in October 1988, called by the African National Congress (ANC), Danie Craven, the patriarch of Afrikaner rugby, agreed to a top-to-bottom integration of South African rugby. This was a major victory for the ANC and for integrated sport in South Africa (Kidd 1989, 18).

INTERNATIONAL DEVELOPMENTS IN TENNIS

Developments on the international sport scene, however, were to result in some concrete measures about tennis professionals competing against South Africans. After many years of lobbying, tennis finally became a sport at the Summer Olympics in Seoul in 1988. Since the distinction between professional and amateurs had long disappeared in tennis, many countries were represented by touring professionals. Indeed, the top women's professional tennis player in the world, Steffie Graf, competed for West Germany and won the gold medal in the Seoul Olympics. Because South Africa had been banned from the Olympic movement in 1970 after a long struggle, whether South Africans could compete in these Games was not at issue.

But the attitude in the International Olympic Committee (IOC) towards sporting contacts was much different under the leadership of Juan Samaranch than it had been in the 1960s and 1970s, when, to say the least, it had been a cautious one. International pressure was brought to bear on the ITF because, like all other international sport federations, it controlled the playing regulations and eligibility rules for Olympic tennis. In return for tennis being included in the Seoul Olympics, the ITF had been required to withdraw its sanction for the South African Open Tennis Championships and to ban any further play with South Africa (Kidd 1988, 647). For the reasons noted above, the latter requirement meant only that international team competitions, such as the Davis and Federation cups were affected. Indeed, South Africa had withdrawn voluntarily from Davis and Federation Cup competitions in 1975, after India had defaulted to South Africa in the finals of the Davis Cup rather than compete against that country.[55] However, South Africa still retained its membership in the ITF, and efforts to remove it from the organization had not been successful.

Next, the IOC stipulated that if tennis was to stay on the sport roster for the 1992 Summer Olympics, all sanctioned tournaments in South Africa were going to have to stop (Polyani, 1 September 1989). Since the ATP had won the struggle with the MTC, a newly formed body, called the ATP Tour, was now in control of the international men's tennis circuit. With the IOC's general assembly meetings scheduled for the end of August 1989, the ATP Tour, although having confirmed in July that two of its international tournaments would again be held in South Africa, reversed its decision and withdrew its sanction of these tournaments (*Star* [South Africa], 31 August 1989).

Subsequently, at its general assembly meetings in Puerto Rico, the IOC announced that tennis would be on the official list of events at the 1992 Summer Olympics in Barcelona, but at the same time, it stipulated that any player who competed in South Africa from 31 August 1989 onward would be banned from future Olympic tennis competitions (Polyani, 1 September 1989). The IOC also announced that it supported a motion to bar South Africa from the ITF, a motion that was to be tabled at the ITF at its annual general meetings the following month (*Star* [South Africa], 31 August 1989). The IOC further warned that tennis as an Olympic sport could still be in jeopardy unless the ITF took steps to ban all tennis tournaments under its jurisdiction in South Africa (Polyani, 1 September 1989). In a final resolution, the IOC announced that its South Africa ban would apply in the future to all Olympic sports (ibid.).

Bowing to international pressure, the ITF finally suspended South Africa from its membership list at its annual meetings in September in Buenos Aires, and it cancelled all ITF – sanctioned tournaments in that country (*Citizen* [South Africa], 18 September 1989). The resolution to suspend South Africa was supported by a strong public statement by CTA's chairperson, Robert Wright.[56]

Years of hard work by anti-apartheid sport activists had finally broken down the resistance in international tennis to denying sanctions to tennis tournaments in South Africa. Tennis professionals from that country were, however, still free to compete in Grand Slam events (the four big international tennis championships: the Australian, French, and US opens, and Wimbledon, which were controlled by a separate organization, the Grand Slam Committee), and the ATP Tour circuit events in most countries around the world. Indeed, many non–South African professionals continued to play in lucrative tennis tournaments in

South Africa, despite the fact that these tournaments had lost their sanctions. These players, along with South Africans on passports of convenience, were still free to compete with impunity in virtually every country.

CHAPTER EIGHT

Canadian Sport Initiatives in the Commonwealth

Perhaps the most significant international sport initiative that the government took subsequent to the 1987 cabinet record of decision, which signalled a greater use of sport in Canada's diplomatic endeavours, was the proposal that the secretary of state for external affairs, Joe Clark, put forth in the summer of 1989 to provide assistance to the Commonwealth Games Federation (CGF) and developing countries in the Commonwealth. Because this initiative was tied in part to the resentment that some Commonwealth countries felt when Victoria, B.C., was awarded the 1994 Commonwealth Games, this chapter begins with a brief overview of the events surrounding Victoria's successful bid, and contrasts it with the international embarrassment caused to the Canadian government by the Ben Johnson scandal at the 1988 Seoul Olympics.

THE VICTORIA COMMONWEALTH GAMES BID

The July 1988 federal government announcement of a ban on visas for South African professional sportspersons wishing to compete in Canada (Canada, 29 July 1988) was propitiously timed to have a positive impact on the bid by Victoria for the 1994 Commonwealth Games. This bid was to be considered at the CGF general assembly meetings scheduled for the following September in conjunction with the 1988 Summer Olympics in Seoul, and the visa ban on South African athletes was seen as a measure that would have a favourable effect on delegates from black African nations (*Globe and Mail*, 10 February 1989; Kidd 1988, 658). Indeed, Canadian posts abroad were advised at the end of June that the admission of South African sportspersons to Canada was a very sensitive matter in the light of, among other things, the upcoming Victoria bid.[1] There was some controversy over Victoria's eventually winning this bid. In the competition for the 1990 Games, which was held at the CGF meetings in Los Angeles in conjunction with the 1984 Summer Olympics, the Commonwealth Games Association of Canada (CGAC) was committed to support any significant bid from a third-world country. However, no such submission was forthcoming to the CGF executive by the official deadline, that is, six months before the general assembly meetings in Los Angeles. At the Los Angeles meetings, however, New Delhi made an impromptu bid, and reluctantly the Canadian delegation supported this rather weak presentation.[2] Auckland won out over New Delhi in the final round of voting.

After these Los Angeles meetings, the CGAC tried to ascertain whether New Delhi would be bidding again for the 1994 Games. However, no official word was forthcoming from India, so the Canadian association set about to ensure that there would be a viable Canadian bid for these Games. There had been concern in the CGF ever since the bidding for the 1986 Games (when there had only been one bid, that of Edinburgh) about the shortfall of viable host cities. Some six months before the CGF meetings in Seoul, the CGAC found out that New Delhi was indeed going to make a substantive bid for the 1994 Games. At this point, some Commonwealth countries argued that Canada should drop out of the running to allow for a successful third-world bid. But by this time, the CGAC was committed to support the Victoria bid. The Victoria delegation had put considerable time and effort into winning the Canadian competition over eight other cities, and there was a great deal of civic enthusiasm for staging the Games in Victoria.[3] Both the British Columbia and federal governments had also committed themselves to supporting this bid and, if it was successful, the Games themselves.

All three members of the Indian delegation who spoke on behalf of the New Delhi bid at the CGF meetings in Seoul argued that it was high time the Games were awarded to a city in a developing country, pointing out that only once in the history of the Games had such a city been selected – Kingston, Jamaica, in 1966 (Commonwealth Games Federation, 15 September 1988a). Despite this strong emotional appeal to the voting delegates, Victoria won the bid on the first ballot, garnering 29 votes. New Delhi was second with 18 votes, while Wales trailed with 7 (Commonwealth Games Federation, 15 September 1988b, 8). The Commonwealth Secretariat in London made much of this issue (see Commonwealth Secretariat, 9 February 1989), questions were raised in the press, and there was some bitterness in certain quarters of the Commonwealth over what was seen as yet another snub of developing nations.[4]

If this reaction to the outcome of the bid for the 1994 Games had been widespread in third-world Commonwealth countries, Victoria would not have won the competition. Many sport officials in these developing nations saw that staging the Games in their country would put a tremendous strain on already very limited government support for sport. Building the very expensive facilities required to host events such as swimming and athletics (track and field) would not only divert badly needed funds, but would also make very little contribution to the development of sport in the host country. These sport officials tended to view the controversy about the awarding of the 1994 Games to Victoria more as a political ploy in some developing Commonwealth countries. In addition, Victoria promised much superior facilities and technical support for the Games than did New Delhi, an attraction to many third-world athletes and sport officials.[5]

In contrast to the good news about the success of the Victoria bid, the Seoul Olympics themselves proved to be very traumatic for Canada. The dramatic revelation that Ben Johnson had failed to pass his post-race doping test turned his victory in the 100-metre final from national triumph to national tragedy. The resulting Dubin Commission of Inquiry and the subsequent investigation into the proper role of the federal government in supporting high-performance sport in Canada are stories for another place. Canada's stature in international sport circles was considerably diminished by this incident. Particularly embarrassing was the fact that Canada had played a role in developing international agreements on doping in sport and had some years earlier established its own drug policies for sport. The first such policy had been put into place late in 1983 after two scandals involving Canadian athletes. The first of these incidents occurred at the Pan American Games in Venezuela in August 1983. New drug-testing techniques were introduced at the Games, and many athletes were caught off guard. Some, including two Canadian weight-lifters, tested positive and were disqualified. Many other athletes, particularly from the United States, refused to compete and went home (Ministry of State for Fitness and Amateur Sport [undated]). Shortly after this incident, four Canadian weight-lifters returning from competitions in Eastern Europe were apprehended at Mirabel Airport with steroids in their possession (ibid.). In 1985, minister of state for fitness and amateur sport Otto Jelinek strengthened the 1983 policy and increased the penalty for first-time doping infractions from a minimum of one year's suspension from government funding to lifetime ineligibility (ibid.).

Jelinek, recognizing that efforts on the national scene alone were not likely to solve Canada's problems with doping in sport, also took some international initiatives. In 1985 Canada was able to gain observer status on the Council of Europe's Sport Committee for the Development

of Sport Experts on Anti-Doping in Sport (ibid.). Subsequently, Jelinek
was invited to address the fifth conference of the European Ministers
Responsible for Sport (an arm of the Council of Europe) at the end of
September 1986. In this address he advanced a number of proposals,
including one to establish a world anti-doping charter (Jelinek,
September 1986). His speech built on the Council of Europe's existing
Anti-Doping Charter, adopted in 1984 and considered to be the model
for other regions and countries around the world.[6] Jelinek's proposal
was subsequently endorsed by the European sports ministers. As a result, a charter group, consisting of representatives from Canada, the
Council of Europe, the International Olympic Committee (IOC), and
the United States Olympic Committee, set about to develop an international anti-doping charter (Ministry of State for Fitness and Amateur
Sport [undated]).

In the fall of 1987, sport ministers of the socialist nations also issued
a strong anti-doping statement. Jelinek pursued his initiative at the
Calgary Winter Olympics in February 1988, when he was able to convince the ministers of sport from a number of Eastern bloc countries
to attend a world conference on sport doping policies. Consequently,
the First Permanent World Conference on Antidoping in Sport was
hosted by Canada in Ottawa in June 1988 (ibid.). Jean Charest, who by
this time had taken over Jelinek's Fitness and Amateur Sport portfolio,
was quoted as saying that this initiative allowed Canada to retain at least
some credibility in international sport circles after the Ben Johnson
scandal.[7]

THE CANADIAN
COMMONWEALTH SPORT
INITIATIVE

The bitterness in some developing Commonwealth countries over the
awarding of the 1996 Commonwealth Games to Victoria and the continued threat of a boycott of the Auckland Games were to provide the
opportunity for external affairs minister Joe Clark to take some initiatives in support of the Commonwealth Games and to allay some of the
resentment among third-world countries about inequities in both bidding for, and competition at, the Games. Rugby and cricket were at the
centre of boycott threats again. In the spring of 1989, the national
rugby associations of England, Scotland, Wales, Australia, and France
decided to allow their players to accept an invitation to form a World
xv team to make a centennial tour of South Africa the following
September in celebration of the 100th anniversary of rugby in that
country (Christie, 22 August 1989). Consequently the international
anti-apartheid sport movement was pressing for Australia and Britain

to be barred from the Auckland Games. In the summer of 1989, a planned rebel tour of South Africa by English cricketers had also drawn the ire of black African sport leaders. The vice-president of the CGF, Tanzanian Raphael Kubaga, said that if Britain did not intervene to stop the tour, it might face an African campaign to have it banned from international sport (*Business Day*, 3 August 1989). These tours also prompted the Organization for African Unity to call for a boycott of the 1990 Commonwealth Games in Auckland.[8]

It was in this atmosphere that Clark in July 1989 attended a meeting of the Association of South-East Asian Nations Foreign Ministers, at which the possibility of a sport assistance program for third-world Commonwealth countries was discussed. He had been briefed before these meetings that not only were the Commonwealth Games in political danger, but the CGF itself was experiencing financial difficulties. At the conclusion of these meetings, Clark sent back a note to External Affairs asking for more information on the Commonwealth Games. He was scheduled to go on to New Zealand to confer with his counterpart there, who was concerned about the possibility of a boycott of the Auckland Games. He would then travel to Canberra for the fourth meeting of the Committee of Foreign Ministers on Southern Africa (CFMSA).[9]

At the previous (third) meeting of the CFMSA in Harare in February 1989, Clark had experienced some very uncomfortable moments. Just prior to the Harare meetings, figures had been released that showed substantial year-over-year increases in Canada – South Africa trade during the period 1987–88. According to critics of Canada's foreign policy on South Africa, these figures highlighted the inherent limitations of partial sanctions (Watson, 26 January 1989). During the meetings themselves, the Zimbabwean foreign minister claimed that Canadian companies were "shipping arms and equipment via other countries (to South Africa)." He subsequently issued a rather ambiguous retraction (Newman, 13 February 1989, 29). Canada suffered a further embarrassment at the Harare meetings when news broke of a $600 million loan by the Bank of Nova Scotia to Minorco, a Luxembourg-based, South African–controlled company. This loan certainly seemed to violate the spirit, if not the letter, of the Canadian and Commonwealth ban on new investments in South Africa (ibid.). Although Clark received less well publicized praise for "his clear-headed performance in the chair and his evidently heartfelt commitment to the liberation of South Africa's Black majority" (Ross, 11 February 1989, D3), he was undoubtedly relieved to escape Harare.

Back home, Anne Hillmer, head of International Sports Relations at External Affairs, was charged with the responsibility of preparing the briefing document on sport in the Commonwealth for the external affairs minister. This document was sent off to Clark for his meetings in Canberra,[10] with copies to officials in Fitness and Amateur Sport. By this time the atmosphere in the CFMSA had improved, and the foreign ministers were once again pulling in the same direction, in anticipation of the Commonwealth heads-of-government meetings in the Malaysian capital, Kuala Lumpur, in October. The concluding statement by the Commonwealth foreign ministers covered a wide range of issues and recommendations, but the main focus was on ways and means of strengthening financial sanctions against South Africa (Commonwealth Committee of Foreign Ministers, August 1989).

It was at these CFMSA meetings in Canberra that the "Clark initiative" on possible solutions to the political, financial, and organizational problems facing the Commonwealth Games was first put forward. Among the solutions advanced were establishing a Commonwealth sport trust, providing assistance in hosting for developing countries, setting up a travel subsidization fund, staging regional Commonwealth competitions and an annual Commonwealth sport challenge, establishing scholarships and academic exchanges in physical education and sport, and proposals for strengthening and relocating the Commonwealth Games Federation headquarters in London to another site (DEA, 4 August 1989). The Clark initiative was endorsed by the CFMSA, with plans for a follow-up meeting in London the following month (*Citizen* [South Africa], 10 August 1989).

As for the origins of this initiative, Hillmer says that similar endeavours by the Conference of Ministers of Youth and Sport of French Speaking Countries (in French, CONFEJES) were the model for the Clark proposal. CONFEJES had been sponsoring sport aid programs for third-world francophone countries for some fifteen years.[11] In 1988–89 the budget for this program totalled some $700,000, about two-thirds of which went to bursaries to support post-secondary education in sport and physical education for third-world students in developed countries, with the other one-third to sport development programs in the third-world countries (Canadian International Development Agency 1990, 80). These programs had been initiated long before the first Francophonie Games were held in Rabat, Morocco, in 1989 and, according to Hillmer, were good examples of the type of continuing support that was required in third-world Commonwealth countries in the intervals between the Commonwealth Games.[12]

It should be noted, however, that a proposal for sport assistance to third-world Commonwealth countries had been developed by the CGAC in the early 1980s. A new initiatives committee, chaired by Ivor

Dent, had put together a proposal to develop support programs in specific sports that would help third-world countries improve in these sports to a point where they could be real contenders at the Commonwealth Games. The older, white Commonwealth countries have dominated the Games since their inception. In the 1990 Games, 70 per cent of the athletes came from Australia, Britain, Canada, and New Zealand, and these athletes won 86 per cent of the medals (Working Party Final Report, July 1991, 1). After the new initiatives committee's proposal, entitled *International Sport Development Project* (Commonwealth Games Association of Canada 1984), was approved by the CGAC in 1984, Dent took it to various agencies, including Fitness and Amateur Sport, External Affairs, and the Canadian International Development Agency. All were supportive of the idea, but none was willing to commit any funds to it, so the initiative died.[13]

This Commonwealth initiatives proposal had apparently originated in a more comprehensive document prepared in 1980 by Tom Bedecki under contract with Fitness and Amateur Sport. At that time Bedecki was executive director of the Canadian Association for Health, Physical Education, and Recreation. His report, entitled *Federal Commitment to Assisting Sport Technology Cooperation for the 1980s*, focused on ways in which Canadian sport technology could be used to assist developing countries. It proposed starting with a pilot project and outlined specific measures that the Canadian sport community could take to provide assistance to the Commonwealth countries in the Caribbean. Bedecki presented a modified version of his report to the annual general meetings of the CGAC in Montreal in May 1981.[14]

The question of a boycott of the 1990 Auckland Games was raised again at the CFMSA meetings in Canberra. The foreign ministers wanted the Australian and New Zealand governments to intensify efforts to prevent their rugby players from joining the centennial tour of South Africa. However, Commonwealth secretary-general Sir Shridath Ramphal was quoted as saying, "But I am confident that the Games will go ahead as planned" (*Citizen* [South Africa], 10 August 1989, 2). At the same time, the British sport minister, Colin Moynihan, rejected demands that England withdraw from the Auckland Games in order to avoid an African nation boycott because of the Centennial World xv rugby tour and the rebel cricket tour of South Africa. He advanced the traditional British argument that while his government had defended the Gleneagles Declaration by "discouraging" tours of South Africa, it was "fundamentally objectionable" to consider further, and more dramatic, sanctions such as the withdrawal of passports, fines, or imprisonment in an attempt to stop sporting contacts with South Africa. (Hobbes, 8 August 1989).

Ivor Dent, president of the CGAC, was quoted as saying that the Clark initiative had been instrumental in defusing an anti-apartheid boycott of the Auckland Games. According to Dent, it diverted attention away from the political vulnerability of the Games and focused on the Games as sport rather than as a political platform (Christie, 19 August 1989). Indeed, by the end of August, the black African sport leaders were calling for England and Australia to be banned from the Auckland Games rather than proposing a boycott. However, Bruce Kidd pointed out that this change was part of the more recent strategy in the anti-apartheid sport movement over Gleneagles Declaration violations (Kidd, 22 August 1989) and that, in his view, the Clark initiative had no bearing on defusing the boycott threat.

At any rate, the question of a boycott was not an issue at the CGF general assembly meetings in Auckland, held in conjunction with the 1990 Games. The unanimity of the federation about apartheid, however, was evident when a resolution put forward by Barbados was adopted unanimously. This resolution endorsed the federation's wholehearted commitment to non-racial sport, condemned the rebel English cricket tour of South Africa on the eve of the Auckland Games, endorsed the peaceful demonstrations that were to greet this tour in South Africa, called once again on each federation member to abide strictly by the Code of Conduct, and authorized the chairman to establish forthwith a small committee to monitor the implementation of the code (Commonwealth Games Federation, 23 January 1990).

After the Clark initiative had been presented at the CFMSA meetings in Canberra, it was refined and further developed in External Affairs, and was vetted at a special meeting of Commonwealth officials in London in September. This meeting was chaired by Canadian Peter Daniel, assistant deputy minister for external affairs, and some thirty-five Commonwealth countries were represented. The document was returned to Ottawa for further refinement, and subsequently a two-page memo was sent to all Commonwealth nations by the Commonwealth Secretariat in London. Thus, at the Commonwealth heads-of-government meetings in Kuala Lumpur in October 1989, a resolution came forward approving a Commonwealth sport assistance program and striking a Working Party on Strengthening Commonwealth Sport. Roy McMurtry was subsequently appointed to chair this committee. Besides his experience as a cabinet minister in several Ontario Conservative governments, McMurtry had served as Canada's high commissioner in London and established in the position had good contacts with the Commonwealth Secretariat.[15]

After two formal meetings and a number of informal ones, the working party produced a preliminary report late in 1990. This report was then vetted by a shadow committee of the High Level Appraisal Group. This group, composed of ten Commonwealth prime ministers, had been established at Kuala Lumpur to look at ways of strengthening the Commonwealth. The shadow committee was composed of high-level officials who represented their prime ministers.[16] The report was also vetted by African Olympic, Commonwealth, and government sport officials in Nairobi in January 1991. The working party then presented its preliminary report to the CGF general assembly meetings in Malta in April 1991. Here it met with generally favourable responses. The exception was that of the seven-nation United Kingdom group, who questioned the wisdom of inviting government involvement (i.e., interference) in Commonwealth sport matters.[17] The preliminary report was revised further, and a final report (Working Party Final Report, July 1991) was presented to the Commonwealth heads-of-government meetings in Harare in October 1991.

The final report focused on two broad issues: the need to transfer resources and sport expertise from the developed to the undeveloped Commonwealth countries and the need for a plan to preserve and sustain the Commonwealth Games themselves. The report picked up on many of the proposals in the original memo that had been sent the previous year to Joe Clark from the International Sports Relations desk for his meetings in Canberra. Particular emphasis was placed on the precarious financial condition of the CGF executive office in London, which was operating on a volunteer basis and was dependent almost entirely on the largesse of a French oil company, Elf UK, for its office space and communications expenses and on the British Sports Council for its other operating expenses (ibid., 5). Commonwealth governments, said the working party, should provide modest financial support to the CGF over the short run, until it could develop strategies to raise money on its own.

Although the Commonwealth heads of government had expressed concern at their 1989 Kuala Lumpur meetings about the need to host the Games in all regions of the Commonwealth, the working party could not arrive at any specific formula that would ensure this objective without being too restrictive and that would be acceptable to most countries.[18] Instead, it recommended that the CGF "be encouraged to adopt the *principle* of hosting the Games more widely throughout the Commonwealth ... while ensuring that proper standards prevail" (Working Party Final Report, July 1991, 9).

The report also drew attention to the inequities in competitive opportunities in the Commonwealth Games. Here the working party recommended that Commonwealth sport officials impress upon national and international aid agencies the "importance and value of including sport in aid programmes," and it urged the extension of existing Commonwealth aid programs whenever possible to include sport-related projects (ibid., 11). Besides the disparity between developed and the third-world nations, the report pointed to the inequities in opportunities for women and recommended that leadership programs be developed to rectify these (ibid., 3). In this respect, it drew on a document entitled "Commonwealth Sport and Women" (January 1990), prepared by the Commonwealth Women and Sport Network. This network had been formed at the Auckland Games by women from around the Commonwealth who were concerned over inequities in opportunities for female athletes, coaches, administrators, and federation representatives.[19] This initiative was spearheaded by Canadian Fitness and Amateur Sport Women's Program director Diane Palmason.[20] In making its recommendations about women, the working party also took note of the recommendations of the Commonwealth meetings of ministers responsible for women's affairs, which was held in Ottawa in October 1990 (Working Party Final Report, July 1991, 3).

The Working Party Final Report was presented at the Commonwealth heads-of-government meetings in Harare in October 1991. It did not receive the kind of attention at these meetings that Canadian and Commonwealth sport officials had hoped it would. The meetings were shortened by one day, and the report was placed on the agenda on the last afternoon. Prime Minister Brian Mulroney had made much of the human-rights issue at these meetings and had tied Canadian assistance to third-world countries to their human-rights record (Sallot, 28 February 1992, A13). His comments were not well received by many Commonwealth countries, and attention in the Canadian press focused on this issue. Nevertheless, the heads of government endorsed the working party report. In doing so, they "stressed the special role which sport should play in fostering Commonwealth values" and welcomed sport aid programs that would contribute to reducing the disparities between developed and undeveloped countries (Commonwealth Heads of Government, 21 October 1991, 19). In order to sustain the Commonwealth sport initiative, they also endorsed the working party's recommendation that an ad hoc committee be established with a mandate and membership similar to that of the working party. Roy McMurtry subsequently accepted an invitation to chair this committee. The heads of government also expressed hope that the hosting of the Commonwealth Games would be "shared more equitably among member countries while ensuring that proper standards prevail" (ibid.). In this endorsement of the working party's recommendation, they stepped back from their stronger expression of concern over this matter at Kuala Lumpur in 1989.

Various motives have been attributed to Joe Clark for taking these sport initiatives in the Commonwealth. Certainly they were consistent with Canada's persistent efforts to take over the leadership role in the Commonwealth vacated by Britain when Margaret Thatcher fell out with the other countries over increasing sanctions against South Africa. Clark's initiatives were also consistent with Canada's efforts to bolster its international image as a supporter of third-world causes. His interest in the Commonwealth was tied up with the fact that he had a great deal of latitude in matters relating to the Commonwealth and third-world countries. Prime Minister Mulroney was known to have little interest in this area and indeed in most spheres of international relations and national security. Mackenzie King, Lester Pearson, Pierre Trudeau, and Clark himself in his short stint as prime minister had all demonstrated considerably more interest in, and commitment to, an active Canadian foreign policy and a strong position on third-world issues. The exceptions were Mulroney's sporadic interest in southern African affairs and the central role he played in relations with the United States.

These motives, however, do not explain why the Canadian government selected sport to meet these goals. Some see the sport initiatives as having been taken out of a concern for the welfare of the Commonwealth. According to this view, Clark saw boycotts of the Commonwealth Games and controversy over the sites for these Games as threats to an already fragile Commonwealth, and he believed that putting the Games on a more solid footing would increase the stability and harmony of the Commonwealth. This opinion is supported by Ivor Dent, then the president of the CGAC, who said that Clark could see that the Commonwealth was held together by only tenuous threads and that one of these threads was the Commonwealth Games.[21] This line of reasoning also fits with Roy McMurtry's assessment. According to him, Clark believed strongly in the Commonwealth and had a desire to strengthen it. Sport was one of its most obvious manifestations.[22]

But there appears to be more to the issue than these explanations. Clark seems to have taken a personal interest in sport in the Commonwealth and shown an appreciation and concern for the Commonwealth Games. Indeed, he was an enthusiastic supporter of the Toronto Ontario Olympic Committee's bid for the 1996 Summer Olympics.[23] His reluctant shift, at the end of April 1991, from the External Affairs portfolio to Constitutional Affairs probably marked the end of this era of ascendency for sport in Commonwealth affairs. Without an empathetic minister, it is likely to be given much shorter shrift. Certainly, most senior officials in External Affairs still do not appear to exhibit much interest in sport as a part of Canada's foreign affairs.

Despite Clark's departure from the international affairs post, the sport initiatives that he put forward, if adequately funded by the developed Commonwealth nations, will have a positive impact on the Commonwealth Games and indeed on wider relations among those nations. Assistance and support for a third-world country to stage the 1998 Games would help to alleviate the bitterness felt in many countries about the awarding of the 1994 Games to Victoria. Efforts to improve coaching, facilities, and ancillary services to athletes in third-world countries would also help to remove the stark inequities in Commonwealth sport and make competition at the Games fairer and more exciting. Measures to provide better competitive and coaching opportunities for women would be particularly salutary. Providing the financial wherewithal to put the CGF headquarters on a sound financial footing and moving it to a third-world country would give those countries a greater sense of belonging and ownership of the Games. All these measures would surely contribute to more harmony and accord among Commonwealth nations.

Despite urgings by the working party, there was little indication of such financial support when the Commonwealth heads of government approved its report in October 1991. Canada was one of only a very few countries to commit funds for this purpose. In one of his last acts as secretary of state for external affairs, Clark in April 1991 pledged $1 million on an annual basis for five years for sport aid to third-world Commonwealth countries.[24] These monies, however, were to come from existing budgets: $750,000 from the Canadian International Development Agency (CIDA) and $250,000 from the International Sports Relations section in External Affairs.[25] Britain did increase its support for the operation of CGF headquarters in London by housing it in the British Sports Council's quarters, as well as continuing to provide monies for technical and secretarial assistance.

The wheels of government bureaucracy roll exceedingly slow. By early 1992, only one Commonwealth sport aid initiative had been approved by CIDA. That was to support a swimming coaching development project in Zimbabwe, headed by Canadian swim coach Trevor Tiffany. The money from International Sports Relations did not come on stream until April 1992.[26]

POLITICAL CHANGE
IN SOUTH AFRICA
AND INTERNATIONAL SPORT

Although the whites-only election of F.W. de Klerk as president of South Africa in September 1989 was greeted with a great deal of scepticism abroad, the measures he subsequently introduced to break down apartheid were to have a great effect on attitudes towards sporting contacts with South Africa. Only days before the October 1989 Commonwealth heads-of-government meetings in Kuala Lumpur, de Klerk made a dramatic gesture towards reform in South Africa by releasing eight leading black political prisoners (*Globe and Mail*, 21 October 1989). Even more startling steps, including the lifting of the ban on the African National Congress and the release of Nelson Mandela, were soon to follow.

In the mean time, the CFMSA increased its efforts to obtain the co-operation of major international banks in imposing more stringent financial sanctions on South Africa. But simultaneously with the Commonwealth heads-of-government meetings in Kuala Lumpur, South Africa scored a public-relations victory by announcing an agreement for rescheduling $8 billion in short-term debt (Howard, 20 October 1989). It is noteworthy that none of the major banks involved in these negotiations with South Africa was based in a country represented on the CFMSA. This limited the influence of the committee's efforts to persuade the banks to impose stricter financial sanctions on South Africa. The Commonwealth heads-of-governments meetings in Kuala Lumpur featured yet another dramatic confrontation between Margaret Thatcher and other Commonwealth leaders, notably Brian Mulroney. But the Commonwealth heads did endorse the continuation of the CFMSA under Joe Clark's leadership and laid down the standard of "clear and irreversible change," both as a yardstick for consideration of sanctions relief and for possible Commonwealth assistance to a post-apartheid South Africa (Wood 1990, 289). Signs of this "clear and irreversible change" were soon to come.

Rapid changes towards sporting contacts with South Africa were also taking place. In the late 1980s, the anti-apartheid sport movement raised the possibility of allowing South Africa back into international sport, provided certain sport-specific conditions were met. Up to this time, the movement had maintained that there could be "no normal sport in an abnormal society" (Kidd 1991a, 40). One of the key conditions was the creation of "single, democratic, nonracial, and nonsexist" sport governing bodies in South Africa (ibid., 41).

For a number of years, the IOC had been sending out feelers about the possibility of South Africa being readmitted to the Olympic movement. In December 1990, IOC president Juan Samaranch announced that his organization intended to send an investigative team to South Africa the following March. This team was comprised of some of the members of the IOC's Apartheid and Olympism Commission (AOC), plus a few additional IOC members. It was headed by Kelba M'Baye, former chief justice of the World Court, who chaired the AOC. One month later Samaranch announced that M'Baye's team would negotiate the conditions under which South Africa could return to the Olympic movement.[27]

In March 1991 the anti-apartheid sport leader Sam Ramsamy, chair of the London-based South African Non-Racial Olympic Committee, said that other African nations were likely to allow the lifting of sport sanctions against South Africa on the condition that de Klerk made good his promises of "sweeping" changes in the racist laws of South Africa. Ramsamy, who was also a special advisor to the IOC, held out the promise of an early return of South Africa to the Olympics. He also announced that a new interim non-racial committee had been formed in South Africa, consisting of anti-apartheid South African sport leaders and members of the existing (all-white) South African National Olympic Committee (Christie, 14 March 1991). Commenting on these developments, Fitness and Amateur Sport's liaison officer with External Affairs, Alan Zimmerman, was quoted as saying that Canada's sport sanctions against South Africa would remain in place until there is "a clear signal from the African sport community that the time is right to lift" them (ibid., C14). Zimmerman added, however, that Ramsamy's remarks were the beginning of that signal.

The IOC investigative team visited South Africa in late March 1991. F.W. de Klerk was quoted as saying he thought that the IOC should lift its ban on his country because doing so would send a positive message to South Africans by rewarding his efforts to dismantle apartheid (Wren, 24 March 1991). M'Baye's group met with Nelson Mandela, Chief Mangoseuthu Buthelezi, de Klerk and other government ministers, and leaders of many sport organizations, including the newly formed Interim National Olympic Committee of South Africa (INOCSA) (DeFrantz, 28 May 1991, 12C). The IOC team was informed that the last of the apartheid laws would be dismantled in June. Consequently, it established four criteria, in addition to the dismantling of apartheid, for South Africa's readmission to the IOC: that sport be totally integrated in South Africa, that the structure of INOCSA comply with the conditions of the IOC charter, that INOCSA be recognized by the Association of National Olympic Committees of Africa, and that at least five South African sport governing bodies in Olympic sports be recognized by their respective international sport governing bodies.[28] As part of these negotiations, the IOC gave tentative recognition to INOCSA and committed $2 million to establish training programs, hire coaches, and give scholarships to black athletes in South Africa (Christie, 6 July 1991).

South Africa's acceptance back into international sport came a step closer in April 1991, when the International Amateur Athletic Federation (IAAF) announced that the country would likely be allowed to compete in its World Championships in Tokyo in August. South Africa had not been able to participate in world track and field events since 1974, when it was expelled from the IAAF (Christie, 20 April 1991).

In April 1991, de Klerk followed his promise that the "pillars of apartheid" would be removed with the introduction of a draft bill on 9 April repealing the Population Registration Act (*Globe and Mail*, 10 April 1991). This act, which classified South Africans at birth by racial origin, formed a cornerstone of apartheid. Further legislative measures were introduced to advance reforms in the areas of land distribution, political immunity, and education. Initially the de Klerk government maintained that although it was willing to repeal the land distribution laws, which segregated residential areas and reserved 87 per cent of South African territory for whites, it was "totally opposed to any form of redistribution of agricultural land" and blacks would be expected to buy back lands taken from them as a result of apartheid (*Globe and Mail*, 23 April 1991, A13). This position was softened somewhat in May when planning minister Hernus Kriel established an "all-party advisory commission" to consider land claims (*Globe and Mail*, 21 May 1991).

In further efforts to advance its apartheid reforms, the South African government relaxed the terms of immunity from prosecution for political offenses. On 24 April 1991 justice minister H.J. Coetsee announced that 124 political prisoners would be freed as a result of these changes, which introduced indemnity for those convicted of treason and violent acts, provided these actions had not resulted in injury or death (*Globe and Mail*, 25 April 1991). Quota laws that had permitted racial segregation in universities, but which had never been formally implemented, were also removed at this session of parliament. However, de Klerk's government failed to address the controversial Universities Act, that provided for the establishment of racially separate institutions (*Globe and Mail*, 24 April 1991). The last legal pillar of apartheid fell on 17 June, when the South African parliament repealed the Population Registration Act, marking a dramatic change that was greeted with enthusiasm around the world (Christie, 6 July 1991).

The way was now cleared for the international sport movement to re-admit South Africa. In early July the president of the IAAF, Primo Nebiolo, stated that the new South African Amateur Athletics Association (which replaced three separate organizations that governed the sport under apartheid) "is now in condition to ask the IAAF to be reaccepted as normal members" and that South Africa would be able to compete in the August championships in Tokyo (ibid., A2). However, the IAAF voted shortly before these championships to bar

South African athletes on the grounds that athletics in that country had not yet been sufficiently integrated (Jollimore, 24 August 1991, A12). But Nebiolo's announcement did precipitate immediate action by the IOC. A few days later, in what some observers saw as an effort not to be upstaged by Nebiolo, Juan Samaranch announced that he had decided to "proclaim the outright recognition of the National Olympic Committee of South Africa" (Christie and Van Niekerk, 10 July 1991, A1). This gave the new National Olympic Committee of South Africa the green light to normalize its relationships with the respective international sport federations and the Association of National Olympic Committees of Africa, and allowed for an integrated team of black and white South African athletes to participate in the 1992 Summer Olympics in Barcelona.

Not everyone was pleased with the IOC decision. Leaders of some anti-apartheid organizations felt that the move was premature. Dikgang Moseneke, deputy leader of the hard-line black Pan Africanist Congress, said, "My message is 'Think again, it's far too early'" (ibid., A12). The president of the South African Council on Sport, Joe Ebrahim, said that Samaranch was "wrong to admit South Africa" (ibid.). Indeed, many white sportspersons in South Africa were still opposed to integrated sport. Particularly intransigent were those in tennis and in the non-Olympic sports of golf and rugby, whose South African organizations have tried desperately to keep their all-white sporting ties with Britain, New Zealand, and Australia in defiance of the Commonwealth ban on sporting contacts with South Africa.

The South African education minister greeted Samaranch's announcement by stating that the IOC decision "serves as further proof of international acceptance of the [South] African government's sincere efforts and progress toward creating a democratic dispensation" (ibid., A12). The IOC's announcement was followed shortly by President George Bush's decision to lift the US trade embargo on South Africa.

One of the principal questions that we posed in our introduction was the extent to which transnational sport organizations and activities have an impact on national and international political behaviour. The IOC's position on apartheid in sport is an interesting starting point for such a discussion. When pressure was building in the 1950s and 1960s to isolate South Africa, the IOC took the decision to ban the country from the Olympics only very reluctantly (see chap. 4). On the other hand, it took the lead in accepting South Africa back into the international sport community and perhaps into the international community more broadly defined. In the next chapter, we examine the IOC in the light of current thinking about transnational organizations and activities.

The IOC as a Transnational Organization

To a very great extent, the point of our story is to demonstrate that international sport organizations and, indeed, other international organizations (such as the Organization of African Unity) that have sought to pull down apartheid in South Africa, have had a direct impact on Canada's foreign policy. This view is entirely consistent with the theoretical framework that we introduced in chapter 1. There has been little written from this perspective about the relationship between transnational sport organizations and the policies of national governments. There was a literature that emerged during the 1970s, in particular, a paper by Susan Shaw (1976) and another by Timothy Shaw and Susan Shaw (1977). These articles examined the role that transnational black African organizations played in isolating South Africa in the world of international sport. Concurrently, three papers were written which were concerned more generally with international sport: two preliminary analyses by David Kanin (1976, 1978) of the Olympic movement as a transnational phenomenon and a third by James Nafziger (1978) about the regulation of "transnational" sport competition.

We have documented the increasing attention that has attended international sport events and the international political machinations that have surrounded the Olympic and Commonwealth Games in the last two decades. Our study suggests that organizations such as the International Olympic Committee (IOC) and the Commonwealth Games Federation merit careful examination in the light of current thinking about transnational organizations. In particular, an examination of the IOC might lead to a better understanding of how international sport organizations function and what influence they wield, both within the context of transnational society and in terms of the policies of participant states.

Robert Keohane and Joseph Nye (1974–75) made an important distinction between governmental and non-governmental transnational organizations, that is, that " 'transnational' involves non-governmental actors and 'transgovernmental' refers to sub-units of government when they operate relatively autonomously from higher authority in international politics" (ibid., 41). In this chapter, we focus on the "transnational" dimensions, although there is considerable value in examining the "transgovernmental" activities of national sport officials, such as those of Sport Canada consultants in their dealings with international sport organizations or the activities of the professional staff of Canadian national sport organizations, since the salaries of the latter are subsidized by the government and their respective organizations are dependent largely on funds from the federal government. But first we discuss briefly the development of transnational organizations.

DEVELOPMENT OF TRANSNATIONAL ORGANIZATIONS

Rapid technological development, the growth of economic interdependence, and the relative redistribution of power and influence in the international system have led us to a situation where we can only understand the world if we conceive of it in "trans"national, as well as "inter"national, terms. As we pointed out in chapter 1, the priorities and predispositions of governments have, as a consequence, necessarily changed. Among other things, recent events have diminished the importance of traditional "high politics" issues such as security and elevated "low politics" issues, including those relating to ethnicity, social welfare, culture, and economic well-being. Moreover, the classic distinction between foreign and domestic affairs has become blurred; no longer can we understand domestic policy as the quest for economic security (and equality of opportunity) and foreign policy as exclusively the quest for physical security. World politics has become increasingly less formal, taking place at the transnational and transgovernmental levels rather than exclusively through more formal diplomatic channels.

A number of developments since World War II have accelerated the growth and increased the importance of transnational relations (the material in this section is drawn mainly from Huntington 1981; Keohane and Nye 1974–75; Morse 1970). First, the belief that the UN could simultaneously resolve the political, social, and economic ills of the world and support the doctrine of state sovereignty proved to be overly optimistic. The UN was unable, in the absence of any real extra-state powers, to guarantee collective security; nor was it able, without any real influence, to resolve the growing conflict between north and south. Moreover, the inability to gain co-operation and agreement or financial support from its member nations rendered it largely impotent in its attempts to play the role of global peacemaker. Second, the "fiscal" crisis of the modern welfare state, which started in the United States and Britain in the early 1970s and spread to other Western industrialized nations, meant that individual governments became even more reliant on the private sector and on economic relations with their trading partners. Third, American hegemony has declined steadily since the early 1970s (Kennedy 1988). The debate about the relative decline of the United States has become an important part of the popular discussion surrounding US foreign policy and a critical development in international relations theorizing (see Nau 1990; Nye 1990). The decreasing importance of the traditional US security guarantee is also an important part of this phenomenon. These two developments have meant that the other Western industrialized nations have become increasingly less reliant on the United States for defence and economic leadership. Fourth, the dramatic end of the Cold War has meant that the threat of nuclear conflict (or, more properly, the perception of such a threat) has been significantly reduced. Ironically, and unfortunately, a less structured world may mean an increase in the proliferation of nuclear weapons to third-world powers. However, the decline in the traditional threat and the increased importance of formerly less powerful states point to the logic of both transnational and transgovernmental relations.

Individual nation-states became less able to control either their internal or their external affairs. Thus the need to foster and develop quasi-autonomous, non-governmental organizations (QUANGOs) and activities such as the UN Commission on Transnational Corporations and the Western Economic Summit increased. At the same time, it has become clear that economic co-operation with developing countries is at least as important as military intervention and political control. The international and transnational organizations that were created to meet these needs resulted in more opportunities for government officials to meet with their counterparts from other nations to discuss policies, form alliances, and in some cases to act independently of the official policies of their own countries. This development has, in turn, contributed to less centralized control of foreign affairs by sovereign nations, to the further breakdown of the distinction between domestic and foreign policies, and to the disintegration of any clear policy agenda for most governments. The collapse of Soviet hegemony vis-à-vis its Eastern European, Warsaw Pact allies and the primacy of social and economic issues in this recent "revolution" add additional credence to the logic of transnational relations. In fact, it has been the collapse of the Cold War system that has really provided a window for transnational society to operate and flourish.

THE ORIGINS AND EVOLUTION OF THE IOC

The developments outlined above caused a great growth in the number and influence of transnational organizations, both in business and in the non-profit domain. In the words of Samuel Huntington (1981, 199), there has been "a *transnational organizational revolution* in world politics [Huntington's italics]." In sport this development could be seen in the great increase in the number of sports that have formed global organizations and the increasing number and significance of world championships since World War II. By 1990 the General Association of International Sports Federations, which was established in 1967, had a membership of seventy-five international sport federations and other international organizations (Canada [undated], 23). Correspondingly, with the advent of television and the parallel commercialization and professionalization of international sport, the IOC had taken on an importance and significance that could not have been imagined in the 1940s or 1950s.

The IOC, of course, had its origins before the turn of the century, long before the concept of transnational organizations was born. It was founded in 1894 at the Congress of Paris at meetings to discuss Baron Pierre de Coubertin's dream to revive the ancient Greek Olympic games. The IOC was to be "the final authority on all questions concerning the Olympic Games and the Olympic Movement" (Nafziger 1978, 164). The Olympics, in de Coubertin's view, were to promote peace and understanding among nations by fostering "Victorian" ideals of sportsmanship. This dream came to fruition when the first modern Olympics were held in Athens in 1896.

Because the modern Olympics grew out of Victorian concepts of sport, which themselves were based on idealized views of the ancient Greek games, it is not surprising that the IOC was dominated at its inception by white, upper-class males from industrialized countries in Europe. Members were chosen ostensibly on the basis of their commitment to these Olympic ideals rather than as representatives of any country. However, wealth, status, gender, and race were obviously very important factors in their selection. The composition and *modus operandi* of the IOC changed little through the first half of the twentieth century. In fact, as recently as 1989, the IOC membership could still be seen as "an aging assembly with lords, dukes and even princes among its members" (Polanyi 2 September 1989). The obsession that some members have with such pedigree was evident in memoirs of Lord Killanin, who was president of the IOC in the 1970s (Killanin 1983, 18–19).

But despite Margaret Polanyi's observation about an aging assembly of royalty and nobility, events since World War II have forced considerable changes in the composition of the organization. With the rapid expansion in the number of countries that wished to participate in the Olympic Games, it became necessary to admit members from the Soviet Union and its Eastern bloc allies as well as from many third-world countries. This meant that the membership changed to include persons of different colour, class, race, and outlook from those of traditional members. It has been IOC policy to select members who were not connected with or representative of the governments of their countries. But it was impossible to ensure that members from these two blocs met this criteria, even though the IOC insisted on its right to select members. This expansion of the membership was countered by the practice of having two members on the IOC from countries that had previously hosted the Olympics. This practice, of course, favoured the selection of members from Western European, North American, and other white Commonwealth nations and helped to bolster the "old guard" of the IOC. Nevertheless, the interplay of these new forces has meant that the IOC today is a much more heterogeneous, political, and divisive organization than was the case in the first half of this century.

The selection of members was and still is a self-perpetuating process. Originally, members nominated their own successors. But today, they are elected after screening and nomination by the IOC's executive board. The president plays a central role in the selection process. Members were originally elected for life. But in 1966 the IOC passed a non-retroactive resolution that required new members to retire at age seventy-two (Lyberg 1988–89b, 118). A subsequent initiative in 1977 to raise the age limit to seventy-five was rejected by the IOC's general assembly (ibid., 233), but when the IOC constitution was revised in 1985 in Berlin, the age limit was raised to seventy-five (ibid., 349).

Women had to wait until 1981 before attaining membership in the IOC (ibid., 228), despite the fact that females have competed in the Olympics since the second Olympiad in 1900. In 1989 there were only six women among the ninety-odd members in the general assembly of the IOC and none on its powerful executive board (Polanyi 2 September 1989). Lord Killanin's paternalistic views about women in sport nicely illustrate the barriers that they have faced in gaining membership in the IOC (see Killanin 1983, chap. 10).

Although the IOC general assembly has the constitutional right to decide on such matters as the rules, selecting what sports are to be on the Olympic schedule, and choosing the site of the Games, this group is obviously too large to be able actually to attend to complex matters and the day-to-day business of the organization (Taylor 1986b, 221). Thus these matters fall largely on the nine-member executive board, the president (who holds much discretionary power in the operation of the IOC), and the large staff at IOC headquarters in Lausanne, Switzerland. (This large staff became possible when the television revenues started to escalate in the 1970s.) Three other "groups" make up the Olympic family: the national Olympic committees (NOCs); the various individual international sport federations (ISFs), and the actual games organizing committees (GOCs).

Countries that wish to compete in the Olympic Games must set up a NOC. The NOC must then attest to its willingness to abide by the Olympic rules and belong to a minimum of five recognized ISFs before it can be accredited by the IOC. These NOCs promote the Olympic movement and finance and select the teams, athletes, and officials who attend the Games in their respective nations. NOCs must, according to the Olympic charter, be "structurally separate" from their government, but in practice, as with its own membership, the IOC has not been able to enforce this provision (Kanin 1981, 5–6). In 1990 the IOC recognized 167 NOCs (Canada [undated], 31).

All bids to host Olympic Games must come through the country's NOC, but NOCs have no direct vote on the IOC. In seeking to extend their influence with the IOC, they formed an Association of National Olympic Committees in 1966. Before this time, they had met informally among themselves and with the executive board of the IOC (Killanin 1983, 75). At first, Avery Brundage, then president of the IOC, resisted efforts by the NOCs to formalize their role in the Olympic community (Lyberg 1988–89b, 124–5). But in 1973 the IOC established, on a formal basis, the Tripartite Commission, composed of representatives from the Association of NOCs, the IFSs, and the IOC, in order to improve communications among the three groups (ibid., 199). Subsequently the Tripartite Commission has served a number of useful functions, including the preparation of a manifesto on apartheid. In 1977 this manifesto helped to ward off a Soviet-led attempt by UNESCO to take over the role and functions of the IOC (Killanin 1983, 72–3). Another achievement of the Tripartite Commission was that it convinced the IOC to establish an Olympic Solidarity Aid Program, which distributes funds from the IOC's television revenue to assist developing nations with the advancement of the Olympic movement (Taylor 1986b, 226).

The second important arm of the Olympic movement is made up of the individual ISFs. They are, in fact, more powerful than the respective NOCs because the IOC delegates to each recognized ISF the right to set the eligibility and playing rules and facility standards for its sport. This decentralization of eligibility rules was one of the main reasons for the breakdown of the old amateur code that prevailed through to the 1960s. Avery Brundage was the last great defender of this code, and he held tenaciously to it in his struggles with the International Ski Federation over the commercialization and professionalization associated with the 1968 and 1972 Winter Olympics (see Macintosh, Bedecki, and Franks 1987, 51–2, for an account of these struggles). Although Brundage won some of the battles, it was inevitable that he would lose the war. There was a series of subsequent debates over amateurism between the IOC and a number of ISFs. But by the time of the 1988 Seoul Olympics, any distinction between "amateur" and "professional" in Olympic sport had virtually disappeared. The appearance of the US basketball "Dream Team" in the 1992 Barcelona Olympics brought this reality to the attention of the world in a most forceful manner.

The final member of the Olympic "family" is the group that actually organizes and runs the Olympic Games. These games organizing committees (GOCs) are formed once the IOC has awarded the Games to a particular city. They are placed in the delicate position of having to work both with various levels of government in their respective countries and with the IOC in accomplishing this task. For instance, a critical requirement of the IOC is that the host country issue visas to all persons who can show that they are accredited as a representative of their country. It was this provision that caused the brouhaha between Trudeau and the IOC over the right of Taiwanese athletes to compete in the 1976 Montreal Olympics.

THE POLITICIZATION AND COMMERCIALIZATION OF THE IOC

Although there were numerous political incidents connected with the Olympics during the first third of the twentieth century (see, for instance, Kanin 1981, chap. 2), they attracted little attention because the Olympic Games had not become the international spectacle we know today. The first such incident to attract the attention of leaders world wide was Adolf Hitler's attempt to use the 1936 Games in Berlin as an event to promote his doctrine of the superiority of the "Aryan race." Even then, most politicians and Olympic officials and athletes stuck to the rhetoric that the Games were "above politics," and so the Berlin Games went forward as usual, allowing Hitler to use them to his own ends.

But the social, economic, and political changes that came about after World War II were to have a profound effect on the Olympic movement. First, shortly after the war, the Soviet Union made a deliberate decision to use sport as a vehicle to promote its political ideology abroad and to foster friendship with non-aligned and third-world countries. In order to accomplish these goals, it was necessary for the Soviets and their Eastern bloc allies to gain membership and influence in the various ISFs and the IOC. The successes of the Soviets and their allies in the international sport arena is a story for another place. Here it is important to bear in mind that Soviet bloc representation on the ISFs and the IOC brought delegates with much different views about sport from those to which these organizations had been accustomed. As noted above, these new members also held much closer ties to their respective governments and believed that sport was inexorably tied to politics, a view that was abhorrent to the "old guard" of the IOC.

The second, and perhaps the most significant, post-war change that had an impact on international sport was the advent of television in the early 1950s. Its impact on sport was discussed briefly in chapter 1. The affinity between sport and television was not lost on either national or transnational business concerns. International corporations were increasingly looking to sell their goods and services across national boundaries. What better way than to sponsor international sport events and advertise their products during the telecasts of these events? The myriad advertisements of international corporations that one sees both on the side boards and in the commercials during the televising of the World Figure Skating Championships, for example, are a vivid testimonial to the attractiveness of international sport events to corporate sponsors. After the rights to telecast the such sport events are bought by various national networks, these networks recover the cost by selling spot advertisements to sponsors. In the United States, spot ads for sport events can sell for hundreds of thousands of dollars. A thirty-second advertisement during the 1991 Super Bowl football game cost $800,000 (Martin, 27 January 1991, H29).

The Olympic Games, of course, are central in these commercial enterprises. For instance, ABC charged $285,000 for a thirty-second commercial break during the 1988 Calgary Winter Olympics (Taylor 1988b, 190). A brief history of the sale of Olympic Games television rights vividly illustrates the growth of television revenues (the figures are all in US dollars). In 1956 the major television networks boycotted the Melbourne Olympics, maintaining that sport events were news and, as such, a matter of public interest and that television rights should be given to them free. CBS paid only about $400,000 for the US rights to the Summer Olympics in Rome; the total amount paid for the television rights to these Olympics was around $1.2 million. By 1968 ABC had to pay $4.5 million for the US rights to the Mexico City Summer Games. Those to the 1976 Montreal Summer Games in Montreal went to ABC for $25 million. Then the costs escalated dramatically. The US rights to the 1980 Moscow Games went for $87 million; four years later in Los Angeles, they cost $225 million. For rights to the 1988 Seoul Games, NBC paid $300 million. This latter figure accounted for approximately only three-quarters of the total television rights revenue. Rights to the Winter Games soared from $2 million for the 1968 Grenoble Games to the $309 million ABC paid for the US rights to the 1988 Calgary Games (Irwin 1988, 35).

During the 1960s and 1970s the host GOCs negotiated television contracts with the big American networks. But the IOC was dissatisfied with the manner in which the Seoul GOC carried out the television contract negotiations and with the $300 million finally obtained from NBC. In light of the $309 million received for US rights to the Calgary Winter Games, it had expected more. Henceforth, the IOC decided, it would set up its own television rights committee and negotiate directly with the big American television networks (Taylor 1986b, 231–2). This commission established what amounted to an auction system for the rights to the 1992 Summer Games in Barcelona. In the ensuing bidding among networks, the US television rights to these Games went to NBC for $401 million (Shames 23 July 1989, 24). The television revenue from the 1988 Seoul Games was split three ways: 20 per cent went to the construction of media facilities at the Games site; of the remainder, the host GOC received two-thirds and the other one-third went to the IOC. After providing 10 per cent of its third toward the costs of referees and judges for the Games, the IOC gave one-third of the remainder to the ISFs involved in the Games, one-third went to its Olympic Solidarity Aid Program, and the rest it kept itself (Taylor 1988b, 190).

In 1985 the IOC hired a Swiss firm, International Sports and Leisure, to market the Olympic logo and name (Marotte, 8 February 1992, A10). Since that time, the IOC has been aggressively selling the rights to the Olympic symbol to international business concerns. Some sponsors, such as Coca-Cola and VISA, have bought world-wide rights for both the Summer and Winter Games in 1992. Others, including IBM and Rhinolith, opted to be sponsors for only the Winter Games (Campbell, 25 February 1992, B3). Some of these sponsors have paid up to $30 million (US) for these rights (Marotte, 8 February 1992:

A10). The IOC has also entered into an agreement with five participating countries to issue a series of gold and silver coins in each of the five years leading up to the centennial celebrations of the modern Olympic movement in 1996. Although the NOCs in the participating countries (Canada was the first in 1992) will receive about 3 per cent of the net revenue, the rest will go back to the IOC to be distributed to member nations through its Olympic Solidarity Aid Program (Christie, 18 March 1992, C12). Television revenues and sponsorship royalties have made the IOC a wealthy transnational organization.

The growth of nationalism after World War II also had a great impact on the Olympics. As the industrialized countries of Western Europe gave up their colonies, the latent nationalism in Africa and Asia blossomed. These countries looked for ways in which this nationalism and the accompanying political ambitions could be expressed, and they often turned to sport as a means of achieving these goals. This development was to create another "bloc" in the IOC, that of third-world countries, and the concept of a "non-political" Olympic family was irretrievably lost.

Another important outcome of this growth of nationalism was that the Olympics Games increasingly became a prime target for protests and demonstrations. The student protesters who were killed in Mexico City just before the 1968 Summer Olympics and the demonstration by US black athletes on the victory podium at these Games, the massacre of Israeli athletes at the 1972 Munich Games, and the black African nation boycott of the 1976 Montreal Games are prime examples of this development. The major powers were also to have their turn at exploiting the Olympics for political ends: thus the US–led boycott of the Moscow Games in 1980 and the USSR counter boycott of the Los Angeles Games in 1984.

THE IOC AS A TRANSNATIONAL ORGANIZATION

A transnational organization, according to Samuel Huntington (1981, 198), is characterized by being a "relatively large, hierarchically organized, centrally directed bureaucracy"; performing "a set of relatively limited, specialized, and, in some sense, technical functions"; and performing these "functions across one or more international boundaries and insofar as is possible, in relative disregard of those boundaries." It is clear that the IOC possesses these three characteristics of transnational organizations; with its ties to its "family," it represents a relatively large, hierarchical, centrally directed body with a central purpose that carries out a relatively simple goal, that of promoting the Olympic movement and staging the Olympics. As we will see, the IOC has also been most successful in transcending national boundaries.

In order to further characterize transnational organizations (TOs), Huntington contrasts them with international organizations (IOs). In the first place, IOs require "the identification and creation of a common interest among national groups." On the other hand, a TO "has its own interest which inheres in the organization and its functions, which may or may not be closely related to the interests of national groups." Second, IOs, according to Huntington, "are designed to facilitate the achievement of a common interest among many national units. [In contrast, TOs] are designed to facilitate the pursuit of a single interest within many national units" (ibid., 200). Once again, the IOC can clearly be classified as a transnational organization; it has its own agenda and pursues a single purpose that is not necessarily in accordance with that of individual nations.

The third difference between IOs and TOs, according to Huntington, is that the IO "requires *accord* among nations; the [TO] requires *access* to nations. These two needs, accord and access, neatly summarize the differences between the two phenomena" (ibid.; Huntington's italics). The question of access is central to the success of the IOC. Its product, the Olympic Games, is widely sought after. Despite the financial risk associated with hosting the Olympics, there is always fierce competition among cities (and, in reality, between governments) to win the bid. The payoff is not in immediate monetary terms; rather, it is in more intangible and long-range rewards. In the case of the Winter Olympics, the motivation for hosting them has often been the legacy of winter sport and its ancillary facilities and accommodation that can subsequently be used to attract a lucrative tourist trade. For many developing industrialized nations, the Olympics represent a chance, through world-wide television, to provide a showcase to the rest of the world. Tokyo and then Seoul successfully exploited the Olympics to prove to the rest of the world that they were, indeed, world-class cities and nations. In the case of Japan, its hosting of the 1964 Summer Olympics was coincident with its "full rehabilitation after the Second World War into international life" (Taylor 1988b, 192). The subsequent increase in international recognition and in business and tourism justified the immense expenses incurred by these two countries in staging the Olympics. In the case of Japan, these expenses were estimated to be around £1,000 million (ibid.).

The hosting of the 1980 Summer Olympics in Moscow offered the USSR an opportunity to exploit its athletic triumphs to propagate socialist ideology, both abroad and at home. The US–led boycott of these Games detracted somewhat from this objective, but in many third-world and socialist countries, the absence of the United States and some of its allies were hardly noticed. In contrast, the 1988 Los Angeles Games became a showcase for private enterprise. The first-ever profit from an Olympic Games was widely touted as a victory for the "American" way of doing things.

The attractiveness of the Olympic Games, then, has made it possible for the IOC to cross national borders successfully or, in Huntington's words (1981), to gain access to countries. The line-up of cities that bid for the 1996 Summer Olympics certainly was a clear indication that this appeal is not diminishing. The competing cities, including Toronto, each spent millions of dollars to prepare bids, send delegations to various international sport meetings, and wine and dine as many IOC members as possible. Toronto's unsuccessful bid was estimated to have cost some $16 million, much of it contributed by the provincial and federal governments.

THE IOC'S INFLUENCE ON
SOVEREIGN NATIONS

It is clear that under Huntington's broad definitions, the IOC can be seen as a transnational organization. But a further important hypothesis about transnational organizations is that they are capable of influencing both the foreign and the domestic policies of sovereign nations. Evidence for such a theory is often difficult to gather because of limited access to classified government documents. But there is much in the public domain to show that transnational sport organizations have had an impact on the policies of governments. Our story of "hockey diplomacy" in chapter 2 provides one good example. After Hockey Canada, with the encouragement of the minister of health and welfare, got the International Ice Hockey Federation (IIHF) to agree that teams could use up to nine professionals in the 1970 World Hockey Championships, Avery Brundage, president of the IOC, put pressure on the Soviet Union by threatening to declare the Soviet hockey team ineligible for the 1972 Winter Olympics if it played against professional athletes in these championships. As a result, the Soviets and their Eastern bloc hockey-playing allies reneged on the agreement, and the IIHF reversed its stand and banned all professionals from the upcoming championships, which were to be staged in Winnipeg. Canadian hockey officials, with the full backing of the federal government, reacted by withdrawing from the IIHF and the World Hockey

Championships, and as a consequence, gave up the right to host these championships in Winnipeg and put their status in the Winter Olympics hockey competition at risk.

Another example of the IOC's attempt to influence the policies of sovereign governments was made clear in chapter 3. The IOC used all its resources to make Trudeau back down on his one-China policy, including bringing diplomatic pressure to bear from the United States and its Western allies. At the last minute, Trudeau relented, allowing the Taiwanese team to fly whatever flag and play whatever anthem it wished, but he stuck to his condition that it could not participate under the name "Republic of China." Although Taiwan refused to abide by Trudeau's condition and stayed away from the Montreal Games, the IOC had fought Canada to a standstill on this issue.

Similarly, in 1980 the IOC put pressure on the Canadian government to ignore the US–led boycott of the Moscow Olympics. Both Canadian members of the IOC, James Worrall and Richard Pound, who at that time was also president of the Canadian Olympic Association, met with Canadian cabinet ministers to try to convince them to support sending a team to Moscow. But in this case the IOC efforts were to no avail; the pressure on Canada to stand by its neighbour and ally was too great, and it put its weight behind this US foreign-policy initiative.

But perhaps the most vivid example of the IOC as a force in international politics had to do with the efforts of its president, Juan Antonio Samaranch, to avoid the boycotts that had damaged both the 1980 and the 1984 Summer Olympics and the disruptions that plagued earlier Games. When it was announced in 1981 that Seoul, Korea, would be the site of the 1988 Summer Olympics, there were dire predictions about the future of the Games. Given that there were no formal relations between North and South Korea and given the volatile situation at the border between these two countries, it was hard to imagine that these Games could be carried off without major political incident. Samaranch, however, was the consummate diplomat. He keep the North and South Koreans negotiating over the matter of holding some Olympic events in North Korea until immediately before the Games were to commence. He had to break the IOC rule that the Games must be held in one country even to commence these negotiations. More important, he was able to get assurances from both the Soviet Union and the People's Republic of China that they would not boycott the Games, even though they both had difficult political roles in the Korean peninsula. The importance of this political *coup* could be seen when the Soviet Union formally accepted the invitation to participate in the Seoul Olympics in January 1988. One day later, the Seoul stock exchange soared to an all-time high (Taylor 1988b, 192).

There never was a realistic chance that any part of the Games would be hosted in North Korea. The IOC had no intention of allowing this to happen, and any careful observer knew that it was virtually impossible. In this enterprise, the IOC was aided in that the conditions set by both sides doomed the negotiations from the start (ibid.). Richard Pound, an executive vice-president of the IOC, had aptly coined the phrase for these negotiations: a "dialogue of the deaf."[1]

Samaranch was the first president of the IOC to acknowledge (at least publicly) that sport could not remain apart from international politics and that the world of sport must work in consultation with the world of states (Taylor 1988a, 553). The breakdown of the Cold War in the late 1980s, one of the most important events to signal the effective end to adversarial, state-centred world politics, aided his cause greatly. This new world of interdependence, along with Samaranch's considerable diplomatic skills, allowed him to bring off the Seoul Games without political incident. In the words of Olympic scholar John MacAloon (1991, 32), this "was the greatest single act of diplomacy and statesmanship in Olympic history." (For quite a different view of Samaranch, see Simson and Jennings 1992.)

Over 160 nations participated in the Seoul Games. Only 6, including Albania, Cuba, and North Korea, turned down their invitations (Taylor 1988b, 194). The Games went forward without external political protest, and the South Korean government was able to get opposition parties and student radicals to call off their demonstrations during the Games. As a result, the Seoul Games were seen around the world to be a great success, and world confidence in the Olympic movement was restored. This outcome gave South Korea a tremendous opportunity to promote itself.

South Korea also made political capital from the Games. After forty years of isolation, the doors to the socialist countries of the world opened to South Korea, Hungary and Yugoslavia extended diplomatic recognition, and Poland and Czechoslovakia announced plans to follow suit. Although the Soviet Union did not, it established a trade office in Seoul, and South Korea set up consular offices in Moscow in 1990. By 1990 trade between the People's Republic of China and South Korea reached nearly $4 billion (US) (Park 1991, 357).

Indeed, South Korea was so encouraged by the success of the Games that it renewed efforts in 1989 to be admitted to the UN four decades after its first application (Howe, 15 October 1989, 15). Finally, the negotiations between the two Korean governments that had been instigated by the IOC marked the start of a guarded dialogue between the countries over other matters and, in particular, about access to North Korea by citizens of the South. In the words of the president of the

Seoul Olympic Organizing Committee, Seh-jih Park, "It is difficult to imagine that these amazing developments for my country are not associated with the sporting and diplomatic successes of the Seoul Olympic Games" (Park 1991, 357).

In our final chapter, we examine more closely the impact of the transnational anti-apartheid organizations on international politics in their efforts to isolate South Africa, and the way in which they successfully used sport in these endeavours.

Sport and Foreign Policy in a Transnational World

In this final chapter we return to our transnational theme, connecting it first to the way in which foreign-policy decisions relating to sport were taken in Canada in the 1970s and 1980s. We then turn to the interactions among sovereign states and to transgovernmental and transnational organizations in the politics of international sport, analyzing the events of the 1970s and 1980s in light of the advent of transnational society. Finally, we offer some preliminary speculations on what might develop in the rest of the 1990s.

ISSUES IN CANADA'S SPORT FOREIGN POLICY

In chapter 1 we noted that one important feature of the transnational relations perspective was that it confirmed the practical realization that different views exist among various sub-units in most governments' foreign-policy decision-making process. During the 1970s there was a great deal of discussion in academic circles over the importance of bureaucracies and, in particular, over Graham Allison's book *Essence of Decision* (1971). The Allison argument was both simple and powerful. Political choice is a relational phenomenon, with decisions emerging from a process of conflict, confusion, and ultimately compromise. This logic is particularly suited to the Canadian case, where the power of the chief executive is limited by certain key bureaucratic realities. Kim Nossal identified seven important features of the Canadian system that suggest the applicability of a bureaucratic political approach. These are

1 that the mandates of key government agencies overlap;
2 that a premium is placed on co-ordination, with trade-offs existing as an integral part of such co-ordination;

3 that central agents (such as External Affairs officials) are very powerful in the Canadian case;
4 that the federal public service is very consistent and coherent, rarely swept aside with new governments;
5 that the existence of a cabinet committee system gives additional influence to bureaucrats;
6 that cabinet is a forum where ministers, with their own priorities, their own backgrounds, and their own goals, compete for success; and
7 that there is the reality of federal-provincial concerns. (Nossal 1979, 619–24)

These characteristics together challenge the realist claim that national governments make decisions unilaterally and rationally.

Some scholars see this connection as the crux of the transnational relations perspective. It ran through our account of international sport policy making in Canada and could be seen, for instance, in the negotiations that took place in government circles in the two years preceding the 1978 Edmonton Commonwealth Games. Fitness and amateur sport minister Iona Campagnolo pressed the government to take tougher political and economic measures against South Africa at the same time as it was imposing stricter policies on sporting contacts with South Africans. Certain elements in the government, particularly in the now defunct Department of Industry, Trade, and Commerce, were opposed to this. Bureaucratic and political infighting among External Affairs, Fitness and Amateur Sport, and Employment and Immigration were also evident during the fall of 1988 and the first half of 1989 over the extent to which further restrictions should be placed on South African professional sportspersons' access to Canada and over contacts with South Africans in third-country competitions.

Given the expanded scope of operations for the International Sport Relations section in External Affairs that occurred after the cabinet record of decision in October 1987 and the creation of an International Relations Directorate in Fitness and Amateur Sport early in 1988, it was inevitable that there would be areas of conflict between these two departments. It was especially true in this case, since the Department of External Affairs believes that any and all matters relating to international relations come under its jurisdiction. By the spring of 1988, memos were being exchanged that discussed co-ordination guidelines and put forward the respective departmental perspectives on jurisdictional questions. Indeed, one of these questions arose during the interdepartmental discussions that preceded the policy statement on South African sportspersons in June 1989. During the debate about third-country contacts with South African athletes, the question of who had primary responsibility for enforcing the policy with national sport organizations (NSOs) was raised. Fitness and Amateur Sport claimed that because it provided the lion's share of the monies with which these organizations operated, it should be, in the first instance, both the contact for inquiries about and the enforcer of the new policies on sporting contacts with South Africans in third countries. The June 1989 communiqué tactfully gave both departments as sources for further information.

But there were other sensitive issues that developed because of the increased interest by External Affairs in international sport matters. This should not have come as a great surprise to Fitness and Amateur Sport officials because, as Lane MacAdam, special assistant to the minister for fitness and amateur sport, observed, the Department of External Affairs "spreads it tentacles" into the operations of almost every other government department.[1] Nevertheless, Fitness and Amateur Sport officials were resentful of the relatively large amount of money (some $500,000 in 1989–90) that the International Sport Relations section was able to spend on projects, with little in the way of policy guidelines and what appeared to be a modest level of accountability on the part of the Canadian NSOs that received these monies. This practice stood in marked contrast to the extensive guidelines that Sport Canada had developed for funding the national sport organizations. Indeed, these relatively lax arrangements were attractive to many NSOs because they resented the careful scrutiny and accountability applied by Sport Canada to the monies it gave them.

These problems were confounded further when a third government body, the Canadian International Development Agency (CIDA), became involved in 1991 with international sport aid projects. Like most other international aid organizations, CIDA has shown little interest in sport, seeing it as being irrelevant to the real problems of third-world countries. This attitude, and CIDA's lack of sport expertise, was bound to cause additional problems in co-ordinating Canadian sport aid initiatives and even more resentment on the part of Fitness and Amateur Sport officials.

Another area of conflict between Fitness and Amateur Sport and External Affairs was over sport promotions. External Affairs arranged many such promotions abroad involving Canadian high-performance athletes, teams, and NSOs without keeping Sport Canada informed. The first notice that Fitness and Amateur Sport received about these initiatives often was a copy of the telex External Affairs had sent to the Canadian post involved. According to Fitness and Amateur Sport officials, this state of affairs frequently caused embarrassment. To avoid such occurrences, Fitness and Amateur Sport thought it should be consulted as to the expertise and capabilities of the persons that External Affairs utilized in its sport promotions. In addition, External Affairs projects were often not planned to take into account Fitness and Amateur Sport's international sport plans.

Most of these sport promotions involved the use of professional staff and sportspersons from Canadian NSOs, which depend largely on Fitness and Amateur Sport for financial support. Cases in point were the technical-assistance initiatives in Singapore and Malaysia, taken in 1989 by the International Sports Relations section in External Affairs. Working in conjunction with the Coaching Association of Canada (CAC), External Affairs entered into three-year contracts in which the expertise of the CAC was used to develop coaching certification programs in Singapore and Malaysia.[2] Fitness and Amateur Sport officials raised questions about these kind of initiatives. These officials believed that because organizations such as the CAC were subsidized largely with funds from Sport Canada, decisions about whether such programs were to go ahead should rest first with them. Moreover, Fitness and Amateur Sport could not see what contribution such programs made to Sport Canada's mandate to enhance Canada's international or national sport performances. Such projects, Fitness and Amateur Sport argued, put competing demands on NSOs and thus detracted from their primary mandate, which was to improve domestic and international sport.[3] The NSOs, of course, believed that as organizations at "arm's length" from the government, they should be able to take decisions about sport promotions and technical assistance on their own. As well, such initiatives were attractive to the NSOs because they provided the organizations with some additional revenue and the prestige associated with such ventures. They also allowed NSOs to reward valued professional staff members and coaches by sending them to other countries.[4]

Fundamental to these points of conflict were the different uses to which sport promotions were put by Fitness and Amateur Sport and External Affairs respectively. These differences were articulated in the discussions surrounding the development of the cabinet memoranda that preceded the record of decision of October 1987. Sport Canada's objectives in sport promotions – that is, to improve performance levels and to enhance Canada's stature in international sport circles – often came into conflict with those of External Affairs, which were related to the way sport can be used to further Canada's broader foreign-policy objectives. Such differences were at the heart of the tension between the two departments and were manifested in disagreements over some of the new sport initiatives of the rejuvenated International Sports Relations section in External Affairs.

This discord could clearly be seen in the CAC's coaching certification programs in Singapore and Malaysia. External Affairs was anxious to underwrite these technical initiatives because they met its objectives to "reach out" to third-world countries, especially where it had Commonwealth or francophone interests. These "sport aid" programs could also be mounted in bilateral agreements at a modest cost. Fitness and Amateur Sport, seeking also to enhance its position in international sport circles, probably would have chosen other countries for such initiatives.[5]

In an effort to establish better relations between the two departments, recommendations were advanced on a number of occasions to establish a formal interdepartmental committee to vet sport-promotion and other proposals before they were launched. However, nothing ever came of this suggestion.[6] Part of this reluctance may have been the previous experience that External Affairs had had with interdepartmental committees. An Interdepartmental Committee on External Relations (ICER) had emerged in the aftermath of the Liberal government's 1970 white paper on foreign policy. This committee had included the clerk of the Privy Council, the secretary of the Treasury Board, the deputy ministers of Manpower and Immigration, Trade and Commerce, and Public Works, and the president of CIDA. Although External Affairs maintained the chair, the committee became a major source of conflict among the four departments. By the mid-1970s External Affairs managed to regain its influence and effectively squash ICER. Since that time, interdepartmental committees have been viewed by the department as a direct challenge to its authority on international matters.

Increased interest in sport as part of Canada's foreign-policy initiatives also brought into sharper focus questions about the purpose and value of sport exchanges. The first formal sport-exchange agreement entered into by Canada was that reached with the Soviet Union in 1974. It grew out of the interaction between Soviet sport and diplomatic officials and their Canadian counterparts that surrounded the Canada-Soviet hockey series in 1972 and from discussions that Tom Bedecki, then acting director of Sport Canada, had with Soviet officials when he visited Moscow in 1973 to attend the World Student Games.[7] The agreement, signed between Fitness and Amateur Sport and the Soviet State Committee of Physical Culture and Sport, was part of a larger cultural agreement reached in 1971 between the two countries (Morse 1987b, 9).

The pattern of sport exchanges as part of a larger cultural pact was followed in agreements with the People's Republic of China (PRC) and some Eastern European Socialist countries. Exchanges with Western nations such as Australia, as well as that reached with Cuba, tended to be less formal and were negotiated between Canadian sport organizations and their counterparts abroad.[8]

Shortly after Canada established diplomatic relations with the PRC in 1972, Canadian prime minister Pierre Trudeau visited that country. On this visit the matter of sport exchanges was raised and, in particular, the possibility of Canada's sending a table-tennis team to the PRC. Because of the inferior abilities of the Canadian team, there was little interest in Ottawa in such a tour.[9] Consequently it was agreed that the two countries' badminton teams would exchange visits. The following year the University of British Columbia Thunderbird hockey team visited the PRC, and that country sent its table-tennis team to Canada.[10] These visits marked the beginning of what some have called "ping-pong diplomacy." The next exchange, a tour of the PRC by Canada's swimming team, introduced government officials to the world of international sport politics. They soon found out that it was illegal under International Swimming Federation (FINA) regulations to compete against countries that were not FINA members. The PRC was not a member. Threatened with suspension, the Canadian Swimming Association sent a team of veteran swimmers whose international careers were at an end. These athletes, along with (for good measure) the accompanying CTV television crew, were all subsequently suspended by FINA (Morse 1987b, 10).

This run-in with the international sport establishment confirmed the need for additional expertise in international sport relations in the Canadian sport bureaucracy. Tom Bedecki, who as director of Sport Canada had been instrumental in the signing of the first Canada-Soviet sport exchange agreement, assumed the post of director of International Relations in Fitness and Amateur Sport in 1976. This position, however, disappeared in 1978, evidently because External Affairs was opposed to a proliferation of functions across different governmental departments.[11] It was not re-established until 1988. In the interim, the task of dealing with sport exchanges fell largely to Eric Morse, who worked at the International Sport Relations desk in External Affairs from 1974 to 1986. In 1976 he was appointed as secretary to the interdepartmental committee established by External Affairs and Sport Canada in 1976.[12] It was primarily Morse who, on behalf of Fitness and Amateur Sport, dealt with the subtleties of reaching sport-exchange agreements with other countries and who kept the appropriate Canadian posts informed.

Another early sport-exchange program that was not part of a wider protocol negotiated by the Department of External Affairs was with Cuba. This initiative was part of "Game Plan '76" and came about because of Sport Canada's need to have a warm winter site for Canadian athletes who were training for the 1976 Montreal Olympics. Canadian athletes in some eleven Olympic sports trained in Cuba during the winter of 1975–76. That country, in turn, was interested in using some of Canada's indoor training facilities. Canadian sport officials, however, were apparently quite upset when Cuba wanted to send its very inexperienced synchronized swimmers to Montreal to train with the much more sophisticated Canadian team.[13]

The 1974 Canada-Soviet sport-exchange agreement was renewed in 1979. However, Canadian sanctions imposed in response to the Soviet Union's invasion of Afghanistan in December 1979 resulted in the cancellation of all cultural exchanges with the Soviet Union, including sport. This prohibition lingered long after all the other economic sanctions were removed, probably because of a lack of interest in cultural exchanges (under which sport and academic exchanges were subsumed) by government officials. While the new Liberal government that came to power in 1980 made it clear that it did not object to the continuation of sport exchanges with the Soviet Union, despite the suspension of formal bilateral cultural relations, for the most part they were not restored until the mid-1980s (Morse 1987c, 46). According to Morse, Canadian NSOs "found other fish to fry" (ibid.).

Ironically, it would be left to Otto Jelinek, the minister of state for fitness and amateur sport in the new Conservative government, to revive sport exchanges with the Soviet Union in November 1984 when he signed a second renewal agreement. The Geneva Summit earlier in the year, which had made specific reference to the restoration of US–USSR sport relations, paved the way for this renewal (ibid.). Jelinek was well known for his anti-communist views, and he received a fair amount of ribbing from his colleagues for signing this first exchange agreement with the Soviet Union by the Conservative government (ibid.).

Canadian sport officials, however, were not enthusiastic about renewing sport-exchange programs with the Soviet Union, in part because they were busy elsewhere and in part because they felt they were getting just as much from the exchange agreements that had been signed with what was then the German Democratic Republic (GDR), and without as much red tape (ibid., 46–7). The Canada–GDR sport-exchange agreement grew out of a trip to Eastern Europe in the spring of 1977 by the first minister of state for fitness and amateur sport, Iona Campagnolo, the director of Sport Canada, Roger Jackson, and the head of International Sports Relations in External Affairs, Eric Morse.[14] According to Jackson, this agreement was an exception to those normally concluded with Eastern European countries because it was not part of a larger cultural one, but was simply drawn up by Morse and signed by Campagnolo.[15]

The Canada–GDR agreement, however, soured after Otto Jelinek's trip to the GDR to renew it in September 1986 (Morse 1987c, 47).

According to Lane MacAdam, Jelinek wanted to include in the new agreement a clause stating that both countries would take steps to control athlete doping. GDR officials balked at this clause. For its part, the GDR insisted on making reference in the document to the evils of "professional and commercial misuse of athletes." Neither side would back down, and Jelinek left the GDR without renewing the agreement.[16] Morse, however, attributes the breakdown of these negotiations to the fact that because the 1988 Calgary Olympics were so close at hand, Canada was no longer the attractive partner it had been earlier when the GDR was seeking to train for these Winter Games in Canada (Morse 1987c, 47). Consequently, during the visit to Canada of the Soviet Sport Committee president, Marat Gramov, in conjunction with the "Rendezvous '87" NHL–USSR hockey series in February 1987, interest was renewed in Canada-Soviet sport exchanges. During Gramov's visit, he issued a joint communiqué with Otto Jelinek on sport exchanges between the two countries for 1987. This program was one of the largest to date, including some sixteen separate visits to the Soviet Union by Canadian delegations and twelve corresponding visits by Soviet athletes. Some sixteen sports were involved in all (ibid.).

It is not surprising, given their number, that Canadian sport exchanges have encountered many problems, some because of last-minute planning and poor follow-up and co-ordination and others for larger political reasons. Sport exchanges were often afterthoughts to more general bilateral cultural agreements; consequently sport officials were under pressure to devise specific proposals quickly.[17] In some instances, such as the exchange with Cuba, Canadian NSOs cancelled their commitments with little notice or regard for formal protocol. Sport exchanges, according to Tom Bedecki, were often not a high priority with them.[18] This caused a great deal of international embarrassment. According to a senior External Affairs official, this disregard of External's broader objectives in foreign-policy is a common problem in government. Most other ministries that deal with foreign-policy matters, for instance, in agriculture and sport, are pleased to enter into bilateral agreements with other countries. However, when these "line" departments want to get out of the agreements, they are not sensitive to the wider repercussions their withdrawal might have for Canada's international relations.[19]

On the other hand, Canadian NSOs sometimes entered into agreements with their counterparts that were not part of the formal exchange agreement. This often left Canadian government officials faced with deciding who was financially responsible for the costs of these "unofficial" ventures. There were also difficulties in gaining optimal publicity from the visits of Canadian teams and officials abroad. Predictably, each side blamed the other, External Affairs claiming it had not been properly informed by Canadian sport officials and Fitness and Amateur Sport complaining that External Affairs had neglected to inform appropriate Canadian posts abroad.

Certainly, one cause of these problems was that until recently Fitness and Amateur Sport had no formal mechanisms to deal with these matters. Another was the rapid turnover of ministers of state for fitness and amateur sport since the creation of this post in 1976 (Morse 1987b, 8). The turnover rate was particularly acute in the final two years of the 1980–84 Liberal government (see Macintosh, Bedecki, and Franks 1987, 131) and, more recently, during the Conservative governments of the late 1980s and early 1990s. Moreover, the most competent of these sport ministers often held another, more important cabinet position. These ministerial "problems" not only caused a lack of continuity in leadership for sport exchanges, but reflected the relatively low importance that successive governments have attached to Fitness and Amateur Sport. This ministry had been seen by many incumbents as a jumping-off point for a more prestigious cabinet posting, an attitude that was bound to have an adverse effect on the motivation of officials within Fitness and Amateur Sport to work on international sport exchanges.

The effectiveness of sport exchanges would be greatly enhanced if there was a clearer understanding of, and agreement on, their desired outcomes. Certainly, these goals were difficult to determine before Fitness and Amateur Sport had its own international sport capacity and had to rely extensively on the expertise of External Affairs (Morse 1987b, 8). Richard Pound devoted some time to the question of sport exchanges in his 1987 report to Fitness and Amateur Sport. Among other things, he recommended that a coherent policy for bilateral sport agreements should be reached in consultation with Canadian NSOs, whereby Canada could benefit from foreign expertise and sport technology, as well as offering assistance to other countries in these areas (Pound 1987, 8). Such a policy would need to be co-ordinated with the diplomatic exigencies of External Affairs and with the objectives that External Affairs itself sees for sport exchanges. Once the policy was in place, more careful planning and co-ordination among Fitness and Amateur Sport, External Affairs, and Canadian NSOs would be required to implement it. Finally, many government officials, as well as Pound, have indicated the need for effective evaluation of sport-exchange programs.

These issues point to the difficulty of melding sport with foreign policy. As Morse observed, External Affairs is primarily interested in the problems that sport poses and the opportunities it offers for the pursuit of Canada's foreign policy (Morse 1987b, 9). Sport does not conform particularly well to this model since it does not easily fit into External's organizational structure; nor does it have the cachet that security and economic issues seem to possess. When sport issues such as the 1980 Moscow Olympic boycott invade domestic and international policy agendas, the department's structure has shown itself to be especially unsuited to meet such crises. In addition, Fitness and Amateur Sport's views on what Canada's position should be in international sport are often very different from those of External Affairs. This was demonstrated quite dramatically in 1980.

Despite the problems that surfaced after the cabinet record of decision in 1987, there have been many positive aspects to this increased emphasis on sport as part of Canada's foreign-policy initiatives. Certainly, as was pointed out in the External Affairs memorandum to cabinet, sport promotions have the potential to reach a wider audience than do "high" cultural undertakings or academic exchanges. Former Canadian ambassador to the Soviet Union Robert Ford often decried the poor level of hockey teams that Canada sent to the Soviet Union in the 1960s because hockey was so important to the Soviet public.[20] Sport initiatives also can be undertaken in countries and regions that are not easily accessible to many cultural events. According to a senior External Affairs official, sport is a unique weapon in the department's arsenal because it can reach out to audiences in other countries (especially in the third world) in a way that other cultural ambassadors, such as symphony orchestras and famous authors, cannot.[21]

The International Relations and Major Games Directorate[22] in Fitness and Amateur Sport has certainly met Otto Jelinek's objective of providing the minister with much needed expertise in the realm of international sport. The rapid turnover of ministers in this post in the second half of the 1980s and the early 1990s (with one exception: Otto Jelinek), however, has meant that hardly had a minister been briefed on international sport matters than he or she was replaced by the next one. Nevertheless, this expertise was of value to Canadian NSOs in their efforts to gain better access to, and more influence on, international sport governing bodies. To this end, the International Relations Directorate prepared the publication *The Administration of International Sport and Fitness* (Canada [undated]) for the use of national sport officials. The directorate also provided NSOs with much needed information on the rapidly changing scene in South Africa in the late 1980s and early 1990s.

The infighting between the International Sports Relations section of External Affairs and the International Relations and Major Games Directorate in Fitness and Amateur Sport ended abruptly in February 1992, when the federal government announced that as part of efforts to "streamline" External Affairs, the functions of the International Cultural Relations division were to be transferred to other departments. As a result, International Sports Relations, along with its budget and person-years, was subsumed by the International Relations unit in Fitness and Amateur Sport. According to a senior official in External Affairs, the International Sports Relations section (within International Cultural Relations) was a small, underfunded operation that had little technical expertise in sport. It had no "critical mass" and its reporting function had always been problematic. Thus the transfer of its functions and resources to Fitness and Amateur Sport, where there was a wealth of expertise and direct access to, and knowledge, of Canadian NSOs, made sense. With its much larger budget, Fitness and Amateur Sport would be able to muster more personnel and resources for international sport matters when the occasion arose.[23]

Certainly, this amalgamation means that international sport exchanges and promotions are likely to be better co-ordinated, although CIDA is still responsible for providing sport aid to the Commonwealth under the commitment that Clark made just before leaving his cabinet post in External Affairs. But the Canadian sport community was most upset about the move because of what it perceived as the loss of a very powerful and influential department (External Affairs) in matters of international sport. The assistant deputy minister for culture and communications, Peter Daniel, and Anne Hillmer spoke on behalf of the government decision at the annual meeting of the Canadian Olympic Association (COA) in St John's, Newfoundland, in early April 1992. The COA was not convinced, however, and its board of directors unanimously passed a resolution expressing "unreserved opposition" to the proposed transfer of the International Sports Relations section in External Affairs to Fitness and Amateur Sport. The board stated that the transfer was "not in the best interest of either Canadian sport or Canadian foreign policy" and that it contradicted "important initiatives taken by ... [the] Government over the past five years that have put Canada at the forefront of international sports diplomacy."[24]

Taking a different tack, Bruce Kidd wrote to Prime Minister Brian Mulroney, pointing out that along with the arts, "highly visible sports events have become extremely important sites for diplomacy and foreign policy initiatives."[25] Both the arts and sport contribute significantly to Canada's interests in trade, tourism, human rights, and development in the third-world. Kidd concluded by urging the government to reverse its decision to dismantle the International Sports Relations section in External Affairs.

The demise of the International Sports Relations section, as Kidd points out, may well mean that sport will play a lesser role in Canada's wider foreign-policy objectives and correspondingly that Fitness and Amateur Sport may be inclined to use sport initiatives more often to enhance Canada's stature in the international sport community and to improve Canada's international sport performances. If this happens, it will be regrettable. As Anne Hillmer pointed out, "the challenge (for Fitness and Amateur Sport) is to make sure sport remains a component of Canada's trade and foreign policy and doesn't get marginalized" (Christie, 19 March 1992, C6).

In an attempt to reassure the sport community, Prime Minister Mulroney wrote COA president Carol Anne Letheren that this transfer of responsibilities would not "impinge on the over-riding responsibility of the Secretary of State for External Affairs for the formulation and co-ordination of Canadian foreign and trade policy and for ensuring the coherence and relevance of other government policies and programs which have an international dimension."[26] The government, according to Mulroney, will continue to play a role in international sports relations by creating a small policy and liaison unit for international cultural relations programs.[27] This unit will provide advice and support to those departments (including Fitness and Amateur Sport) that have taken over the various functions of the defunct International Cultural Relations division. It will keep the respective departments informed on the foreign-policy priorities of External Affairs and provide a means of gathering information and requests for help from these departments.[28] The effectiveness of these measures in keeping sport integrated with Canada's trade and foreign-policy initiatives remains to be seen.

In international sport matters of highest import, however, External Affairs will certainly, as it has in the past, take the lead in advising cabinet on policy. For instance, although Canada's sport sanctions against South Africa were lifted in the summer of 1991, it is unlikely that External Affairs would not be central to considerations to reimpose them. If relations between the South African government and the African National Party deteriorate again, the question of sport sanctions may well be on Canada's foreign-policy agenda again. The fight against apartheid in South Africa was certainly a driving force behind Canada's foreign-policy initiatives through much of the 1970s and the 1980s. Next we speculate on developments on the international sport scene in the 1990s that may influence Canada's foreign policy.

INTERDEPENDENCE AND
THE RISE OF TRANSNATIONAL
ORGANIZATIONS —
SOME CONCLUDING REMARKS

In this book we have attempted to relate some of the larger questions that have emerged from the study of world politics and the logic of interdependence to international sport and its related organizations. We argued in chapter 1 that to understand the relationship between sport and foreign policy, it is necessary to understand the activities of such transnational organizations as the International Olympic Committee (IOC) and that we must understand them in "trans-national," as opposed to "inter-national," terms.

Kalevi Holsti (1980, 23) has argued that interdependence is "the most pervasive and fundamental result of the rapidly growing transactions between societies" and that "the development of these multidimensional contacts represents one of the essential forms of systems change in the 20th century." Unfortunately, much of the literature on interdependence has focused either on the attempt to measure interdependence (with particular reference to the problems of determining when simple dependence becomes complex interdependence and how to distinguish between sensitivity and vulnerability) or on the debate over whether interdependence is a process or a condition. Little attention has been paid to the rich "world" of interdependence.

We have begun with the assumption that interdependence is both real and important. Furthermore, our focus has been on the influence of transnational organizations (and transgovernmental relations) on national governments. What our examination of sport and foreign policy suggests is that there are a number of direct consequences of transnational relations for the formulation and implementation of Canadian foreign policy, for transgovernmental organizations such as the Commonwealth heads of government and the (Commonwealth) Committee of Foreign Ministers on Southern Africa (CFMSA) and for non-governmental, transnational sport organizations such as the Commonwealth Games Federation and the IOC.

Of the consequences that result from the greater level of transnational and transgovernmental transactions, perhaps the most important (and admittedly the most general) is the increasing national sensitivity to external decisions. We suggested in chapter 9 that national governments are more and more constrained in their actions by the decisions taken by the IOC. This is in part due to the fact that the IOC has become a much wealthier, and therefore more independent, organization and in part to the tremendous attraction to governments and business of hosting the Olympics. A related consequence of the increasing importance of transnational relations is the inability of national governments to use the Olympics to promote national goals or achieve national purposes. In the post–World War II, Cold War era, nation-states were in a position to use international sporting events to serve their particular ideological positions or national priorities. Now, in a world where ideological differences are less obvious and where market forces play a larger role in the "sponsorship" of international sporting events, the latitude for state action is considerably reduced. It is most unlikely that we will see again the type of "bloc" political boycotts of the Olympics that the superpowers were able to muster in 1980 and 1984, although in the rapidly changing international political environment, anything is possible.

On the other hand, transnational organizations such as the IOC are also constrained in their actions by the positions taken by individual states and coalitions of states. The IOC took a cautious approach to supplications for membership from Baltic nations and, subsequently, other parts of the Commonwealth of Independent Republics and the breakaway republics in Yugoslavia. It elected to wait until these new "nations" had received diplomatic recognition from Western European nations and the United States before taking any action on their applications. For instance, the IOC invited Croatia and Slovenia to send teams to the 1992 Winter and Summer Games only after these new "republics" had been recognized by the European Community and several other nations, including Canada (*Globe and Mail*, 18 January 1992, A16). The political stakes were too high and the situations too volatile for it to do otherwise. To grant membership earlier in these situations would have risked the ire of the powerful nations in the world. As Taylor (1988a) notes, organizations such as the IOC seek to act independent of government. In so doing, they run the danger of "the erosion or collapse of their own authority and significance," and they must keep in touch with the changes in the modern world and adapt to them (ibid., 547–8).

In contrast, the IOC took the lead in welcoming South Africa back into its fold. Here the political risk of being out in front of the rest of the world was much less than in the volatile political situation in Yugoslavia and the former Soviet Union. The Soviet Union was preoccupied with its own disintegration, and the United States and Britain had never been in the forefront of the anti-apartheid campaign. By taking this lead, the IOC put considerable pressure on the nations of the world and the various transgovernmental and transnational organizations that had imposed sport sanctions against South Africa. One of the first signs of this pressure came in February 1991, when the CFMSA resolved that although arms and economic sanctions would be maintained until there were real changes in the apartheid system, the Commonwealth should support the development of non-racial sport in South Africa and that in this it would be guided "by international governmental and sports-federation supporters of the anti-racial sports movement" (Secretary of State for External Affairs, 16 February 1991, 2).

The announcements in the summer of 1991, by both the IOC and the International Amateur Athletes Federation (IAAF), welcoming South Africa back to the international sport movement applied further pressure. The Canadian government was in a particularly awkward position. Under its existing policy, Canadian athletes would have been prohibited from competing in the IAAF World Championships in Tokyo in August 1991 if South African athletes were present. Given that the athletes of many countries, including the United States, would most likely have competed, banning Canadian athletes would have been a most unpopular decision with the sport community and the general public. Hurried meetings among officials from Fitness and Amateur Sport and External Affairs were required to put in place a contingency plan for participation in these championships. Certain elements in External Affairs argued that Canada should maintain its right to determine when Canadian athletes should compete against those from South Africa, deciding on its own when a particular sport federation from South Africa had met the criterion of full integration. Not only would this have been a most difficult arrangement for Canadian officials to monitor, but it could have put Canada in a most precarious position if the country were to bar its athletes from competitions where a majority of nations were participating with South Africans.[29] Ultimately, the Canadian government went along with international developments and announced that it would be guided in its South African sport policies by the actions of transnational and transgovernmental organizations (Canada, 29 July 1991).

The rapid move by the IOC to readmit South Africa put other Commonwealth nations, and the organization's Gleneagles Declaration and Code of Conduct, in the same kind of jeopardy. Not allowing Commonwealth athletes to compete in the 1992 Olympics against South African athletes was a most unwelcome prospect. But the Commonwealth was reluctant to lift its economic sanctions on South Africa. Many black African and third-world Commonwealth countries were opposed to such a move until there were clearer signs of the end of apartheid and progress towards a universal franchise. The importance of the issue of these sporting bans in the Commonwealth can be seen by the fact that it was not left up to the Commonwealth Games Foundation. It was placed on the agenda of the CFMSA again at its meeting in New Delhi in September 1991. Although the foreign ministers still did not recommend the lifting of the arms embargo or economic sanctions, they did follow up their earlier communiqué by proposing that "people to people" sanctions, including sport, be removed. To this end, the CFMSA recommended that all Commonwealth restrictions (in respect to each particular sport) be lifted once the following criteria were met: racial integration of the sport had been recognized as achieved by the appropriate representative non-racial sport organization in South Africa, the sport had been readmitted to its parent international sport federation (ISF), and the appropriate non-racial South African sport organization had agreed to resume international competition (Commonwealth Committee of Foreign Ministers, 13–14 September 1991, 4–5). These criteria followed closely those that had been laid down by the IOC earlier in the year. Indeed, the first recommendation meant that transnational sport organizations (that is, the relevant ISF) would play a crucial role in determining when Commonwealth athletes would be able to compete against South Africans. These recommendations on sporting contacts with South Africa were approved at the Commonwealth heads-of-government meeting in Harare in October 1991 (Commonwealth Heads of Government, 21 October 1991, 5–6).

Our analysis has also shown that transgovernmental organizations such as the Organization of African Unity and its sport arm, the Supreme Council for Sport in Africa, along with allied non-governmental organizations such as the South African Non-Racial Olympic Committee, can have a significant effect on governmental foreign policy. For instance, the boycott of the 1976 Montreal Olympics that these organizations engineered was to have a great impact, not only on the Canadian government, but also on the Commonwealth heads of government. The Gleneagles Declaration, reached by the heads of government in 1977 after concerted efforts by the Canadian government to save the 1978 Edmonton Commonwealth Games, is a prime example of this influence. That the efforts of these anti-apartheid organizations were not always politically successful can be seen in Margaret Thatcher's refusal to back down in face of their threats of a massive boycott of the 1986 Edinburgh Games. In this instance, Thatcher's convictions about not tightening economic sanctions on South Africa were stronger than her concern for harmony in the Commonwealth or the welfare of the Edinburgh Games.

Several other implications arise from this analysis. First, it seems clear that both rational choice and the planning function are severely inhibited by the increasing prominence and independence of the IOC. The balance of power between, on the one hand, the IOC, the national Olympic committees, and the ISFs and, on the other, national governments is clearly shifting in the direction of the IOC and the ISFs. National governments can, as we have seen in the case of the Moscow Olympics boycott, take draconian measures aimed specifically at national non-participation. But it seems to be increasingly difficult today to garner public support for such a position, and any such proposals for non-participation clearly would draw protests from domestic groups capable of exerting strong pressure, such as the television networks and the large sport television audience.

Governments are, in short, becoming increasingly unable to control the activities of transnational actors such as the IOC. Strict compliance with the rules of membership and steadily increasing reliance on television rights and other royalties make the IOC especially impervious to the pressures of national governments. Before the Seoul Olympics, for example, the IOC took over from the Korean Games Organizing Committee the responsibility for issuing official invitations to those Games. At the same time, it instituted a rule that if a country accepted its invitation and then withdrew, the officials of that country would be banned from future Games. In Los Angeles, officials from Eastern bloc nations attended the Games in spite of the absence of their athletes (Taylor 1988b, 193). The same was true of officials from the US and other boycotting nations at the Moscow Olympics (Coghlan 1990, 249). In fairness to these officials, their presence at the IOC and associated ISF meetings held in conjunction with the Games was essential if they were to maintain their influence in these organizations.

Although the IOC's influence in international politics is ascendant and it is less likely to be subjected to the political influence of powerful blocs of nations, its future is not without peril. Certainly, it will come under increasing pressure from its international sponsors, the television industry, and other transnational business concerns, to adapt to their wishes and requirements. This will include more demands to adjust playing schedules, the timing of events, and the rules of competition in order to make them more attractive to a large viewing audience and to put less emphasis on, or even eliminate, those events that do not meet this criterion. Indeed, at the general assembly of ISF in Sydney in October 1991, IOC official Gilbert Felli said that the "Olympics will have to reshape its format by the year 2000 to have a greater television appeal" and that the television networks should have a role in this reshaping (*Whig Standard*, 19 October 1991, 20). He continued that although many sports were pushing for greater numbers of competitors and several non-Olympic sports wanted to be admitted, only proposals that led to a reduction in the numbers would be acceptable.

The IOC will also face demands from its sponsors to allow them advertising access to the Olympic venues themselves, a practice that is commonplace at virtually all other national and international sport competitions. The present prohibition on commercial enterprises and sponsorships on Olympic sites is one of the last vestiges of the IOC's resistance to the complete professionalization and commercialization of the Olympic Games. According to Richard Pound, this prohibition means that the IOC "leaves millions of sponsorship dollars 'on the table'" (Pound 1990, 7).

Another commercial threat to the IOC is likely to come from high-profile ISFs, who will want to take a greater share of the television and sponsorship revenues from the Olympics. The IOC will find these demands hard to deny because in high-profile Olympic sports such as athletics (track and field), gymnastics, and aquatics, the international sport federations hold the threat of withdrawing from the Games, thus decreasing the attraction of the Games to television networks and sponsors. The growing appeal of the World Championships in these sports can be seen in the four-year, $91 million (US) contract that the IAAF signed with the European Broadcast Union in May 1992 (Christie, 30 May 1992, A17). The absence of such sport federations as the IAAF from the Olympics would make their own World Championships even more attractive to television and commercial sponsorship than they are at present.

The Ben Johnson scandal and the subsequent Dubin Commission of Inquiry raised questions about the current values in international sport. Indeed, commission chair Charles Dubin decried what he saw as a moral crisis in sport. This issue has revived interest in restoring the values that Pierre de Coubertin envisaged for the Olympics when he conceived them in the late nineteenth century. Bruce Kidd (1991b, 370) has written eloquently about integrating athletic, artistic, cultural, and intellectual activities into an Olympic "festival of sports, intercultural exploration, and service." For the many reasons we have outlined in this and the previous chapter, we see little hope of this change occurring from within the IOC. In fact, Kidd himself cites IOC executive vice-president Richard Pound as saying in 1990 that the Olympic Games are now more successful than ever before and that "no new orientation is necessary" (ibid., 373). Pressure for the laudable changes that Kidd enunciates in his article, in our opinion, will have to come from outside the established sport structure. Some political scientists (for instance, Watts 1991), see a counter force to the inevitable alienation of further political and economic integration in the new world of interdependence. This counter force will manifest itself in a search for "smaller political units more sensitive to their electorates and capable of expressing regional distinctiveness and ethnic, linguistic or historically derived diversity" (ibid., 16). It is in this development that we see the greatest hope for a reorientation of today's dominate sport values of record and performance. Television magnate Ted Turner's promotion of the Goodwill Games in Seattle in 1990 indicated that he perceived there to be some public interest in a different orientation to international televised sport spectacles.

Another global development that may have an impact on international sport is the effort of the United States to develop a North American trading bloc with Mexico and Canada in order to counter the growing economic power of the European Community and the rapidly expanding Pacific Rim trading consortium. The leaders of these economic blocs, who will be intent on gaining international media attention and building regional allegiances, may decide to use sport to their ends. The use of sporting events to promote *national* unity was commonplace in the post-war era, for instance, in the Canada Games and Spartakiad, the all-Soviet games. Perhaps there will be an increase of attention and importance attached to *regional* sport events in the 1990s. This tendency could be seen in the 1980s; European championships grew in number and importance and the 1990 Asian Games that were staged in Beijing and the 1991 All-African Games in Egypt assumed major proportions. The Pan-American Games might well be used in a similar way by any new North (and South) American economic consortium. Certainly, the 1991 Pan-American Games in Cuba were used to good advantage by Fidel Castro in his attempts to stave off the collapse of communism in his country. The development of, and the greater importance attached to, these regional games and single-sport World Championships have already been seen by sport officials in the Commonwealth as a threat to the continued existence of the Commonwealth Games (Commonwealth Games Federation, 17 October 1991).

In his book *Bound to Lead*, Joseph Nye (1990) has suggested that the United States, faced with its declining economic and military hegemony, will attempt to use culture to maintain its place of primacy in the world. In fact, he argues strenuously that the concept of this "soft power" is critical in the formulation and implementation of foreign policy. Certainly, the influence of us "low culture" is increasingly felt around the world. Perhaps the United States will move to use sport more formally in this way. Global interest in sport by North American professional cartels is increasing. The start-up by the National Football League in 1991 of the World Football League, with franchises in Canada and Europe, is one such example. Developments such as this and those outlined in preceding paragraphs could pose additional threats to the IOC's hegemony in international sport and cause new problems and concerns for sovereign states.

Finally, the whole business of interdependence is self-perpetuating. At the systemic level, as status hierarchy declines, interdependence grows. At the national level, as national governments lose the leverage of ideological consensus to support the formulation and predisposition of their foreign policies, interdependence grows. At the level of the organization, as more organizations operate across national borders rather than between them, interdependence grows. At the same time, national governments and national organizations will attempt to retain their authority.

It is not at all clear today whether increased communications, cultural and economic convergence, and what appears to be the end of the post-war great-power rivalry will lead to reduced levels of international conflict. It is just as plausible to assume that decreased stability (order) will result from the "pluralization" of the international system. The Gulf War, as well as the breakup of the Soviet Union and Yugoslavia and the subsequent chaos and violence in these regions, suggests that a reduction of international conflict may be too optimistic a view. What we do know, however, is that the world cannot be understood in terms of simple state-to-state models and that the foreign policy of sport must be understood in terms of this new transnational world – despite the fact that, on the surface, it is still clearly organized along territorial lines.

List of Interviewees

NAME	RELEVANT POSITION(S)
Adams, Harry	Held a temporary position at the sports desk, Department of External Affairs, 1973–74.
Bedecki, Tom	Held various positions within the federal government sport bureaucracy from the late 1960s to 1980, including director of Sport Canada and director of International Relations, Fitness and Amateur Sport.
Bergbusch, Eric	Special co-ordinator, Edmonton Commonwealth Games, Department of External Affairs, 1978.
Campagnolo, Iona*	Minister of state for fitness and amateur sport, 1976–79.
Daniel, Peter	Assistant deputy minister, Culture and Communications, External Affairs, and International Trade Canada, 1988– .
Dent, Ivor	Mayor of Edmonton, 1968–74; a Canadian delegate to the Commonwealth Games Federation general assembly, 1978–83; president of the Commonwealth Games Association of Canada, 1983–90.
Deschênes, Leo*	Professor, School of Human Kinetics, University of Ottawa; worked with the Conference of Ministers of Youth and Sport of French-Speaking Countries in the 1980s.
Dickenson, Laurence*	Director-general, International Cultural Relations Bureau, External Affairs and International Trade Canada, 1986–88.

Fisher, Douglas   Freelance journalist; advisor to the federal government on sport issues in the late 1960s and the 1970s.

Gotlieb, Allan   Under-secretary of state for external Affairs, 1977–81.

Gowan, Geoff* **   President, Coaching Association of Canada, 1980– .

Hillmer, Anne   Head, International Sports Relations, External Affairs and International Trade Canada, 1986–92.

Hoffman, Abby   Director-general of Sport Canada, 1981–91.

Jackson, Roger**   Held various positions in the federal sport bureaucracy during the 1970s, including director of Sport Canada, 1976–78; involved in international sport exchanges, 1973–78.

Kidd, Bruce   Professor and director, School of Physical and Health Education, University of Toronto; sport scholar and political activist.

Lang, Chris**   Director of administration for the Task Force on Sports for Canadians, 1968–69; secretary-treasurer and board member of Hockey Canada in the 1970s.

Lefaive, Lou   Held various positions in the federal sport bureaucracy from the late 1960s to 1981, including director of Fitness and Amateur Sport, director of Sport Canada, and president of Hockey Canada.

MacAdam, Lane   Special (and executive) assistant to respective ministers of state for fitness and amateur sport, 1984–91.

MacAloon, John   Professor of anthropology, University of Chicago; sport scholar.

Makosky, Lyle   Assistant deputy minister, Fitness and Amateur Sport, 1986– .

McMurtry, Roy   Chair, Working Party to Strengthen Sport in the Commonwealth, 1990–91.

Moffatt, Bob   Executive-director (1988–89), president (1989–   ), Canadian Tennis Association.

Morse, Eric   Head, International Sports Relations, External Affairs and International Trade Canada, 1974–86.

Paquet, Guy   Deputy-director (francophone institutions), External Affairs and International Trade Canada, 1985–93.

Palmason, Diane* **	Director of the Women's Program, Fitness and Amateur Sport, 1986–90.
Pope, Jeremy	Head of the Legal Affairs Division, Commonwealth Secretariat, London, 1990.
Pound, Richard	President, Canadian Olympic Association, 1977–82; member (1978–), executive vice-president (1983–91), executive board member (1992–), IOC.
Regan, Gerald	Minister of state for fitness and amateur sport, 1980–82.
Robertson, Ian*	Director of the Commonwealth Division, Department of External Affairs, 1978–81.
Scott, John	Acting director of International Relations and Major Games, Fitness and Amateur Sport, 1988– .
Skrabec, Ed	Head, Special Olympics Coordination Unit, Department of External Affairs, 1975–76.
Smith, Ken*	Secretary of the Commonwealth Games Association of Canada, 1987– .
Worrall, James	Member (1967–89), member of executive committee (1974–78), IOC.

*Written communication
**Telephone communication

GLENEAGLES DECLARATION

The member countries of the Commonwealth, embracing peoples of diverse races, colours, languages and faiths, have long recognised racial prejudice and discrimination as a dangerous sickness and an unmitigated evil and are pledged to use all their efforts to foster human dignity everywhere. At their London Meeting, Heads of Government reaffirmed that apartheid in sport, as in other fields, is an abomination and runs directly counter to the Declaration of Commonwealth Principles which they made at Singapore on 22 January 1971.

They were conscious that sport is an important means of developing and fostering understanding between the people, and especially between the young people, of all countries. But, they were also aware that, quite apart from other factors, sporting contacts between their nationals and the nationals of countries practising apartheid in sport tend to encourage the belief (however unwarranted) that they are prepared to condone this abhorrent policy or are less than totally committed to the Principles embodied in their Singapore Declaration. Regretting past misunderstandings and difficulties and recognising that these were partly the result of inadequate inter-governmental consultations, they agreed that they would seek to remedy this situation in the context of the increased level of understanding now achieved.

They reaffirmed their full support for the international campaign against apartheid and welcomed the efforts of the United Nations to reach universally accepted approaches to the question of sporting contacts within the framework of that campaign.

Mindful of these and other considerations, they accepted it as the urgent duty of each of their Governments vigorously to combat the evil of apartheid by withholding any form of support for, and by taking every practical step to discourage contact or competition by their nationals with sporting organisations, teams or sportsmen from South Africa or from any other country where sports are organised on the basis of race, colour or ethnic origin.

They fully acknowledge that it was for each Government to determine in accordance with its law the methods by which it might best discharge these commitments. But they recognised that the effective fulfilment of their commitments was essential to the harmonious development of Commonwealth sport hereafter.

They acknowledged also that the full realisation of their objectives involved the understanding, support and active participation of the nationals of their countries and of their national sporting organisations and authorities. As they drew a curtain across the past they issued a collective call for that understanding, support and participation with a view to ensuring that in this matter the peoples and Governments of the Commonwealth might help to give a lead to the world.

Heads of Government specially welcomed the belief, unanimously expressed at their Meeting, that in the light of their consultations and accord there were unlikely to be future sporting contacts of any significance between Commonwealth countries or their nationals and South Africa while that country continues to pursue the detestable policy of apartheid. On that basis, and having regard to their commitments, they looked forward with satisfaction to the holding of the Commonwealth Games in Edmonton and to the continued strengthening of Commonwealth sport generally.

London, 15 June 1977

CODE OF CONDUCT

AS ADOPTED BY THE FEDERATION IN

GENERAL ASSEMBLY AT BRISBANE, 6 OCTOBER 1982

1. In this code the expression "a breach of the Gleneagles Declaration" means:
   For individual commonwealth sportsmen:
   > competing in a sports event in a country which practises apartheid or competing elsewhere in a sports event in which an individual from such a country is competing in a representative capacity for his country or sports body.

   For commonwealth sportsmen as members of teams:
   > participating in a sports event which includes a team from a country which practises apartheid.

   For commonwealth sports administrators:
   > planning or facilitating such competition or participation by commonwealth sportsmen as noted above.

2. In discharging its duty to secure effective implementation of the Gleneagles Declaration, each Commonwealth Games Association shall so conduct its affairs and shall require that each of its affiliated national governing bodies shall so conduct their affairs as to ensure that no approval, recognition, support or facility is given to sports contact between sportsmen and sports administrators from their countries and those of any country which practises apartheid.

3. If a Commonwealth Games Association becomes aware of an impending or actual breach of the Gleneagles Declaration involving a sportsman or administrator of a *non-Commonwealth Games sport* from its country, it shall promptly:
   (a) notify either the sportsmen or administrator or the national governing body concerned in writing as to the full implications both personal and in respect of the sport in general of the actions contemplated and make known its opposition.
   (b) in the event of an actual breach, require its affiliated national governing bodies to declare those involved ineligible to participate in the Commonwealth Games whether as a competitor or administrator and failing such action by all national governing bodies, it shall itself declare those involved ineligible to participate in the Commonwealth Games.
   (c) notify the Hon Secretary of the Commonwealth Games Federation of the position giving details of the action taken or planned by the Commonwealth Games Association and its affiliated national governing bodies in the discharge of their duties under this code of conduct.
   (d) notify its government of the implications of the action contemplated or taken and request its government to take all steps necessary in the discharge of its obligations under the Gleneagles Declaration.

4. If a Commonwealth Games Association becomes aware of an impending or actual breach of the Gleneagles Declaration involving a sportsman or administrator of *a Commonwealth Games sport* from its country, it shall promptly:
   (a) notify either the sportsman or administrator or the national governing body

concerned in writing as to the full implications, both personal and in respect of the sport in general, of the actions contemplated and make known its opposition thereto and require the national governing body of the sport concerned to do likewise;

(b) in the event of any impending breach take steps with a view to securing the abandonment of the actions in contemplation and shall request that each of its affiliated national governing bodies shall do likewise;

(c) in the event of an actual breach:

(i) require its affiliated national governing bodies to declare those involved ineligible to participate in the Commonwealth Games whether as a competitor or administrator until further notice and failing such action by all national governing bodies, it shall itself declare those involved ineligible to participate in the Commonwealth Games.

(ii) require that such other action as may be appropriate in the particular circumstances is promptly taken against the individual concerned by the appropriate national governing body;

(iii) where the national governing body has given official approval or support to such breach, shall forthwith by due process suspend that national governing body from affiliation and notify the appropriate international federation of its action.

(d) notify the Hon Secretary of the Commonwealth Games Federation of the position giving details of the action taken or planned by the Commonwealth Games Association and the national governing body concerned in the discharge of their duties under this code of conduct.

5. A person who, after the date on which this code of conduct was adopted, is party to a breach of the Gleneagles Declaration or who is a member of the national governing body of any sport which commits or condones such a breach shall not be eligible to compete or act in any official capacity in the Commonwealth Games or to hold office in the Commonwealth Games Federation or any Commonwealth Games Association unless and until the general assembly shall otherwise decide.

6. No form of sports exchange shall take place between any Commonwealth Games Association and a Commonwealth Games Association or the governing body of a Commonwealth Games sport which has been suspended or individual sportsmen declared ineligible to participate in the Commonwealth Games.

AND, THE FEDERATION BY SPECIAL RESOLUTION IN GENERAL ASSEMBLY FURTHER AGREED THAT:

in the expectation that this code will be faithfully complied with and in view of the constitutional powers conferred upon the Federation to deal with gross non-fulfilment of the Gleneagles Declaration, the Games should not in future be jeopardised.

Notes

1 Department of External Affairs files, National Archives of Canada, Record Group 25, vol. 19, file 8137–40, parts 1 and 2. For further references to Department of External Affairs (DEA) files located in the National Archives of Canada (NA), the abbreviated citation used is DEA files, NA, RG 25, ... For files located in External Affairs, the abbreviation is DEA files, ...

2 DEA files, NA, RG 25, vol. 19, file 8137–40, part 1.

CHAPTER TWO

1 Fitness and Amateur Sport Directorate files, National Archives of Canada, Record Group 29, vol. 1329, file 13. For further references to Fitness and Amateur Sport Directorate (FASD) files located in the National Archives of Canada (NA), the abbreviated citation used is FASD files, NA, RG 29, ... For files located in Fitness and Amateur Sport, the abbreviation is FAS files, ...

2 Personal communication with Lou Lefaive, 22 November 1989.

3 FASD files, NA, RG 29, vol. 1329, file 13.

4 DEA files, NA, RG 25, vol. 19, file 8137–40, parts 1 and 3.

5 DEA files, NA, RG 25, vol. 19, file 8137–40, part 3.

6 DEA files, NA, RG 25, vol. 19, file 8137–40, parts 1 and 2.

7 FASD files, NA, RG 29, vol. 1331, file 6.

8 Ibid.

9 Personal communication with Lou Lefaive, 22 November 1989.

10 Ibid.

11 FASD files, NA, RG 29, vol. 1333, file 5.

12 FASD files, NA, RG 29, vol. 1357, file 2.

13 Personal communication with Douglas Fisher, 18 September 1989.

14 FASD files, NA, RG 29, vol. 1333, file 5.

15 FASD files, NA, RG 29, vol. 1357, file 2.

16 FASD files, NA, RG 29, vol. 2075.

17 FASD files, NA, RG 29, vol. 1352, file 4.

18 Personal communication with Douglas Fisher, 9 January 1990.

19 Personal communication with Douglas Fisher, 18 September 1989.

20 FASD files, NA, RG 29, vol. 1357, file 2.

21 "Confidential source" in this and all subsequent instances in the endnotes refers to government documents to which we were given access on the condition of non-attribution, or to interviews with central actors who wished their comments to remain anonymous. A list of the central actors interviewed in this work appears as appendix A.

22 Personal communication with Douglas Fisher, 18 September 1989.

23 Personal communication with Lou Lefaive, 22 November 1989.

24 Confidential source.

25 Confidential source.

26 Confidential source.

27 Confidential source.

28 Confidential source.

29 Confidential source.

30 Confidential source.

31 Personal communication with Lou Lefaive, 22 November 1989.

32 DEA files, no. 55–26–Hockey–1–USSR, vol. 2.

33 FASD files, NA, RG 29, vol. 1352, file 10.

34 DEA files, no. 55–26–Hockey–1–USSR, vol. 2.

35 Personal communication with Lou Lefaive, 22 November 1989.

36 DEA files, no. 55–26–Hockey–1–USSR, vol. 4.

37 FASD files, NA, RG 29, vol. 1353, file 1.

38 DEA files, no. 55–26–Hockey–1–USSR, vol. 4.

39 Personal communication with Douglas Fisher, 18 September 1989.

40 DEA files, NA, RG 25, vol. 3054, file 10.

CHAPTER THREE

1 DEA files, NA, RG 25, vol. 3061, file 96.

2 Ibid.

3 DEA files, NA, RG 25, vol. 3061, file 106.

4 DEA files, NA, RG 25, vol. 3059, file 60.

5 DEA files, NA, RG 25, vol. 3061, file 96.

6 DEA files, NA, RG 25, vol. 3062, file 106.

7 DEA files, NA, RG 25, vol. 3054, file 7.

8 Ibid.

9 DEA files, NA, RG 25, vol. 3059, file 65.

10 DEA files, NA, RG 25, vol. 3054, file 22.

11 Ibid.

12 Ibid.

13 Personal communication with James Worrall, 24 March 1990.

14 DEA files, NA, RG 25, vol. 3061, file 96.

15 DEA files, NA, RG 25, vol. 3056, file 36, part 1.

16 Ibid.

17 Confidential source.

18 Personal communication with Ed Skrabec, 30 November 1989.

19 DEA files, NA, RG 25, vol. 3055, file 27.

20 DEA files, NA, RG 25, vol. 3056, file 36, part 1.

21 Personal communication with James Worrall, 24 March 1990.

22 Ibid.

23 Personal communication with Ed Skrabec, 4 November 1989.

24 DEA files, NA, RG 25, vol. 3056, file 36.

25 Personal communication with Ed Skrabec, 4 November 1989.

26 Confidential source.

27 Confidential source.

28 Confidential source.

29 Personal communication with Ed Skrabec, 4 November 1989.

30 Personal communication with James Worrall, 24 March 1990.

31 Ibid.

32 Confidential source.

33 DEA files, NA, RG 25, vol. 3056, file 36, part 1.

34 Ibid.

35 Ibid.

36 Ibid.

37 Ibid.

38 Ibid.

39 Ibid.

40 Ibid.

41 Ibid.

42 Ibid.

43 DEA files, NA, RG 25, vol. 3061, file 96.

44 DEA files, NA, RG 25, vol. 3056, file 36, part 1.

45 Personal communication with Ed Skrabec, 3 November 1989.

46 Personal communication with James Worrall, 24 March 1990.

47 DEA files, NA, RG 25, vol. 3062, file 104.

CHAPTER FOUR

1 Personal communication with Eric Morse, 24 August 1989.

2 Confidential source.

3 DEA files, NA, RG 25, vol. 3054, file 22.

4 Ibid.

5 Ibid.

6 Personal communication with Eric Morse, 24 August 1989.

7 Confidential source.

8 DEA files, NA, RG 25, vol. 3060, file 78.

9 Ibid.

10 Ibid.

11 DEA files, NA, RG 25, vol. 3054, file 22.

12 FAS files, no. 7112–1, vol. 1.

13 Confidential source.

14 Confidential source.

15 Confidential source.

16 Confidential source.

17 Confidential source.

18 Confidential source.

19 Confidential source.

20 Confidential source.

21 Personal communication with Iona Campagnolo, 1 December 1990.

22 Personal communication with Allan Gotlieb, 18 February 1991.

23 Personal communication with Iona Campagnolo, 1 December 1990.

24 Personal communication with Allan Gotlieb, 18 February 1991.

25 Personal communication with Jeremy Pope, November 1990.

26 Confidential source.

27 Confidential source.

28 Personal communication with Iona Campagnolo, 1 December 1990.

29 Confidential source.

30 Confidential source.

31 Confidential source.

32 Personal communication with Iona Campagnolo, 1 December 1990.

33 Personal communication with Eric Morse, 17 October 1990.

34 FAS files, no.7112–5–1, vol. 20.

35 Ibid.

36 Personal communication with Iona Campagnolo, 1 December 1990.

37 Confidential source.

38 Personal communication with Ivor Dent, 18 October 1990.

39 Personal communication with Iona Campagnolo, 1 December 1990.

40 Confidential source.

41 Personal communication with Iona Campagnolo, 1 December 1990.

42 Confidential source.

43 FAS files, no.7112–5–1, vol. 20.

44 Personal communication with Eric Morse, 17 October 1990.

45 Personal communication with Iona Campagnolo, 1 December 1990.

46 Personal communication with Eric Morse, 17 October 1990.

47 Confidential source.

48 Confidential source.
49 Personal communication with Eric Morse, 17 October 1990.
50 DEA files, NA, RG 25, vol. 3060, file 78.
51 Confidential source.
52 Confidential source.
53 FAS files, no.7037–2, vol. 1.
54 Ibid.
55 Personal communication with Iona Campagnolo, 1 December 1990.
56 Ibid.
57 Confidential source.

CHAPTER FIVE

1   Personal communication with Allan Gotlieb, 18 February 1991.
2   DEA files, no.55–26–OLYMP–SUMMER–80, vol. 6.
3   DEA files, no.55–26–OLYMP–SUMMER–80, vol. 5.
4   Personal communication with James Worrall, 9 October 1990.
5   DEA files, no.55–26–OLYMP–SUMMER–80, vol. 7.
6   Personal communication with Richard Pound, January 1989.
7   Confidential source.
8   Personal communication with Eric Morse, 24 August 1989.
9   Ibid.
10 Personal communication with Gerald Regan, 1 May 1990.
11 Personal communication with Allan Gotlieb, 18 February 1991.
12 Personal communication with Eric Morse, 24 August 1989.
13 DEA files, no.55–26–OLYMP–SUMMER–80, vol. 4.
14 Personal communication with Allan Gotlieb, 18 February 1991.
15 Personal communication with Gerald Regan, 1 May 1990.
16 Personal communication with James Worrall, 9 April 1990.
17 Confidential source.

CHAPTER SIX

1   In 1982, following the Liberal Party's return to power, the Department
    of External Affairs was reorganized and enlarged to include a trade
    function. This "new" ministry, which encompassed the old trade wing of
    International Trade and Commerce, was called External Affairs and
    International Trade Canada (EAITC). Later in 1982 a further reorgan-
    ization occurred, giving EAITC three ministers: a secretary of state for
    external affairs, an international trade minister, and an external relations
    minister. The first two are senior members of government, whereas
    the third is a junior post. For the sake of convenience, we will continue
    to refer to the ministry as the Department of External Affairs.
2   Personal communication with Bruce Kidd, 21 February 1991.

3 Letter from Robert Fowler, assistant secretary to cabinet, foreign and defense policy, to Bruce Kidd, 16 November 1981.

4 Letter from Eric Morse to Peter Lesaux, assistant deputy minister, Fitness and Amateur Sport, 6 January 1982.

5 Personal communication with Bruce Kidd, 21 February 1991.

6 Ibid.

7 Confidential source.

8 DEA files, no.55–26–OLYMPICS–SUMMER–1984, vol. 2.

9 Letter from Abraham Ordia to D.M. Dixon, honourary secretary, Commonwealth Games Federation, 26 April 1984.

10 Memo from Eric Morse to Abby Hoffman, 10 January 1985.

11 Personal communication with Ivor Dent, 31 January 1991.

12 Memo from Eric Morse to Abby Hoffman, 10 January 1985.

13 Personal communication with Ivor Dent, 31 January 1991.

14 Memo from Eric Morse to Abby Hoffman, 14 January 1985.

15 Personal communication with Eric Morse, 20 February 1991.

16 Personal communication with Abby Hoffman, June 21 1990.

17 Letter from Gerald Regan to Bruce Kidd, 8 May 1981.

18 Letter from Bruce Kidd to Gerald Regan, 28 July 1982.

19 Ibid.

20 Ibid.

21 Letter from Bruce Kidd to Raymond Perrault, 16 August 1983.

22 Letter from Eric Morse to Bruce Kidd, 1 June 1984.

23 Quoted in a letter from Iain Angus, MP, Thunder Bay–Atikokan, to Joe Clark, 23 July 1986.

24 Letter from Eric Morse to Guy Wright, 20 December 1985.

25 Letter from Bruce Kidd to Joe Clark, 25 February 1985.

26 FAS files, no.7112–7, vol. 1.

27 Ibid.

28 Personal communication with Ivor Dent, 31 January 1991.

29 Personal communication with Lane MacAdam, 28 March 1991.

30 Personal communication with Ivor Dent, 31 January 1991.

31 Personal communication with Lane MacAdam, 28 March 1991.

32 Confidential source.

33 Confidential source.

34 Personal communication with Eric Morse, 20 February 1991.

35 Personal communication with Lane MacAdam, 28 March 1991.

36 Personal communication with Ivor Dent, 31 January 1991.

CHAPTER SEVEN

1 Personal communication with Lane MacAdam, 29 March 1991.

2 Ibid.

3 Ibid.
4 Confidential source.
5 Personal communication with Anne Hillmer, 28 November 1990.
6 Ibid.
7 Ibid.
8 Ibid.
9 Personal interview with Lane MacAdam, 28 March 1991.
10 Confidential source.
11 Personal communication with Anne Hillmer, 28 November 1990.
12 Confidential source.
13 Confidential source.
14 Personal communication with Anne Hillmer, 28 November 1990.
15 Confidential source.
16 Confidential source.
17 Confidential source.
18 Personal communication with Anne Hillmer, 28 November 1990.
19 Confidential source.
20 Confidential source.
21 Personal communication with Anne Hillmer, 28 November 1990.
22 Confidential source.
23 Personal communication with Abby Hoffman, 26 March 1991.
24 Personal communication with Lyle Makosky, 21 August 1991.
25 Personal communication with John Scott, 8 March 1991;
   with Lane MacAdam, 28 March 1991.
26 Personal communication with Lyle Makosky, 21 August 1991.
27 Personal communication with John Scott, 13 June 1991.
28 Letter from Bruce Kidd to Joe Clark, 5 July 1987.
29 Ibid.
30 Letter from Joe Clark to Bruce Kidd, 28 August 1987.
31 Personal communication with Bruce Kidd, 21 February 1991.
32 Telegram from Sam Ramsamy to Harry Arthurs, 26 June 1988.
33 Letter from Bob Wright to Harry Arthurs, 15 July 1988.
34 Letter from Bob Moffatt, president, CTA, to John Scott, 13 October 1989.
35 Ibid.
36 Memo from Joe Clark to Barbara McDougall, 8 September 1988.
37 Letter from Barbara McDougall to Joe Clark, 15 May 1989.
38 Ibid.
39 Letter from Jean Charest to Joe Clark [no date].
40 Memo from Lyle Makosky, assistant deputy minister, Fitness and Amateur Sport, to Jean Charest, 1 May 1989.
41 Notes of the Working Group meeting, South Africa sporting policy review, 24 January 1989.
42 Letter from Joe Clark to Bruce Kidd, 28 October 1988.

43 Letter from John Scott to Bruce Kidd, 14 December 1988.

44 Memo from John Scott to Lane MacAdam, spokesperson for the minister of state for fitness and amateur sport, 18 October 1988.

45 Memo from John Scott to Lyle Makosky, 10 August 1989.

46 Letter from Bob Moffatt to John Scott, 13 October 1989.

47 Memo from John Scott to Lane MacAdam, 18 October 1988.

48 Personal communication with Bob Moffatt, 21 March 1991.

49 Letter from Bob Moffatt to John Scott, 13 October 1989.

50 Notes of Working Group meeting, South Africa sporting policy review, 24 January 1989.

51 See letter from Bruce Kidd to Joe Clark, 5 June 1989.

52 Letter from Bruce Kidd to Jean Charest, 18 December 1989.

53 Memo from John Scott to Lyle Makosky, 31 January 1989.

54 Personal communication with John Scott, 6 March 1991.

55 Personal communication with Bob Moffatt, 21 March 1991.

56 Letter from Bob Moffatt to John Scott, 13 October 1989.

CHAPTER EIGHT

1 Confidential source.

2 Personal communication with Ivor Dent, 25 October 1990.

3 Ibid.

4 Ibid.

5 Personal communication with John Scott, 13 June 1991.

6 Ibid.

7 Personal communication with Lane MacAdam, 28 March 1991.

8 Personal communication with Anne Hillmer, 28 November 1990.

9 Ibid.

10 Ibid.

11 Ibid.

12 Ibid.

13 Personal communication with Ivor Dent, 25 October 1990.

14 Personal communication with Tom Bedecki, 29 January 1991.

15 Personal communication with Anne Hillmer, 28 November 1990.

16 Ibid.

17 Personal communication with Anne Hillmer, 30 January 1992.

18 Personal communication with Roy McMurtry, 26 January 1992.

19 Personal communication with Diane Palmason, 13 March 1991.

20 Personal communication with John Scott, 6 March 1991.

21 Personal communication with Ivor Dent, 25 October 1990.

22 Personal communication with Roy McMurtry, 26 January 1992.

23 Personal communication with Lane MacAdam, 13 June 1991.

24 Letter from Joe Clark to David Dixon, honorary secretary, CGF, 10 April 1991.

25 Personal communication with John Scott, 30 January 1992.
26 Personal communication with Anne Hillmer, 30 January 1992.
27 Personal communications with Richard Pound, 2 July 1991; 6 August 1991.
28 Personal communication with Richard Pound, 2 July 1991.

CHAPTER NINE

1 Personal communication with Richard Pound, 2 July 1991.

CHAPTER TEN

1 Personal communication with Lane MacAdam, 28 March 1991.
2 Personal communication with Geoff Gowan, 13 August 1991.
3 Memo from Lyle Makosky, assistant deputy minister, Fitness and Amateur Sport, to John Scott and Abby Hoffman, 21 March 1989.
4 Personal communication with Geoff Gowan, 13 August 1991.
5 Confidential source.
6 Personal communication with John Scott, 13 June 1991.
7 Personal communication with Tom Bedecki, 29 January 1991.
8 Personal communication with Tom Bedecki, 20 September 1989.
9 Personal communication with Tom Bedecki, 29 February 1991.
10 FAS files, no.7037–1, vol. 1.
11 Personal communication with Tom Bedecki, 29 January 1991.
12 FAS files, no.7037–2, vol. 1.
13 Personal communication with Tom Bedecki, 20 September 1989.
14 FAS files, no.7037–2, vol. 1.
15 Personal communication with Roger Jackson, 25 September 1989.
16 Personal communication with Lane MacAdam, 13 June 1991.
17 Personal communication with Tom Bedecki, 29 January 1991.
18 Personal communication with Tom Bedecki, 8 August 1991.
19 Confidential source.
20 Personal communication with Eric Morse, 2 August 1991.
21 Confidential source.
22 The co-ordination of major games was added to the responsibilities of the International Relations Directorate early in 1991.
23 Confidential source.
24 Letter from COA president Carol Anne Letheren to Brian Mulroney, 20 April 1992.
25 Letter from Bruce Kidd to Brian Mulroney, 5 March 1992.
26 Letter from Brian Mulroney to Carol Anne Letheren, 21 July 1992.
27 Ibid.
28 Confidential source.
29 Confidential source.

Bibliography

Allison, G.T., 1971. *Essence of Decision: Explaining the Cuban Missile Crisis*. Boston: Little-Brown.

Anglin, D., and S. Godfrey, 1987. "Unfinished business: Canadian support to the FLS and SADCC." Paper presented to the Parallel Commonwealth Conference, Vancouver, 9–11 October.

Baka, R., and D. Hoy, 1978. "Political aspects of Canadian participation in the Commonwealth Games." *CAHPER Journal*, 44(4):6–14, 24.

Bateman, D., and D. Douglas, 1986. *Unfriendly Games. Boycotted and Broke: The Inside Story of the 1986 Commonwealth Games*. Great Britain: Mainstream and Glasgow Herald.

Bayer, J., 1988. "Domestic politics and Canadian sanctions: The case of Afghanistan." Paper presented at the Workshop on Canada, the Soviet Union, and Economic Sanctions: The Lessons to be Learned. Toronto: Centre for Russian and East European Studies, University of Toronto.

Beltrame, J., 21 June 1989. "Govt. seeks ban on golfers violating South African policy." *Ottawa Citizen*.

Blouin, G., 1978. "Canadian policy toward Southern Africa: The decision-making process." In D. Anglin, T. Shaw, and C. Widstrand, eds., *Canada, Scandinavia and Southern Africa*. Uppsala: Scandinavian Institute of African Studies.

Brutus, D., 1978. "International declaration against apartheid in sport: Draft convention against apartheid in sport: United Nations action." *Journal of Sport and Social Issues*, 2(2):1–3.

Buckwold, S.L., A. Caouette, B. Holliday, R. Lasalle, and S. Leggatt, 1977. *Report by the Committee on International Hockey to Iona Campagnolo*. Ottawa: Government of Canada.

Burrows, S.J., 1978. "The Growth Pattern of International Sports Boycotts against South Africa." MA thesis, Carleton University, Ottawa.

Business Day, 3 August 1989. "Black Africa's warning to Britain." Johannesburg.

Byers, R.B., 1978. "Defence and foreign policy in the 1970s: The demise of the Trudeau doctrine." *International Journal*, 33(2):312–38.

Cady, S., 3 July 1976. "US makes threat to quit Games over Taiwan ban." *New York Times*.

Calamai, P., 7 December 1976. "British aid sought for Games." *Edmonton Journal*.

Calgary Herald, 31 July 1987. "Golf."

– 2 February 1988. "South Africa faces chaos: Clark."

– 15 February 1989. "Kidd says tennis lobby is pushing to ease restrictions."

Campagnolo, I., 11 May 1977. Letter sent to all national sport governing bodies regarding the issue of sporting contacts with South Africa.

Campbell, N., 22 February 1992. "Competing off the slopes." *Globe and Mail*. Toronto.

Canada, (undated). *The Administration of International Sport and Fitness*. Ottawa: Fitness and Amateur Sport.

– 1970. *Foreign Policy for Canadians*. Ottawa: Information Canada.

– 1974. *Exchange Agreement between Canada and the Union of Soviet Socialist Republics*. Treaty Series 1971, no. 40. Ottawa: Queen's Printer.

– 8 July 1985. "Canadian government policy regarding sporting contacts between Canada and South Africa." Ottawa.

– 1986. *Improved Program Delivery: Health and Sports. A Study Team Report to the Task Force on Program Review*. Ottawa: Minister of Supply and Services.

– 28 October 1987. "International sports relations." Speech by Joe Clark, secretary of state for external affairs, Ottawa.

– 28 October 1987. "Higher profile for Canada in international sport relations." *Press Release*. Ottawa.

– 29 July 1988. "Canada tightens ban on sporting contacts with South Africa." *Press Release*. Ottawa.

– 28 June 1989. "Canada tightens ban on sporting contacts with South Africa." *Press Release*. Ottawa.

– 29 July 1991. "Canadian policy on sporting contacts with South Africa." Ottawa: Fitness and Amateur Sport.

Canada Report, 22 July 1976. "Olympics and Taiwan." Ottawa.

Canadian International Development Agency, 1990. *Annual Report 1988–9*. Ottawa: Ministry of Supply and Services.

Canadian News Facts, 4 August 1976. Vol.10(13). Toronto: Marpep.

Canadian Olympic Association (COA), 1983. "Minutes of the 3rd annual meeting of COA athletes advisory council." Montreal, 22–24 April.

Canadian Olympic Organizing Committee (COJO), 1978. *Montreal 1976: Games of the XXI Olympiad Official Report*. Vol. 1. Ottawa.

Canadian Tennis Association, January 1990. *Special Report: Sporting Contacts with South Africa*. Toronto: National Tennis Centre.

Cantelon, H., 1984. "The Canadian absence from the XXIInd Olympiad –

Some plausible explanations." In M. Ilmarinen, ed., *Sport and International Understanding*. New York: Springer-Verlag.

Carr, E.H., 1946. *The Twenty Years Crisis: 1919–1939*. London: Macmillan.

Carter, J., 1982. *Keeping Faith: Memoirs of a President*. New York: Bantam Books.

Chan, S., 1990. *Exporting Apartheid: Foreign Policies in Southern Africa, 1978–1988*. London: Macmillan.

Christie, I., 1986. "Politics in the modern Olympic Games up to 1980." *Physical Educator*, 43(1):44–55.

Christie, J., 19 August 1989. "Commonwealth Games body grateful to Canadian plan." *Globe and Mail*. Toronto.

– 22 August 1989. "Great Britain, Australia facing ban from Games." *Globe and Mail*. Toronto.

– 12 December 1989. "PGA's South African loophole remains Open sore for Canada." *Globe and Mail*. Toronto.

– 14 March 1991. "Sport world set to embrace South Africa." *Globe and Mail*. Toronto.

– 20 April 1991. "South Africa to compete at world track meet." *Globe and Mail*. Toronto.

– 6 July 1991. "Welcome mat out for South Africa." *Globe and Mail*. Toronto.

– 18 March 1992. "IOC launches five-year party." *Globe and Mail*. Toronto.

– 19 March 1992. "International relations section thrown out." *Globe and Mail*. Toronto.

– 30 May 1992. "U.S. faces dilemma after Reynolds ruling." *Globe and Mail*. Toronto.

– and P. Van Niekerk, 10 July 1991. "South African athletes to return to world stage." *Globe and Mail*. Toronto.

Citizen (South Africa), 10 August 1989. "Commonwealth pledge to protect games."

– 18 September 1989. "Tennis out in the cold."

Clark, J., 26 September 1988. "Notes from a speech by J. Clark, Secretary of State for External Affairs." Le Centre de ressources universitaires en developpement international. Université Laval, Québec.

Coghlan, J., 1990. *Sport and British Politics since 1960*. New York: Falmer Press.

Coleman, J., 1987. *Hockey Is Our Game: Canada in the World of International Hockey*. Toronto: Key Porter Books.

Commonwealth Committee of Foreign Ministers (on Southern Africa), August 1989. "Concluding statement." Canberra.

– 13–14 September 1991. "Commonwealth news release." London: Commonwealth Secretariat.

Commonwealth Games Association of Canada, 1984. "International sport development project." Ottawa.

Commonwealth Games Federation, 5 May 1982. "Minutes of the extraordinary meeting of the general assembly." London.

– 6 October 1982. "Minutes of the general assembly meeting." Brisbane.
– 26 July 1984. "Minutes of the general assembly meeting." Los Angeles.
– 4 June 1985. "Statement by African countries." Edinburgh.
– 1988. *Constitution of the Commonwealth Games Federation*. London.
– 15 September 1988a. "Minutes of general assembly meeting." Seoul.
– 15 September 1988b. "general assembly 1988; 1994 bids; speeches." Seoul.
– 23 January 1990. "Resolution tabled by Barbados and adopted unanimously." General assembly meeting, Auckland.
– 17 October 1991. "News release." London.

Commonwealth Group of Eminent Persons, 1986. *Mission to South Africa: The Commonwealth Report*. Harmondsworth: Penguin Books for the Commonwealth Secretariat.

Commonwealth Heads of Government, 21 October 1991. "The Harare communiqué." Harare.

Commonwealth Secretariat, 1987. *The Commonwealth at the Summit*. London.

– 9 February 1989. "CWG at the crossroads or giving developing nations chance to host 'friendly games.'" London.

Commonwealth Secretary-General, 1989. *Report of the Commonwealth Secretary-General*. London: Commonwealth Secretariat.

Commonwealth Women and Sport, January 1990. "A report prepared by a Commonwealth women and sport network." Auckland.

Cooper, A.F., ed., 1985. *Canadian Culture: International Dimensions*. Toronto: Canadian Institute of International Affairs.

Cox, R.W., 1979. "Ideologies and the NIEO." *International Organization*, 33(2):257–302.

Cruickshank, J., J. Sallot, and M. Valpy, 17 October 1987. "Leaders urge new sanctions." *Globe and Mail*. Toronto.

DeFrantz, A., 28 May 1991. "Apartheid just one of issues to be settled." *USA Today*. Arlington, Va.

Department of External Affairs (DEA), 1947–76, 1979–80, 1984. Department of External Affairs files. Ottawa. For files located in the National Archives of Canada, the citation is DEA files, NAC.

– 4 August 1989. "International sport relations." Ottawa.

Devoir, 12 February 1980. "Jeux de Moscou: Les USA demandent au CIO de ne pas hâter sa décision." Montréal.

Dougherty, J. and R. Pfaltzgraff Jr., 1990. *Contending Theories of International Relations*. 2nd ed. New York: Harper and Row.

Dryden, K., and R. MacGregor, 1989. *Home Game: Hockey and Life in Canada*. Toronto: McClelland and Stewart.

Edmonton Journal, 1 September 1976. "Kiwi policy may spoil Games."
– 29 October 1976. "1978 Games concern to Manley."
– 18 November 1976. "New Zealand gets Games deadline."
– 10 December 1976. "New Zealand questions South African sports links."

- 14 October 1977. "Van Vliet feels boycott improbable."
- 24 October 1977. "Tour valuable, says Van Vliet."
- 26 July 1978a. "Games president 'shocked.'"
- 26 July 1978b. "Nigeria pulls out of Games."
- 1 August 1978. "Athletes, officials urged to take pride in Canada."
- 3 August 1978. "'No point' in taking action against Nigerian pullout."

Facts on File, 24 July 1976. Vol. 36(1836). New York: Facts on Files, Inc.

Ferrabee, J., 12 October 1977. "Van Vliet still lacking a firm yes from all Africans." *Edmonton Journal.*

Fitness and Amateur Sport (FAS), 1973, 1976–78, 1982, 1985, 1986. Fitness and Amateur Sport files. Ottawa.

- 1984–85. *Annual Report.* Ottawa: Minister of Supply and Services.

Fitness and Amateur Sport Directorate (FASD), 1966–73. Fitness and Amateur Sport Directorate files. Ottawa: Department of National Health and Welfare. For files located in the National Archives of Canada, the citation used is FASD files, NAC.

Forbes, M., 18–24 July 1986. "Australia remains South Africa's secret target." *National Times.*

Ford, R.A.D., 1989. *Our Man in Moscow: A Diplomat's Reflections on the Soviet Union.* Toronto: University of Toronto Press.

Fox, B., 6 July 1976. "Olympic principle at stake." *Ottawa Citizen.*

Franks, C.E.S., M. Hawes, and D. Macintosh, 1988. "Sport and Canadian diplomacy." *International Journal*, 42(Autumn):666–82.

Fraser, J., 6 August 1986. "Commonwealth balances on edge of doom." *Globe and Mail.* Toronto.

Freeman, L., 1988. "Rescuing credibility? Canadian policy towards South Africa, 1988." *Southern Africa Report*, 4(3):3–8.

Freeman, S., and B. Penrose, 13 May 1984. "Commonwealth Games threat! England to be expelled." *Sunday Times.* London.

Gilbert, D., 22 May 1975. "China question to be big Olympic headache." *Montreal Gazette.*

Gilpin, R., 1981. *War and Change in World Politics.* Cambridge: Cambridge University Press.

- 1987. *The Political Economy of International Relations.* Princeton, N.J.: Princeton University Press.

Globe and Mail, 24 May 1975. "International Olympic Committee defers decision on China entry." Toronto.

- 19 October 1976. "Kiwis plan to dissuade groups from touring South Africa." Toronto.
- 10 November 1976. "Change of heart by New Zealanders." Toronto.
- 15 November 1977. "African countries renew boycott threat against New Zealand." Toronto.
- 1 May 1980. "Putting aside the Canada Cup." Toronto.

- 24 July 1986. "Canada committed to staying in Games." Toronto.
- 5 January 1987. "Swedish apartheid proposal debated." Toronto.
- 9 July 1988. "Canada rejects softball enthusiast." Toronto.
- 10 February 1989. "Sports and South Africa." Toronto.
- 21 October 1989. "DeKlerk takes a big step and a big risk." Toronto.
- 10 April 1991. "Bill to end pillar of apartheid formally proposed in South Africa." Toronto.
- 23 April 1991. "South African clergy press for land reform." Toronto.
- 24 April 1991. "Another segregation law to die." Toronto.
- 25 April 1991. "S. Africa broadens amnesty." Toronto.
- 21 May 1991. "South African blacks to get some land taken by Pretoria." Toronto.
- 18 January 1992. "2 countries recognized." Toronto.

Goodbody, J., 31 July 1986. "Thatcher cancels arts festival visit." *Times*. London.

Granatstein, J. L., and R. Bothwell, 1990. *Pirouette: Pierre Trudeau and Canadian Foreign Policy*. Toronto: University of Toronto Press.

Guelke, A., 1986. "The politicisation of South African sport." In L. Allison, ed., *The Politics of Sport*. Manchester: Manchester University Press.

Haas, E., 1976. "Turbulent fields and the theory of regional integration." *International Organization*, 30(2):173–212.

Hain, P., 1982. "The politics of sport and apartheid." In J. Hargreaves, ed., *Sport, Culture and Ideology*. London: Routledge and Kegan Paul Limited.

Halifax Chronicle Herald, 28 July 1976. "Two foreign policies."

Halliday, F., 1991. "International relations: Is there a new agenda?" *Millenium Journal of International Studies*, 20(1):57–72.

Hawes, M., 1989. "Canada–US relations in the Mulroney era: How special the relationship?" In B. Tomlin and M. Molot, eds., *Canada among Nations 1988*. Toronto: James Lorimer.

Hayes, F., 1982. "Canada, the Commonwealth, and the Rhodesian issue." In K. Nossal, ed., *An Acceptance of Paradox*. Toronto: Canadian Institute of International Affairs.

Hillmer, A., 1987. "Sport in diplomacy." *bout de papier*, 5(4):25–26.

Hobbes, I., 8 August 1989. "UK minister rejects games boycott threat." *Daily Mail*. London.

Hoberman, J., 1986. *The Olympic Crisis: Sport, Politics, and the Moral Order*. New Rochelle, N.Y.: Caratzas Publishing Company.

Holsti, K., 1980. "Change in the international system: Interdependence, integration and fragmentation." In O. Holsti, R. Siverson, and A. George, eds., *Change in the International System*. Boulder, Colo.: Westview Press.

House of Commons (HC), 1936, 1960, 1976–77, 1980–81, 1985, July 1988. *Debates*. Ottawa.

Houston Chronicle, 16 July 1976. "Taiwan unsure of Olympic role in spite of compromise."

Howard, M., 1980. "Return to the Cold War." *Foreign Affairs*, 59(3):459–73.

Howard, R., 24 January 1989. "Canada broke pledge, South Africans say." *Globe and Mail.* Toronto.

– 20 October, 1989. "South Africa sidesteps squeeze on debt." *Globe and Mail.* Toronto.

Howe, M., 15 October 1989. "Seoul renews bid to gain U.N. seat." *New York Times.*

Hoy, D.C., 1979. "The Proposed African Boycott of the XI Commonwealth Games." MA thesis, University of Alberta, Edmonton.

Hunter, M.G., 1980. "The United Nations and the anti-apartheid in sport movement." *Canadian Journal of History of Sport and Physical Education,* 11(1):19–31.

Huntington, S., 1981. "Transnational organizations in world politics." In M. Smith, R. Little, and M. Shackelton, eds., *Perspectives on World Politics.* London: Croom- Helm.

Ingram, D., 26 January 1977. "Future of Commonwealth Games at stake." *Ottawa Journal.*

International Campaign Against Apartheid Sport, 25 June 1989. "Golf's friends of apartheid not welcome." London.

International Journal, 1970–71. "Canada's foreign policy." Vol. 26(1).

– 1978. "Trudeau and foreign policy." Vol. 33(2).

International Olympic Committee (IOC), January-February 1976. "Minutes of the meeting of the IOC executive board – Innsbruck." Lausanne: International Olympic Committee.

– July 1976a. "Minutes of the meeting of the IOC executive board – Montreal." Lausanne: International Olympic Committee.

– July 1976b. "Minutes of the meeting of the 78th session of the IOC – Montreal." Lausanne: International Olympic Committee.

– October 1976. "Minutes of the meeting of the IOC executive board – Barcelona." Lausanne: International Olympic Committee.

Irwin, W., 1988. *The Politics of International Sport – Games of Power.* New York: Foreign Policy Association.

Jackson, P., 22 April 1978. "Keep Amin out: Dief." *Edmonton Journal.*

– 1 May 1978. "Idi's Games plan a bluff, Dief. told." *Edmonton Journal.*

Janigan, M., 17 July 1976. "How the Taiwan issue erupted." *Toronto Star.*

Jelinek, O., 1986. "Sport should 'build bridges between nations and people.'" *Champion*, 10(3):52–5.

– 30 September 1986. "Doping in sport: The need for an expanded campaign against the use of drugs in sport." Ottawa: Ministry of State for Fitness and Amateur Sport.

– 26 October 1987. "Open letter to presidents, executive directors, technical directors, national sports and fitness organizations." Ottawa.

Jollimore, M., 24 August 1991. "Track and field picture permeated with politics." *Globe and Mail.* Toronto.

The Journal (CBC Television), 13 February 1980. "Soviet Games will go ahead, IOC tells us."

Kaiser, R.G., 1980. "US Soviet relations: Goodbye to detente." *Foreign Affairs,* 59(3):474–99.

Kanin, D., 1976. "The role of sport in the international system." Paper presented at the Annual Convention of the International Studies Association. Toronto.

– 1978. "The Olympic system: Transnational sport organization and the politics of cultural exchange." In B. Lowe, D. Kanin, and A. Strenk, eds., *Sport and International Relations.* Champaign, Ill.: Stipes Publishing Company.

– 1981. *A Political History of the Olympic Games.* Boulder, Colo.: Westview Press.

Keenleyside, T.A., 1983. "Canada–South Africa commercial relations, 1977–1982: Business as usual?" *Canadian Journal of African Studies,* 17(3):449–50.

Kennedy, P., 1988. *The Rise and Fall of the Great Powers: Economic Change and Military Conflict from 1500–2000.* London: Unwin and Hyman.

Keohane, R., and J. Nye Jr., 1972. *Transnational Relations and World Politics.* Cambridge: Harvard University Press.

– 1974–75. "Transgovernmental relations and international organizations." *World Politics,* 27:42–62.

Kereliuk, S., 1986. "The Canadian boycott of the 1980 Moscow Olympic Games." In G. Redmond, ed., *Sport and Politics.* Champaign, Ill.: Human Kinetics Publishers.

Kidd, B., 1983. "Boycotts that worked: The campaign against apartheid in the Commonwealth." *CAHPER Journal,* 49(6):8–11.

– 1987. "Canada and the sports boycott." A report to the International Conference Against Apartheid Sport, Harare, Zimbabwe, November 5–7.

– 1988. "The campaign against sport in South Africa." *International Journal,* 43(4):643–64.

– 1989. "Adjusting the sports boycott." *Southern Africa Report,* 4(4):18.

– 10 February 1989. "Sports and South Africa." Letter to the *Globe and Mail.* Toronto.

– 22 August 1989. Letter to the editor. *Globe and Mail.* Toronto.

– 1991a. "From quarantine to cure: The new phase of the struggle against apartheid sport." *Sociology of Sport Journal,* 8:33–46.

– 1991b. "A new orientation to the Olympic Games." *Queen's Quarterly,* 98(2):363–74.

– and J. Macfarlane, 1972. *The Death of Hockey.* Toronto: New Press.

Killanin, Lord, 1983. *My Olympic Years.* New York: William Morrow.

Korea Times, 3 July 1976. "Montreal Games threatened: IOC blasts Canada decision on Taiwan."

Krasner, S., 1985. *Structural Conflict: The Third World against Global Liberalism.* Berkeley: University of California Press.

Langdon, S., 1978. "The Canadian economy and Southern Africa." In D. Anglin, T. Shaw, and C. Widstrand, eds., *Canada, Scandinavia and Southern Africa.* Uppsala: Scandinavian Institute of African Studies.

Lapchick, R.E., 1975. *The Politics of Race and International Sport: The Case of South Africa.* London: Greenwood Press.

– 1976a. "Apartheid sport: South Africa's use of sport in its foreign policy." *Journal of Sport and Social Issues,* 1(1): 52–79.

– 1976b. "Apartheid and the politics of sport." *African Report,* 21(5):37–40.

– 1979. "South Africa: Sport and apartheid politics." *Annals of the American Academy of Political and Social Science,* 445(Sept.):155–65.

Legge, G., C. Pratt, R. Williams, and H. Winsor, 1970. "The Black paper: An alternative policy for Canada toward Southern Africa." *Behind the Headlines,* 30(1–2):1–18.

Library of Parliament, 29 October 1990. "Notes for remarks by the Right Honourable P.E. Trudeau." Ottawa.

Lyberg, W., 1988–89a. *The IOC Sessions: 1894–1955.* Stockholm: National Olympic Committee of Sweden.

– 1988–89b. *The IOC Sessions: 1956–88.* Stockholm: National Olympic Committee of Sweden.

MacAloon, J., 1991. "The turn of two centuries: Sport and the politics of intercultural relations." In F. Landry et al., eds., *Sport ... The Third Millenium.* Sainte-Foy, Qué.: Presses de l'Université Laval.

Macfarlane, N., 1986. *Sport and Politics: A World Divided.* With M. Herd. London: Willow Books.

Macintosh, D., 1988. "The federal government and voluntary sport associations." In J. Harvey and H. Cantelon, eds., *Not Just a Game.* Ottawa: University of Ottawa Press.

– T. Bedecki, and C.E.S. Franks, 1987. *Sport and Politics in Canada.* Kingston and Montreal: McGill-Queen's University Press.

Manning, P., 1974. *The Organizational Development of Hockey Canada: January 1969 to December 1973.* Edmonton: M. and M. Systems Research.

Manthorpe, J., 18 February 1991. "Commonwealth chains itself to ANC's aspirations." *Ottawa Citizen.*

Marotte, B., 8 February 1992. "Lords of the rings." *Whig Standard.* Kingston.

Martin, D., 27 January 1991. "No football? No problem." *New York Times.*

Martin, P., 27 July 1986. "Guaranteed! New Zealand demand '1990 boycott free.'" *Mail on Sunday.* London.

Matthews, R., and C. Pratt, 1978. "Canadian policy towards Southern Africa." In D. Anglin, T. Shaw, and C. Widstrand, eds., *Canada, Scandinavia and Southern Africa.* Uppsala: Scandinavian Institute of African Studies.

Mays, K., 3 August 1989. "Black Africa's warning to Britain." *Business Day.*

McCabe, N., 10 August 1985. "Bar South Africans, Kidd says." *Globe and Mail.* Toronto.

McKee, K., 21 June 1989. "Protest group has wrong guy, Price insists." *Toronto Star.*

McMillan, C., 1988. "The economic effects of Canada's 1980 sanctions against the Soviet Union." Paper presented at the Workshop on Canada, the Soviet Union, and Economic Sanctions: The Lessons to be Learned. Toronto: Centre for Russian and East European Studies, University of Toronto.

Minister of State for Fitness and Amateur Sport, (undated). "Doping and anti-doping in sport in Canada." Ottawa.

– 14 July 1978. "Canada defines policy for South African sportspeople." *News Release.* Ottawa.

– 1989. "Doping in sport: International developments." Ottawa.

Molot, M., 1977. "Canada's relations with China since 1968." In N. Hillmer and G. Stevenson, eds., *Foremost Nation: Canadian Foreign Policy and a Changing World.* Toronto: McClelland and Stewart.

Monnington, T., 1986. "The politics of black African sport." In L. Allison, ed., *The Politics of Sport.* Manchester: Manchester University Press.

Montreal Gazette, 19 July 1976. "PM puzzled by US anger."

– 22 July 1976. "Taiwan still hot Washington issue."

Morgenthau, H., 1948. *Politics among Nations: The Struggle for Power and Peace.* New York: Knopf.

Morrison, R., 1982. *Government Documents Relating to the 1980 Olympic Games Boycott.* Champaign, Ill.: Graduate School of Library and Information Science, University of Illinois.

Morse, E., 1970. "The transformation of foreign policies." *World Politics,* 22(3):371–92.

Morse, E.S., 1987a. "Successfully blending politics and sport." *Champion,* 11(2):18–20.

– 1987b. "Sport and Canadian foreign policy." *Behind the Headlines,* 45(2):1–18.

– 1987c. "Charting new directions in an old relationship." *Champion,* 11(1):46–8.

Mulroney, B., 23 October 1985. *Statement at UN General Assembly.* Provisional verbatim record of the 47th meeting A/40/PV47:26–7.

Munro, J.A., and A.I. Inglis, eds., 1973. *Mike: The Memoirs of the Right Honourable Lester B. Pearson.* Vol. 2. Toronto: University of Toronto Press.

Nafziger, J.A.R., 1978. "The regulation of transnational sports competition: Down from Mount Olympus." In B.Lowe, D. Kanin, and A. Strenk, eds., *Sport and International Relations.* Champaign, Ill.: Stipes Publishing Company.

– 1980. "Diplomatic fun and the Games: A commentary on the United States boycott of the 1980 Summer Olympics." *Willamette Law Review,* 17(1):67–81.

– and A. Strenk, 1978. "The political uses and abuses of sports." *Connecticut Law Review,* 10(2):259–89.

Nau, H., 1990. *The Myth of American Decline: Leading the World Economy into the 1990s.* London: Oxford University Press.

New York Times, 29 May 1959. "Olympic body ousts Chinese Nationalists."

– 3 June 1959. "U.S. scores ban on Taiwan team."

– 4 June 1959. "Brundage denies pressure by Reds."

– 1 August 1959. "Taiwan may rejoin Olympics."

– 4 July 1976. "us drops threat to quit Olympics."

– 13 July 1976. "Olympics betrayal."

Newman, P., 13 February 1989. "Apartheid and the Canada connection." *Maclean's Magazine.* Toronto.

Newnham, T., 1978. "Some aspects of the role of the New Zealand prime minister, R.D. Muldoon, in the apartheid sports boycott 1974–77." *Journal of Sport and Social Issues,* 2(2):31–34.

Nichols, G., 1 April 1977. "Sports boycott: Edmonton Games could be marred unless compromise reached at UN." *Ottawa Journal.*

North-South Institute, 1987. "Canada's foreign policy: Testing our resolve." *Review '86–Outlook '87.* Ottawa.

Nossal, K.R., 1979. "Allison through the (Ottawa) looking glass: Bureaucratic politics and foreign policy in a parliamentary system." *Canadian Public Administration,* 22(4):610–26.

– 1988a. "Knowing when to fold: The termination trap in international sanctions." Paper presented at the Workshop on Canada, the Soviet Union, and Economic Sanctions: The Lessons from Experience. Toronto: Centre for Russian and East European Studies, University of Toronto.

– 1988b. "The 'idiosyncratic' variable and Canadian foreign policy: The case of the Mulroney government and sanctions against South Africa." Paper presented to the annual meeting of the Canadian Political Science Association, University of Windsor, 11 June 1988.

– 1988c. "Out of steam? Mulroney and sanctions." *International Perspectives,* 17(6):13–15.

– 1989a. *The Politics of Canadian Foreign Policy.* 2nd ed. Scarborough: Prentice-Hall.

– 1989b. "International sanctions as international punishment." *International Organization,* 43(2):301–22.

Nye, J.S., 1990. *Bound to Lead: The Changing Nature of American Power.* New York: Basic Books.

Olafson, G.A., 1988. "The Gleneagles Agreement: Canada's Influence, Contribution, and Involvement." Unpublished manuscript, University of Windsor, Windsor.

– and C.L. Brown-John, 1986. "Canadian international sport policy: A public policy analysis." In G. Redmond, ed., *Sport and Politics.* Champaign, Ill.: Human Kinetics.

– 1988. "The efficacy of economic sanctions: Canadian sport policy and South Africa." Paper presented at the International Society of Comparative Physical Education and Sport Conference, Hong Kong.

Ormsby, M., 13 August 1989. "Ottawa's attempt to beat apartheid just a foolish game." *Toronto Star.*

Ottawa Citizen, 17 July 1976. "Taiwan could lose all Olympic status."

Ottawa Journal, 13 July 1976. "A 'damnable' position."

– 17 July 1976. "At last the Games."

Ottawa Letter, 1985–86. "Mulroney still a key in South Africa debate?" CCH Publishing, 17(82):666.

Page, S., 1988. "Soviet foreign policy since 1979: A volte-face?" Paper presented at the Workshop on Canada, the Soviet Union, and Economic Sanctions: The Lessons from Experience. Toronto: Centre for Russian and East European Studies, University of Toronto.

Park, S., 1991. "The experience of Seoul: Toward a world without barriers." In F. Landry et al., eds., *Sport … The Third Millenium.* Sainte-Foy, Qué.: Presses de l'Université Laval.

Parliamentary Debates, 1969–70. *Hansard.* 5th series, vol. 801. London.

Payne, A., 1991. "The international politics of the Gleneagles Agreement." *Round Table,* 320: 417–30.

Pearson, L.B., 1972. *Memoirs.* Vol.1, 1897–1948. Toronto: University of Toronto Press.

Pentland, C., 1990. "Integration, interdependence, and institutions: Approaches to international order." In D. Haglund and M. Hawes, eds., *World Politics: Power, Interdependence and Dependence.* Toronto: HBJ–Holt.

Pfaff, W., 1989. *Barbarian Sentiments: How the American Century Ends.* New York: Hill and Wang.

Polyani, M., 1 September 1989. "IOC toughens anti-apartheid regulations." *Globe and Mail.* Toronto.

– 2 September 1989. "IOC aware of need to shed old image." *Globe and Mail.* Toronto.

Pound, R., 1984. "The Olympic Boycott: How US President Jimmy Carter tried to ruin the Olympic Games." Unpublished manuscript, Montreal.

– 1987. "Development of an international sport policy." A special report prepared for the minister of state, fitness and amateur sport. Ottawa.

– 1990. "A new orientation to the Olympic Games." Paper presented at the conference After the Dubin Inquiry: Implications for Canada's High-Performance Sport System. Kingston: Sport and Leisure Studies Research Group, Queen's University.

Powers, D., 13 January 1977. "Games officials buoyed by optimism." *Edmonton Journal.*

– 31 December 1977. "Year saw threat to Games of African boycott dwindle." *Edmonton Journal.*

– 20 April 1978a. "Nigeria entry in Games uncertain." *Edmonton Journal.*
– 20 April 1978b. "African claims N.Z. ignoring pact on sports." *Edmonton Journal.*
– 19 May 1978. "No Ugandan team will attend Games." *Edmonton Journal.*
– 15 July 1978. "Gov't bars South Africans." *Edmonton Journal.*
– 31 July 1978a. "Nigerian athletes 'furious' over pullout." *Edmonton Journal.*
– 31 July 1978b. "Arrival ends boycott fear." *Edmonton Journal.*
– 2 August 1978. "Political trouble predicted for future Games." *Edmonton Journal.*
Pratt, R.C., 1983. "Canadian policies towards South Africa: An exchange between the secretary of state for external affairs and the taskforce on the churches and corporate responsibility." *Canadian Journal of African Studies,* 17:497–525.
Questor, G., 1980. "Consensus lost." *Foreign Policy,* 40(Spring): 18–32.
Quick, S., 1990. "'Black knight checks white king': The conflict between Avery Brundage and the African nations over South African membership in the IOC." *Canadian Journal of History of Sport,* 21(2):20–32.
Radwanski, G., 1978. *Trudeau.* Toronto: Macmillan of Canada.
Ramphal, S., 5 August 1981. "How Muldoon let the side down." *Times.* London.
Ramsamy, S., 1984. "Apartheid, boycotts and the Games." In A. Tomlinson and G. Whannel, eds., *Five-Ring Circus: Money, Power and Politics at the Olympic Games.* London: Pluto Press.
– 1991. "Apartheid and Olympism: On the abolishment of institutionalized discrimination in international sport." In F. Landry et al., eds., *Sport ... The Third Millenium.* Sainte-Foy, Qué.: Presses de l'Université Laval.
Redekop, C., 1982. "Trudeau at Singapore: The Commonwealth and arms sales to South Africa." In K. Nossal, ed., *Acceptance of Paradox.* Toronto: Canadian Institute of International Affairs.
– 1984–85. "Commerce over conscience: The Trudeau government and South Africa, 1968–1984." *Journal of Canadian Studies,* 19(4):82–105.
– 1986. The Mulroney government and South Africa: Constructive disengagement."*Behind the Headlines,* 44(2):1–16.
Rosenau, J., 1982. "Order and disorder in the study of world politics: Ten essays in search of order." In R. Maghroori and B. Ramberg, eds., *Globalism Versus Realism: International Relations Third Debate.* Boulder, Colo.: Westview Press.
– 1990. *Turbulence in World Politics.* Princeton, N.J.: Princeton University Press.
Ross, O., 24 October 1987. "Canada emerging as Commonwealth head, Mugabe says." *Globe and Mail.* Toronto.
– 6 February 1988. "Can Canada do enough for Africa?" *Globe and Mail.* Toronto.
– 11 February 1989. "Calling Canada to account." *Globe and Mail.* Toronto.
Rothstein, R., 1981. "On the costs of realism." In M. Smith, R. Little, and M. Shakleton, eds., *Perspectives in World Politics.* London: Croom-Helm.

Sallot, J., 28 Feburary 1992. "Time to tighten the strings on aid." *Globe and Mail.* Toronto.

Saul, J., 1988. "Militant Mulroney? The Tories and South Africa." Paper presented to the annual meeting of the Canadian Association of African Studies, Kingston.

Schrodt, B., G. Redmond, and R. Baka, 1980. *Sport Canadiana.* Edmonton: Executive Sport Publications.

Secretary of State for External Affairs, 22 April 1980. "Afghanistan and the Olympics." Statement in the House of Commons. Ottawa.

– 16 February 1991. "Commonwealth Committee adopts programmed management approach to sanctions on South Africa." Ottawa: External Affairs and International Trade Canada.

Shaikin, B., 1988. *Sport and Politics: The Olympics and the Los Angeles Games.* New York: Praeger Publishers.

Shames, L., 23 July 1989. "CBS has won the world series ... Now it could lose its shirt." *New York Times Magazine.*

Shaw, S., 1976. "Sport and politics: The case for South Africa." *CAHPER Journal,* 43(1):30–8.

Shaw, T., and S. Shaw, 1977. "Sport as transnational politics: A preliminary analysis of Africa." *Journal of Sport and Social Issues,* 1(2):54–79.

Simpson, J., 30 January 1980. "Games boycott move ineffective: Trudeau." *Globe and Mail.* Toronto.

– 1 February 1980. "Role in Iran not enough: Trudeau." *Globe and Mail.* Toronto.

Simson, V., and A. Jennings, 1992. *The Lords of the Rings: Power, Money and Drugs in the Modern Olympics.* Toronto: Stoddart Publishing.

Smith, H., 1989. "The foreign policy of the Mulroney government toward South Africa: Continuity or change?" Paper presented to the annual meeting of the Canadian Political Science Association, Université Laval.

South Africa Sporting Policy Review, 24 January 1989. Notes of the Working Group meeting. Ottawa.

Southern Africa Report, 1988. "South Africa confidential: Document underscores Canadian backsliding." 4(3):9–12.

Sportcom International Inc., December 1986. "Development strategy for Canadian sport diplomacy." Ottawa.

Star (South Africa), 31 August 1989. "Another blow for SA."

Stead, J., 2 August 1986. "Thatcher pelted at Games." *Guardian.* London.

Strenk, A., 1978. "Back to the very first day: Eighty years of politics in the Olympic Games." *Journal of Sport and Social Issues,* 2(1):24–36.

Task Force, 1969. *Report of the Task Force on Sports for Canadians.* Ottawa: Department of National Health and Welfare.

Taylor, T., 1986a. "Sport and international relations: A case of mutual neglect."

In L. Allison, ed., *The Politics of Sport*. Manchester: Manchester University Press.

– 1986b. "Politics and the Olympic spirit." In L. Allison, ed., *The Politics of Sport*. Manchester: Manchester University Press.

– 1988a. "Sport and world politics: Functionalism and the state system." *International Journal*, 43(4):531–53.

– 1988b. "Politics and the Seoul Olympics." *Pacific Review*, 1(2):190–5.

Tennyson, B., 1982. *Canadian Relations with South Africa*. Washington: University Press of America.

Thompson, R.H.T., 1978. "Sporting competition with South Africa: New Zealand policy." Paper presented at the International Conference on the History of Sport and Physical Education in the Pacific Region. Dunedin, New Zealand.

Toronto Star, 15 January 1980. "We may consider Soviet hockey ban MacDonald says."

Toronto Sun, 12 February 1980. "We'll sever all ties."

Trueman, M., 12 January 1980. "Clark would consider moving the Olympics to Montreal." *Globe and Mail*. Toronto.

Trumbull, R., 16 July 1976. "US, Canada: Diplomatic rift." *New York Times*.

United Nations, 1989. *Register of Sports Contact with South Africa*. New York: Centre Against Apartheid.

Valpy, M., 31 January 1987. "Mulroney in Africa: Superb fluff and a stunning revelation." *Globe and Mail*. Toronto.

– 1988. "An interview with Stephen Lewis." *Southern Africa Report*, 4(3):13–15.

von Riekhoff, H., 1986. "The impact of Trudeau on foreign policy." In J.L. Granatstein, ed., *Canadian Foreign Policy: Historical Readings*. Toronto: Copp Clark Pitman.

Waltz, K., 1954. *Man, the State and War*. New York: Columbia University Press.

Watson, P., 26 January 1989. "Our South African imports up 68 % in 1988." *Toronto Star*.

Watts, R.L., 1991. "Canada's constitutional options: An outline." In R.L. Watts and D.M. Brown, eds., *Options for a New Canada*. Toronto: University of Toronto Press.

Wederell, D., 25 September 1976. "The 1978 Commonwealth Games: Canada drops heavy hints to N. Zealand." *Guyana Chronicle*.

Whig Standard, 19 October 1991. "Olympics face changes to appease TV, IOC says." Kingston.

Whitelaw, P., 21 July 1976. "Carter hits out at Canada for Taiwan stand at Games." *Vancouver Sun*.

Wilson, M., 1982. "An examination of the events surrounding the decision of Canada to support a boycott of the 1980 Moscow Olympic Games." MA thesis, University of Western Ontario, London.

Wilson, N., 25 July 1986. "Superstars can't cover those gaps." *Daily Mail.* London.

Wilson, W.A., 22 July 1976. "Trudeau government blamed even when it does well." *Ottawa Journal.*

Winnipeg Free Press, 20 April 1980. "Athletes demand hockey boycott."

Wood, B., 1990. "Canada and southern Africa: A return to middle power activism." *Round Table,* 315:280–90.

Working Party Final Report, July 1991. "Strengthening Commonwealth sport." Ottawa: External Affairs and International Trade Canada.

Wren, C., 24 March 1991. "Olympic panel in South Africa, weighing a return to Games." *New York Times.*

Young, S., 1976. *War on Ice: Canada in International Hockey.* Toronto: McClelland and Stewart.

Index